# Hunting

# Hunting

**A New Zealand History**
**KATE HUNTER**

RANDOM HOUSE
NEW ZEALAND

**For Chris and Rick**

**. . . and maybe one day for my own Flynn and Lil.**

creativenz
ARTS COUNCIL OF NEW ZEALAND TOI AOTEAROA

The assistance of Creative New Zealand is gratefully acknowledged by the publisher.

A RANDOM HOUSE BOOK published by Random House New Zealand
18 Poland Road, Glenfield, Auckland, New Zealand

For more information about our titles go to www.randomhouse.co.nz

A catalogue record for this book is available from the National Library of New Zealand

Random House New Zealand is part of the Random House Group
New York   London   Sydney   Auckland   Delhi   Johannesburg

First published 2009

© 2009 Kate Hunter; illustrations as credited on page 301

The moral rights of the author have been asserted

ISBN 978 1 86979 154 4

This book is copyright. Except for the purposes of fair reviewing no part of this publication may be reproduced or transmitted in any form or by any means, electronic or mechanical, including photocopying, recording or any information storage and retrieval system, without permission in writing from the publisher.

Cover photograph: QW (Joe) Hansen
Design: Anna Seabrook
Map: Janet Hunt
Printed in Asia by Everbest Printing Co Ltd

# Acknowledgements

The success of a project such as this is so heavily reliant on the goodwill, hospitality and generosity of others. This is a humble attempt to thank all those who have assisted. I am very grateful.

For financial support I wish to thank Fish & Game New Zealand, the office of the deputy vice-chancellor (research) at Victoria University of Wellington, together with the university's Faculty of Humanities and Social Sciences and my colleagues in History who facilitated my research and study leave.

For permission to reproduce images and text, and to use oral histories, I am grateful to Alexander Turnbull Library, Archives New Zealand, John Barkla, Merrilyn Bartram, Ian Buchan, Viv and Din Collings, Department of Conservation head office, Department of Conservation Canterbury Conservancy, Department of Conservation Otago Conservancy, Department of Conservation Southland Conservancy, Tui de Roy, Rachel Egerton, John Fogden, Marianne Foster, Athol Geddes, Joe Hansen, Dave Hansford, Muriel Henderson, Invercargill Public Library, Nancy Jordan, Jonathan Kennett, Jack Lasenby, Alan Mark, National Library of Australia, National Library of New Zealand, Nelson Provincial Museum, Queen Elizabeth the Second Trust, South Coast Productions, Ronny Tankersley and family, Museum of New Zealand Te Papa Tongarewa, Wairarapa Archive, Brian and Anne Woodley and David Young.

For expert assistance of all sorts I am in the debt of Sandy Bartle, Robert Cross, Charles Dawson, Sarah Ell, Gillian Headifen, Sean Hushir, Raelene Inglis, Barbara Lyon, Jeremy Rolfe, Lynette Shum, John Sullivan, Murray Williams, Kirsty Willis, Gareth Winter and the many research assistants who collected information and didn't look at me sideways too often. The staff of the National Library's Oral History Unit and the Alexander Turnbull Library are especially thanked for their expertise, interest and support.

For their time and tolerance in being interviewed I thank Viv Collings, Grant Fitz-William, John Fogden, Dave Marino and Jocelyn Rae.

For encouragement and enthusiasm, questions and answers I am especially indebted to Heather Goodall, Jenny Hellen, Doug and Jan Hunter, Jim McAloon, Charlotte Macdonald, Fiona McKergow, Marion Maddox, Kirstie Ross, Sydney Shep, Michael Symons, Lydia Wevers, Jo Williman and David Young.

For keeping a stew on the stove, the billy boiling and so much more, my deepest thanks to Chris Cosslett.

# Contents

| | |
|---|---|
| Preface | 10 |
| Introduction | 17 |
| 1  Swarming with game | 29 |
| 2  Hunting for the pot | 75 |
| 3  Bringing home the bacon | 123 |
| 4  Sportsman's paradise | 187 |
| 5  Collecting and conserving | 237 |
| Epilogue | 283 |
| Endnotes | 289 |
| Illustration credits | 301 |
| Bibliography | 303 |
| Index | 314 |

# Kermadec Is.

**PACIFIC OCEAN**

Three Kings Is.

**TASMAN SEA**

**NORTH ISLAND**

**SOUTH ISLAND**

Chatham Is.

**STEWART ISLAND**

Bounty Is.

Snares Is.

Antipodes Is.

Auckland Is.

Campbell Is.

⑪ ⑫

Nelson

Blenheim

**NELSON/ MARLBOROUGH**

⑬

Greymouth

**WEST COAST**

⑭

**NORTH CANTERBURY**

CHRISTCHURCH

**TASMAN SEA**

SOUTHERN ALPS

⑮

⑯

⑰

Milford Sound

Wanaka

Timaru

**SOUTH CANTERBURY**

⑱

DUNEDIN

Dusky Sound

**OTAGO**

Invercargill

**SOUTHLAND**

Stewart Island

**NORTHLAND**

Dargaville

PACIFIC OCEAN

AUCKLAND

TASMAN SEA

HAMILTON

**AUCKLAND /WAIKATO**

Rotorua

**EASTERN**

Lake Taupo

Gisborne

New Plymouth

**TARANAKI**

Napier

**HAWKE'S BAY**

Wanganui

Wairarapa

Kapiti Island

Masterton

WELLINGTON

**WELLINGTON**

---

**FISH & GAME REGIONS**

National and Forest parks

**NATIONAL AND FOREST PARKS**
National and Forest Parks referred to in the text

1. Raukumara Forest Park
2. Urewera National Park
3. Egmont National Park
4. Tongariro National Park
5. Kaimanawa Forest Park
6. Kaweka Forest Park
7. Ruahine Forest Park
8. Tararua Forest Park
9. Rimutaka Forest Park
10. Haurangi Forest Park
11. Kahurangi National Park
12. Abel Tasman National Park
13. Nelson Lakes National Park
14. Arthur's Pass National Park
15. Westland Tai Poutini National Park
16. Aoraki Mt Cook National Park
17. Mt Aspiring National Park
18. Fiordland National Park

# Preface

**H**unter on hunting? 'Inevitable, I suppose' or 'Of course', people quipped. But all jokes aside, many were surprised I was writing this book. Why a history of hunting? Some people were genuinely mystified, some curious, some appalled. Others, many of them interviewed in the course of writing this book, wanted me to tell them why they should talk to me and to prove that I would treat what they said in a fair way. I don't think I answered this question the same way twice.

First, there were personal reasons for pursuing this project. I had married into a hunting family, where the ethics of conservation and shooting sat comfortably beside one another. In this family, hunting as a form of provisioning was important, and the meat that came into the house was wild, organic, and delicious. I learned to cook venison steak (or hop out of the way while it was done properly). I also had to learn to dodge the meat as it hung in the woodshed up near the clothes line — that took a bit of getting used to, I'll admit.

I came to think of hunting as ethical and conservation-minded; it brought me and my children closer to the food chain, distancing us from industrially produced meat wrapped in cling film. I was all too aware, however, that in the wider population hunting was considered to be, if not barbaric, certainly distasteful and politically suspect. Hunting was, until recently, a very common part of many New Zealanders' lives, yet with increased urbanisation and a general distrust of firearms, it had become marginalised, along with those who participated in it. For most New Zealanders, hunting is now something other people do, and game is something other people eat unless they buy it at great expense from specialist butchers or order it at a restaurant. More than that, in less than 30 years, hunting has become detached from its conservation role in most people's minds; venison and wild pork have become less a symbol of the devastation of our forests and more a gourmet delicacy.

There are professional reasons for my interest, too. As a historian of rural life, leisure, manliness and masculinity, and with an interest in the history of cooking and eating, it was inevitable that I was going to run across hunting at some stage. And I did keep running across it: in reminiscences of early settlement in New Zealand; in rural women's recollections of farm life; in obituaries and death notices of World War One soldiers — 'guns and dogs were his constant companions'. But when I went looking for hunting in histories of rural life and of men in New Zealand, or even in histories of tourism and the outdoors, it was curiously absent.

There are metres of shelves filled with books about hunting in New Zealand bookstores and libraries, so someone was writing and reading about it, but it wasn't the historians. Some historians have touched on hunting in their work: Ross Galbreath in his history of the Wildlife Service and his biography of Walter Buller; David Young's history of conservation in New Zealand; Paul Star's work on the movement from preservationist ideas to conservation in the late nineteenth century. Acclimatisation and hunting had been examined seriously by historians, geographers and ecologists in a few meticulously researched reports for the Waitangi Tribunal concerned with the effects of the laws around game birds and animals. Besides evidence from Maori informants, they relied largely on historical newspaper reports, parliamentary debates and acclimatisation records. Other environmental historians have focused on introduced species, especially rabbits and other feral animals as exotic invaders that have ravaged the countryside. Ecologists too have studied the ecological damage wrought by browsing mammals, wildfowl populations and predators, and the contribution of hunting to conservation. But it seemed to me that there was a gap. Social historians, those of us interested in people, families, communities and the everyday life of the past, had not tried to understand this important facet of New Zealand culture.

I began this project hoping to show that hunters have a place in the history of New Zealanders at work and play in the outdoors. I found much more. While researching this book it seemed as if everywhere I looked I found hunting and hunters. Old cookery books instructed cooks how to stew kereru; children's books made heroes of hunters as well as naturalists and frontiersmen; popular magazines from the 1870s to the 1940s carried stories, debates and opinions about hunting and the relative merits of hunting tourism and conservation, along with advertisements for fur coats. Old catalogues from sports shops were full of firearms and ads for taxidermy services; cigarette cards celebrated the 'outdoors' with pictures of bird-hunting parties, glamorous chamois and tahr hunters, and bushmen with pigs; entries by trampers in hut books recorded numbers of deer shot and venison stews eaten; the walls of clubs, hotels and pubs were adorned with mounted heads.

Sources about hunting are not hard to find. People involved in hunting are not as silent on the topic as historians. In this respect, researching the twentieth-century history of hunting was far easier than the nineteenth. A wide range of oral histories recorded from the 1980s onwards captured the recollections of large numbers of hunters, as part of regional histories, histories of forests and islands, bush workers' stories and conservation histories. Hunting was discussed by many as part of a life spent in the bush. Because of the depth of this existing record, I did not need to interview very many hunters, but those I talked to provided invaluable, detailed information about techniques and processes.

Government department archives also contain fulsome records. As well as Galbreath's excellent history of the Wildlife Service, the extensive Department of Internal Affairs files relating to its Deer Control Section and the records of the Forest Service are remarkably human. They contain letters from all over the country from men and women who perhaps would not normally have written to a government department — anxious wives wanting some idea of when their culler-husbands would be coming out of the bush and paying the landlord; grocers looking to have their accounts with government shooters settled; rural workers, shepherds and musterers asking for work in the off-season. There are petitions objecting to closed seasons on birds in various regions, listing the main occupations of hunters and their families and their opinions on bird species and populations. Far from being strictly bureaucratic, these extensive files provided a detailed window into working lives in the early twentieth century.

The other great advantage when researching the twentieth century is the more abundant photographic sources, in both public archives and private collections. An astonishingly rich photographic record of hunting in New Zealand exists. The increasingly common ownership of cameras, as well as the employment of official photographers by the government, meant that hunting by both private individuals and government employees is well documented. The earliest photographs I found were from the 1860s, of a recently released deer, clearly reluctant to embrace its freedom, loitering on a residential lawn in Wanganui. As photographic technology improved in the later 1890s, posed studio portraits of hunters with their shotguns, dogs and bagged birds gave way to outdoor photographs, as well as to images of domestic interiors showing mounted heads over fireplaces and skins on the floors. As the twentieth century progressed, 16mm then 8mm film recorded hunting trips — again, both private expeditions in 'home movies' and government work in official (National Film Unit) productions.

The nineteenth century was in no way a closed book, however. The difference with this period was that hunting was a part of everyday life: it appeared alongside travel, exploring, bush-clearing, hut- and house-building, logging and farming. Descriptions of hunting are extremely common in reminiscences of colonial life, both published and unpublished. The provision and preparation of food was central to what could be a precarious existence and so commanded attention, but these records also provide evidence of the colony's abundance and the comfortable life an immigrant could have. In the diaries and letters of explorers and surveyors and settlers, hunting appears as part of their daily lives. Settlers' letters and other writings mention the freedom to hunt as one of the privileges bestowed by their immigration and encourage others to come to the colonies and enjoy it.

Documentary evidence is only one part of the hunting record, but it is the one that lends itself to books. Many times during this project I have wished that pages could be three-dimensional so as to incorporate the objects that survive to tell us of the history of hunting. Apart from the obvious equipment of hunting — firearms and knives — there is a built heritage that survives in the form of huts. There is also a more domestic record connecting hunting to our past. Bone-handled knives, ivory piano keys, paintings, skin and fur rugs, mounted heads and birds of all sorts, fur collars, feather muffs, huia-beak brooches, glasses and crockery bearing Sir Edward Landseer's *Monarch of the Glen* all reflect a culture intimately connected to hunting. It is this culture and the lives of those who created, shaped and participated in it that I hope this book illuminates.

Opposite: Many everyday objects reflect hunting as a part of New Zealand culture. Bone-handled knives, ivory piano keys, art and furnishings have all made hunting a part of domestic life.

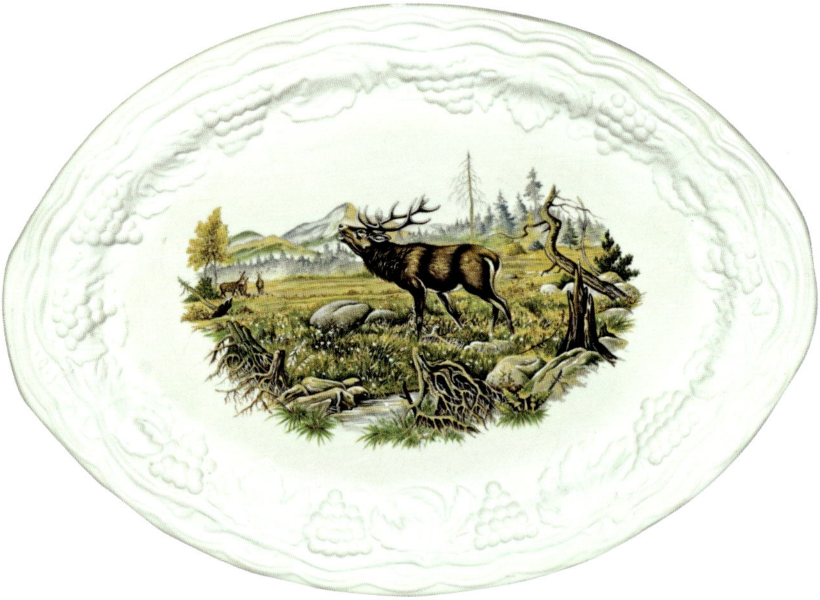

# Introduction

**H**unting tells us many things about culture and society, about changing ideas of and relationships to nature, animals and food. The New Zealand experience of hunting differs from that of other countries in one significant way: with the exception of two species of bat, all mammals here are introduced. This quirk of Gondwana's separation meant that when many other countries were protecting their browsing game, New Zealand was lifting protection on them and, indeed, sinking state resources into their destruction. At a time when hunting was becoming increasingly restricted to the wealthy in Canada and the United States, as well as other British colonies, in New Zealand licence fees and seasonal restrictions on deer, tahr and chamois were all removed. Native forest birds were protected by the 1930s and acclimatisation societies maintained controls over other bird hunting, but the hunting of deer — the symbol of nobility and aristocratic hunting — was not only free to all on public lands, but strongly encouraged. This unusual state of affairs alone makes New Zealand's hunting history worth writing, but there are other reasons for pursuing it.

In recent years, New Zealand historians have examined aspects of pakeha attitudes towards and relationships with nature and 'wilderness'. Environmental historians and historical geographers such as Eric Pawson, Peter Holland, Tom Brooking and James Beattie have all attempted to understand the attitudes of colonists and settlers to the New Zealand landscape and the effects of the environment on these people. They have described the complex tensions between the settlers' emotional response to the beautiful and awe-inspiring, heavily forested land and the Biblical and scientific imperatives to develop it for agriculture and exploit its resources.

In the twentieth century, the big change in attitudes towards nature was the shift to seeing it as a place of recreation. Advances in railway travel and increasing numbers of cars made the outdoors accessible to many more people. By the 1930s, New Zealanders of all classes had embraced tramping with vigour. Histories of tourism, tramping, botanising and 'going bush' have highlighted recreational interaction with the bush and have also, in Kirstie Ross's phrase, attempted to understand 'how pakeha have translated the nature of New Zealand into a national culture'.[1]

Part of the aim of these histories has been to repopulate the historical outdoors. Post-1930s tramping and mountaineering post Hillary's ascent of Everest have come to dominate the image of outdoor activities in New Zealand, yet the bush was filled with people before these activities became popular, with New Zealanders experiencing nature in a whole range of ways.

Above: Hunting has been a family- and community-building activity in New Zealand. Young Neil Foster (in short pants) was photographed with his father, grandfather, cousins and family friends on the opening day of the season in the early 1940s. He still remembers the photo being taken at the 'big pond'.

**20　Hunting**

Hunting was ubiquitous. Parties of bush and alpine trampers often carried at least one rifle and when they did not, they often shared huts with those who did. Venison stew was a remarkably common trampers' dinner. Hunters were arguably the largest section of our historical bush population.

Hunters and hunting have made more of an appearance in histories of conservation in New Zealand. The gradual and tangled movement towards an ethic of native bush and bird conservation has been ably and elegantly analysed by historians such as David Young, Paul Star and Ross Galbreath. Approaches to natural history in the nineteenth century allowed for and encouraged specimen hunting; most of New Zealand's eminent ornithologists, such as Walter Buller, were enthusiastic hunters of native birds. In the twentieth century, the rise of 'conservation', with its focus on indigenous flora and fauna, demanded the hunting of introduced mammals: deer, chamois, tahr, goats, pigs and possums. The killing of animal and plant pests underpins all conservation efforts in New Zealand. Ironically, however, while conservation became a mass social movement, and has become an integral component of the national story, hunting and firearms have become less socially acceptable. Despite this, the link between conservation in all its forms and hunting has been, and remains, strong.

The history of hunting in New Zealand is not only a national story. People, animals and attitudes all link this far-flung corner of empire to a wider world. New Zealanders' attitudes to nature and the trends towards conservation paralleled those in other white settler colonies. Several features of the history of conservation and hunting in Canada, America and other British dominions resonate with the New Zealand experience. Across colonial regimes, the dispossession of indigenous people of their lands and hunting grounds created significant tensions and hardships. Customary harvests of wildlife were generally subordinated to European — more specifically, English — notions of hunting, and legal frameworks surrounding access to game animals very often made indigenous people poachers in their own lands. Tina Loo describes the focus on science and ecology and increasing state intervention to boost wildlife numbers in Canada as a process that marginalised 'local customary use of wildlife, and in that sense was part of the colonisation of rural Canada'.[2] Louis Warren has argued similarly that in the United States where, like New Zealand, native game became the property of the government, the 'conservationist polemic often decried the "wasteful" and "greedy" hunting practices of certain ethnic and social groups'. Hunting meant vastly different things to urban conservationists and to poorly paid rural labourers to whom it was provisioning, recreation and community building.[3] Tensions between different groups of hunters were a common feature of colonial societies, and New Zealand was no different.

The animal species themselves also provide connections with a wider world. Along with the majority of European immigrants to New Zealand, red deer were imported from Britain. They came only in their tens, a handful at a time but, like their human counterparts, they found New Zealand filled with better food and more comfortable living conditions than their homeland. Pheasants and other game birds had a harder time of it, vulnerable as they were to predators and loss of habitat. Tahr, chamois, six species of deer, quail and mallard ducks came from all over Asia, the United States and Europe, and succeeded here.

Scientists and scientific ideas also bound the natural environments of New Zealand with those of other parts of the world. Acclimatisation resulted in massive movements of species around the world. On the whole, plant introductions were more successful than animal ones, but where animals were successfully acclimatised, the ecological effects could be devastating.

There was also an international trade in dead animals and birds. Specimens were a kind of scientific currency used by museum curators, naturalists and collectors. Millions of bird and animal skins and skeletons were traded internationally in the nineteenth century, and New Zealand's museum collections were built up through this process. As will be seen, these movements of people, animals and birds between New Zealand and Britain, other British dominions, Europe and North America was two-way traffic, and with the people came and went ideas about nature.

Hunting is a process. It is not just the killing of an animal or bird, and the link between hunting and killing is not straightforward. To define hunting as simply killing is the narrowest interpretation, and although hunters might be loath to admit it, much hunting does not result in killing.

The link between killing and hunting has changed over time and with circumstances. Killing was essential in those relatively rare instances when wild game was a vital source of food, and when it became clear that New Zealand's native bush and birds could be protected only by killing introduced predators. By and large, many experienced hunters find the act of killing distasteful; the attraction of hunting lies in the chase. The challenge that is relished by hunters is of pitting themselves against an opponent whose entire physiology and behaviour is designed to protect it from predators.

When hunters tell stories, the kill is the smallest part of the narrative. Time is spent describing the anticipation, planning and preparation. Travel, sometimes for days or weeks, occupies more time, especially when the terrain is difficult or beautiful. Locating animals is an important part of the story. Knowing where and when to find them leads to descriptions of early mornings, hours spent watching and waiting and late evenings sometimes toppling into night, catching hunters unawares. If an animal or bird is killed there are more parts of the story, usually quickly and perfunctorily told — gutting, skinning, breasting or plucking, the walk out, the return home

Above: New Zealand's back country has never been empty. Maori and pakeha explored and travelled through the bush and across mountain ranges, hunting as they went. Historians have recently begun repopulating the bush, attempting to understand how people responded to, connected with and were changed by the outdoors.

with meat, storing and hanging. Then perhaps selling, but certainly cooking and eating. The emphasis hunters place on locating animals indicates the importance to them of understanding their behaviour, habits and habitat. Several times in this book there are instances of hunters' reluctance to pull the

Above: Everywhere I looked when researching this book, I found hunters and hunting. Here the Cobb & Co coach, on the road between Nelson and Blenheim, transports a red stag's head, presumably en route to the taxidermist, along with other passengers.

trigger, but never is there regret that they have outwitted the animal on that particular occasion.

It is not my aim to romanticise hunting, but I do want to place it in the wider social context that explains why thousands of New Zealanders have hunted in the past and continue to hunt today. This book examines hunting as work as well as recreation, and draws in the associated processes and expertise supporting hunters. A range of people who may never have carried a rifle, knife or trap into the bush appear in this story: furriers, guides, porters, cooks, families and diners. Hunters themselves appear in multiple roles, as providers, earners, trampers, explorers, as bush- and bird-lovers and as conservationists. This book is about a very ordinary part of everyday New Zealand life.

Chapter 1 describes the intellectual and cultural environment in nineteenth-century New Zealand that provided the backdrop to hunting. Lower-class immigrants were thrilled by the hunting environment that existed when they arrived — one that was free and where native birds and wild pigs were abundant — but the upper-class idea that New Zealand was a country that could only be improved by the introduction of game animals and birds resulted in a great many importations. These introductions were to have enormous repercussions for Maori and pakeha alike. The change to the physical environment was only one part of this; a legal framework was also developed to define legal and illegal hunting. While many initially celebrated freedom from Britain's punitive game laws, restrictions on hunting in New Zealand began to tighten from the 1870s onwards.

Chapters 2, 3 and 4 discuss three motivations behind hunting: the need to eat, earning an income and the pursuit of leisure. Hunting for food was essential for European explorers, surveyors and some settlers. While not always vital to survival, hunting for the pot was seen by some as a measure of economy, and reduced the monotony of the colonial diet. For a variety of reasons the provisioning ethic outlasted the rise of plentiful supplies of farmed meat.

Hunting also provided thousands of New Zealanders with an income in a wide variety of ways. Private individuals hunted for bounties, skins, pelts and meat. From the 1930s, government shooters earned their wages in the bush in the service of the Deer Control Section of the Department of Internal Affairs, then the Forest Service, and finally the Department of Conservation. Supporting these professional hunters and creating the demand for their work were a diverse range of people, from gunsmiths, colonial museum administrators, furriers and taxidermists to game meat processors and Chinese merchants exporting deer velvet and tails for traditional medicines. As the fur industry lost favour with international consumers in the 1960s, the game meat export industry took off. Commercial meat-recovery operations employed shooters, pilots and butchers, peaking in a decade of frenzied activity. For the first time in hunters' lives, venison was too valuable to be eaten in their own homes.

Chapter 4 draws out the more recreational aspects of hunting in New Zealand, although it is a somewhat false distinction in that it is very difficult to separate hunters' motivations. This chapter looks at the creation of New Zealand as 'the sportsman's paradise' through government encouragement of deer- and wapiti-stalking as tourist attractions. It also discusses examples of local trophy hunters, and some who travelled overseas for shooting holidays or safaris. While New Zealand has a tradition of democratic hunting, aristocratic hunting was alive and well here also. This chapter also looks at the range of recreational activities that surround hunting, particularly tramping, photography and writing and reading about hunting.

Chapter 5 returns to the physical environment and ideas about it. In order to further understanding of the natural world, nineteenth-century naturalists used hunting to collect specimens. The shift to more modern ideas of ecology and the conservation of species in their habitats (rather than preservation in museums) saw, in New Zealand, an intensification of the need for hunters and hunting — the complete opposite to what happened in most other parts of the world. In New Zealand, the primary objects of conservation fervour were indigenous birds and plants, and introduced bush-browsers had to go. It was not these ideas of conserving indigenous species that really shifted government opinion, however. In fact it was the erroneous assumption that browsing mammals reduced land-stabilising vegetative cover, and so accelerated erosion. Whatever the motivation, decades of government-sponsored hunting ensued.

This book is by no means a comprehensive history of hunting. There will be parts of the hunting experience that some readers will feel I have skimmed over or not given due prominence to. Some legends have been ignored, some 'big names' perhaps do not appear. What this book demonstrates is what a historian sees when she looks beyond the 'good keen men' of hunting, beyond the current ambivalence about firearms and before recent notions of conservation. It is a broad-brush overview, and there are many leads that I hope others will be encouraged to pursue.

New Zealanders like to think of themselves as a nation of 'can-do' people. The national legend is populated by physically capable, self-reliant men and women. That legend used to be based on pioneers and farmers, and has now come to encompass our identity as outdoor adventurers and conservationists. Hunters belong in this national story as well.

Hunting was essential to successful colonisation. It touched the core need to eat and the human desire to share meals. It served as a form of community building, of family cohesion; it involved inter-generational knowledge being handed down. Cutting across racial and class differences, hunting tells us about different groups and their perspectives on the natural world. Hunting makes explicit a range of attitudes towards nature and assumptions about how it works as well as being essential to the development of scientific knowledge about the natural world. It has also been a significant way that New Zealanders have experienced, closely observed and understood the bush. Hunting ties New Zealand to the world, yet the particular shape of hunting here makes it remarkably distinctive. If there is a 'national culture' in New Zealand, then hunting and hunters are at its core.

# 1

# Swarming with game

Early travellers to New Zealand arrived armed with rumours and imaginings, hopes and dreams. The Pacific was already formed in their minds by their expectations and culture, and they set about making familiar what was alien. When early visitors such as whalers and seafarers looked at the southern oceans and forests they saw a limitless bounty of oil, skins and timber. Wealthy settlers and visitors, such as Charles Hursthouse, who came to New Zealand in the 1850s, saw the land as a vast estate-in-waiting, a place to be owned, developed and improved. Hursthouse also declared that the country 'should swarm with game', an attitude taken up with practical fervour by acclimatisation societies from the 1860s. Formed by professionals and upper-middle-class landowners, acclimatisation societies wanted to improve the colony by introducing animals and plants beneficial for trade and industry, but also for hunting. As well as increasing sources of food, the societies wanted to increase opportunities for gentlemen's sport, and so improve the character of the population.

Other settlers, of lower standing, were quite happy with the bush as it was, with its native birds and wild pigs which had been introduced from the 1760s and had become widespread. Working-class settlers saw in New Zealand a chance to escape deprivation and class-based inequalities. To them, New Zealand was a common, an idea with powerful intellectual and cultural roots. Many immigrants wrote back to family and friends celebrating their freedom to hunt and fish, unrestricted by Britain's centuries-old game laws designed to exclude all but the aristocracy.

But the New Zealand environment was not an estate or a common, and its resources were not limitless. An intellectual environment favourable towards

32 Hunting

hunting led to the introduction of a variety of exotic animals by private individuals, acclimatisation societies and the government. It also fostered a legal framework that governed access to both exotic and native game.

This management of access to native game had far-reaching implications for Maori. From the introduction in the 1860s of such laws, Maori access to native game was restricted, at least on paper. The laws developed to protect kereru, for example, illustrate many of the tensions. In the later nineteenth century, Maori found themselves battling both sportsmen who wanted to hunt kereru and conservationists who wanted to protect them. During the first two decades of the twentieth century Maori access to kereru was completely eroded, and by 1922 it was illegal for either Maori or pakeha to kill the birds. This process of protecting birds through laws illuminated broader changes taking place in the nineteenth and twentieth centuries, for example in attitudes to environmental change, Treaty rights and indigenous rights more generally, including pushes for Maori to modernise and cease relying on wild food sources.

While the intellectual and legal environment in New Zealand in the nineteenth century encouraged certain types of hunting, then regulated that activity, the introduction of animals for hunting (as well as for the fur industry, in the case of possums) had significant consequences for the physical environment. The precise changes to New Zealand's bush and alpine environments are hard to establish, but by the 1920s the remnants left after widespread destruction of native forests for agriculture and forestry were under serious threat by introduced browsing mammals.

## Nothing to shoot?

Nineteenth-century New Zealand was part of a hunting empire. Hunting was a prominent theme in British art and literature. It also influenced land use, architecture and interior design. Queen Victoria and the Prince Consort stalked stags in the Scottish highlands; their favourite artist was Sir Edwin Landseer, who painted various 'aristocratic' animals, from deer, dogs and horses to polar bears and tigers.

Opposite: Wairarapa hunter Neville Spooner's 1936 sketch of 'The Monarch of the Glen', after Edwin Landseer. Landseer(1802–73) was the son of an artisan but his talent for drawing and painting animals gave him entrée into aristocratic circles. He met Queen Victoria in 1837 and secured his position in her court by making a sketch of her favourite dog. He was the royals' favourite artist, spending every autumn in the Scottish Highlands from which he drew a great deal of inspiration. He produced his most famous painting, *The Monarch of the Glen*, in 1851.

### The empire of New Zealand

The empire of hunting was alive and well in New Zealand in the nineteenth century. Canterbury runholder Lady Mary-Anne Barker (whose husband had been friends with John Everett Millais, the painter and big-game hunting grandfather of early New Zealand conservationist Perrine Moncrieff) found similarities between New Zealand expeditions and those mounted in South Africa during her year living in Natal in the 1870s. One of Lady Barker's neighbours in New Zealand was James Dupré Lance, who first came to New Zealand on health leave from the British Army after service in Tibet, then was recalled to active service during the Indian Mutiny of 1857. He returned to New Zealand, with a new bride, in 1859 and bought the Four Peaks station in Canterbury, where he liberated pheasants.[1]

In his reminiscences of growing up in Nelson in the early twentieth century, Newton McConochie wrote that when he was nine years old, he and his brother were looking for ways to hunt pigs without a rifle. The solution came from South Africa.

'In 1900 a man came to our place who had just returned from the war in South Africa. He had with him an assegai such as are used by the African Zulu. Seeing this weapon provided the inspiration that was needed. Why not get our old trustworthy friend the blacksmith to make a spearhead that could easily be fitted to a wooden shaft, so readily attainable from the young growth of the forest.' The blacksmith did indeed make a spearhead for them: it was 3 inches (75mm) long with a tapered shaft 18 inches (460mm) long, with two holes in the shaft and a half-inch (12mm) lug to nail into the handle. 'Our weapon was not assembled until the first pig was bailed, and of course it was hidden again before we returned to the house.'[2]

Wilderness, the countryside and open spaces generally came to be highly valued in the English-speaking world as the nineteenth century progressed. Cities were seen as debilitating the physical and moral health of the population, and for good reason. Many people lived and worked in overcrowded conditions in towns and cities that were poorly planned and unsanitary. Farmers and rural workers were noticeably healthier and better fed; colonials were healthier still. Being closer to nature was seen as desirable by everyone from poets to doctors. Woods, highlands and seashores were available in Britain, but genuine 'wilderness' existed only in the colonies —

India, Africa and North America — and that genuine wilderness contained large, ferocious and magnificent creatures. The aristocratic enthusiasm for hunting in these places developed to such an extent during the 1900s that it became a 'hunting cult'.[3] In Britain, this fervour for hunting was far-reaching enough to influence land use (as in the case of creating deer forests or moors for grouse) as well as interior design, art and architecture. Country houses were remodelled and fitted out as hunting lodges, interiors decorated with artefacts of the Empire such as spears and skins, and walls were adorned with

Above and page 36: Stories of the freedom to hunt and the abundance of game in New Zealand filled the letters of immigrants of all classes. As photographic technology developed, images became another way to communicate this good fortune. This Nelson settler is standing amidst his vegetable garden and fruit trees, with his shotgun and gundog as evidence of New Zealand's bounty. Sitting in the cart, Mr Morton had his 'catch' photographed to carry much the same message of success and good fortune. He may have shot the dozens of birds in the preceding days, but the stag's head included in this image of hunting prowess has already been mounted. To an English audience these images carried a powerful message that may have encouraged others to emigrate.

**Swarming with game 35**

prints of hunting scenes. A trade in trophy heads and 'useful' items such as elephant-foot umbrella stands developed so that the Victorian middle class could emulate the aristocracy. Popular literature and books held up hunters as lovers of travel and adventure, and as courageous explorers with unfailing bushcraft.

The benefits for mind and body of being in the outdoors were complemented by the rise of natural science. At its most extreme, this new science justified extraordinary specimen- or sport-hunting expeditions throughout the British Empire. For example, in 1909, at the very end of the heyday of specimen collecting, former United States president Theodore Roosevelt spent 11 months on safari in East Africa, during which time he killed 512 animals, including nine rare white rhino. He hunted on behalf of the Smithsonian Institute and deposited all of his specimens there. With the justification of natural science, hunting came to be seen as intellectually improving as well as healthful and manly.[4]

It is easy to underestimate the importance of big-game hunting to the

British Empire, but the trade in ivory subsidised wars of conquest and the salaries of British soldiers and colonial administrators throughout Africa, and hunting tourism was extremely important to maintaining British power in India. British aristocratic superiority was displayed during tiger hunts, and the lure of exotic game was a motivation for many British soldiers to go to India. Hunting for meat also underpinned British exploration and surveying, military campaigns, the establishment of mission stations and farms, and the building of railways in British colonies. Throughout British culture the hunting of lions, tigers and elephants was celebrated. During the mid- to late nineteenth century safaris became a staple of aristocratic tourism, and adventure stories featuring the Great White Hunter as the hero became standards of children's fiction.

New Zealand was not immune from these notions about hunting. It was in this wider context that writers like Charles Hursthouse, who declared New Zealand the 'Britain of the South', saw New Zealand as an almost empty landscape into which game animals and birds could — and should — be transplanted. Introduced game would improve not only the New Zealand landscape but the existing fauna as well, even to the extent of making it more cooperative. '[English] Wood-pigeons would find New Zealand a paradise,' Hursthouse predicted, 'and breeding with the native bird, would probably tempt this forest recluse to sun his beauty more in the open country, where men could see and shoot him'.[5] Another English visitor to New Zealand speculated that every farm-servant's 'beau ideal of a new country' was a gentleman's park to which they had access. In a society with centuries of game laws designed to keep the park — and its wildlife — safe from the riff-raff, this ideal had powerful connotations of freedom and independence. And coming from a society where all but the eldest sons of genteel families had to make their own way, the idea of an 'estate' in New Zealand was alluring for the educated classes as well.[6]

Many among those educated classes complained that there was too little to shoot in New Zealand. John Bradshaw, who published his travel book on New Zealand in 1883, found it unlikely that 'true sons of Great Britain could be found ready to dwell in a country in which there is so little to shoot, and where some half-wild pigs . . . [and] a few ducks gave the only chance of a fair day's sport'.[7] Julius von Haast, a geologist and the driving force behind the establishment of the Canterbury Museum, was also an enthusiast for the introduction of deer, tahr and chamois to New Zealand. He thought Canterbury 'eminently fitted for the maintenance of deer, and one felt almost annoyed in traversing these vast wastes to find none there'. (As his son quipped 60 years later, Haast would probably have been still more annoyed 'to find them everywhere destroying the bush'.)[8]

Acclimatisation societies, which were established on a provincial basis between the 1860s and the 1880s, saw the introduction of game as essential to creating the ideal society, and as an improvement to an otherwise dull landscape. The founders of the Nelson Acclimatisation Society (the first to introduce red deer to New Zealand) thought that New Zealand could be an improvement not only on England, but on other British hunting colonies in

Above: Working men of all generations enjoyed hunting in New Zealand. These men photographed during the interwar period were obviously revelling in the lifting of protection on deer from 1930, but 60 years earlier, working-class immigrants to New Zealand had taken as much pleasure in the freedom to hunt birds and pigs.

India and Africa. They celebrated 'the inducement offered to the sportsman who in chasing [deer], could roam about our hills and valleys without even the shadow of a fear of the presence of any dangerous animal'.[9] The improvement of the colony was uppermost in the minds of men of this class, who were convinced that 'a number of well-to-do youth' had been discouraged from visiting New Zealand because of the lack of sport. They were equally convinced that when it became known in the 'Home Country' that Nelson offered deer-stalking it would not only attract wealthy young men, but would make New Zealand 'a favourite resort for tourists'.[10]

The upper-class notion of hunting as a sport that was ennobling and character-building was strong in New Zealand and survived throughout the nineteenth century. Even in the early decades of the twentieth century, Wellington solicitor and president of the national association of acclimatisation societies Leonard Tripp recommended deer-stalking as 'a fine, healthy sport for our young men [that] should be encouraged'.[11] Commentators from Hursthouse in the 1850s through to newspaper reporters in 1914 considered hunting and bushcraft to be essential for good citizenry, and especially important for national defence. Hursthouse urged the introduction of game animals because 'good shots are made by good shooting' and cited America as having 'the raw material for the finest soldiers in the world mainly because her abundance of game makes every tenth man a crack rifle shot'.[12] Robert Baden-Powell, in his 1908 *Scouting for Boys*, declared that the 'whole sport of hunting animals lies in the woodcraft of stalking them' and saw it as essential that boys learn to live in the open, including knowing how to kill, cut up and cook their food.[13] Good hunters made good citizens and good soldiers.

The view among the elite that New Zealand was somehow deficient because of the absence of deer and other game animals was not borne out by letters from young men to their friends and families. Young men of all ranks, but especially the lower classes, revelled in the opportunities to hunt not only unmolested by gamekeepers and police, but with the active encouragement of landowners. John Deans, of the wealthy pioneering Canterbury family, wrote home to his father in 1842, remarking in passing that 'there are a good many wild ducks among the swamps here'.[14] But to his contemporary and friend, Gavin Brackenridge, young Deans enthused about the hunting in New Zealand:

> We can have splendid shooting although there is no grouse, hares nor partridges there are as fine wild ducks as I ever saw in Scotland. They are very plentiful . . . There

*is also a large sort called Paradise ducks, but they are not so fine eating as the common sort. There are lots of quail in the Middle Island [South Island]. In the woodlots we have pigeons very like Cushats at home, but not so wild. If you come upon a dozen or two sitting on a tree you may shoot them all, one after another, as the shot does not put them away unless they are wounded . . . But what you would count as the best sport of any is wild pig hunting. There are thousands of them within twenty miles of [my brother] William's house. He has the best dog I ever saw . . . I believe he has killed some hundreds of them . . .* [15]

Deans ended his letter as many immigrants did, urging his friend to join him. 'When all things fail at home Gavin, come out to New Zealand. You can live as happy and comfortable here as anywhere in the world'.[16]

Immigrants of the labouring and working classes especially found much to please them in New Zealand. They were not at all worried by the absence of aristocratic game. It has been argued that punitive game laws were a 'push factor', encouraging lower-class families to immigrate to New Zealand. 'Hunting and shooting [in England] were class sports which became more and more fashionable throughout the [nineteenth] century. While the villagers craved for meat, they saw the wild creatures about them protected by the Game Laws to provide sport for their "betters".'[17] Punitive game laws had been in force in England from the 1670s, restricting hunting to those with substantial incomes, large land-holdings or other hunting resources. The British countryside was a place of great social antagonism and unrest because 'commoners relished hunting, coursing, and fishing as much as their social superiors and resented any attempt to restrict these pursuits to the gentry'.[18] The persistence of poaching in England and Scotland, even in the face of terrible punishments, is evidence of the widespread resistance to these restrictions.

It is not surprising then, that working-class immigrants' letters home from New Zealand enthused about the opportunities for hunting. George Goodwin, who emigrated to Dunedin in the early 1870s, wrote to his siblings, 'the policemen [don't] stop you when coming into town if your pockets are a bit bulky or you have a bag on your back. . . . You may shoot plenty of rabbits here'. Emigrant Thomas Green took a bush job near Picton and wrote home in July 1874, 'Don't be afraid of the seas, my fellow working men . . . I must tell you that I brought a good double-barrel gun with me, and am not afraid to use it in this country. I can go out and shoot pigs, and all kinds of wild fowls . . .' Many urged their families and friends to join them, saying, 'George . . .

Top: New Zealand's acclimatisation societies were formed in the 1850s, soon after those in London and Paris. The societies formed a worldwide network that was responsible for enormous movements of plants and animals. These wagons transported red deer shipped from Warnham Court in Sussex onto the Mount White Station in Canterbury to form the basis of the Poulter River herd.

Above: Accustomed to human company after the long voyage from England, deer were sometimes reluctant to embrace their freedom. This fallow hind was photographed in Wanganui in the 1860s.

**Swarming with game**

Get the horse whip at my brother Thomas's and drive him with you to Mr Simmons at once. This place would just suit him for there are thousands of rabbits here and wild ducks, and swamp turkeys [pukeko], and the farmers are pleased to see anyone shoot them — any amount of rabbits'. Richard Harwood, a 21-year-old gardener working near Foxton, wrote to his father and brother in this same period emphasising his living conditions, telling them he was 'revelling in shooting pigs, pigeons and ducks, and fishing for eels, the latter under Maori tuition'. Even Joseph Arch, the president of the National Agricultural Labourers' Union in England, when farewelling immigrants in December 1873, 'exulted in the plenitude of wild pigs, cattle, goats, rabbits, pigeons and ducks in New Zealand'.[19] Indeed, in Wellington in the 1840s and '50s, 'fishing, swimming and boating were freely indulged in and for those who liked shooting, there were plenty of native pigeons in the bush and also a fair number of wild pigs . . . This was a good way of adding to the family larder'.[20] Thomson W Leys also made a point of hunting opportunities in his *Brett's Colonists' Guide* of 1883:

> Hunting the wild boar was a favourite pursuit of kings and nobles in Britain, France, Germany and other countries, in ages gone by. In New Zealand, these animals running wild in the bush, descendants of those introduced in the early days, have afforded some exciting sport to the settlers, the dangers encountered in some instances being as great as those read of in medieval times, but without their accessories of pomp and grandeur, unless we consider those supplied by Nature in the beautiful scenery of the forest primeval.[21]

It is clear from the parliamentary debates in 1861, when the first New Zealand legislation was proposed to protect game, that maintaining this freedom to hunt was a deliberate policy here. In 1846, customs legislation had removed duty from the importation of all live animals to facilitate the movement of livestock, but also to encourage the introduction of exotic species. Parliament's concern in the 1860s was that introduced game birds in particular were being hunted throughout the year and not being given a chance to nest and breed freely. The stock of game birds was not increasing and so a proposal came before Parliament to protect birds and animals during the breeding season. All the MPs were at pains to point out that these were not 'game laws'. William Fox said he 'would be sorry' to see game laws introduced which gave some classes hunting privileges over others. William Colenso 'hoped the game-laws would never be introduced in New Zealand' and Edward Stafford, the Colonial Secretary, 'agreed with honourable gentlemen that it was not right to enact game-laws [such as existed in Britain] for New Zealand . . . but this measure has nothing in common with them'. The aim was simply to protect the animals so they had a chance to multiply for the benefit of all.[22] This was, however, the beginning of tightening access to game and never again would Maori or colonists have such freedom to hunt as they had enjoyed in those early years.

## The mania for acclimatisation

If Hursthouse and his peers were the 'ideas men', acclimatisation societies handled the production side of things. The societies were the main, though certainly not the only, drivers of the deliberate introduction of exotic species to New Zealand. Their various motivations centred on the introduction of 'beneficial' flora and fauna — an idea that covered many notions. The founders of the Otago Acclimatisation Society, for example, outlined their aims in terms that Paul Star describes as 'sentiment combined with utility'. After the introduction of game species, fur species and beneficial birds, 'the sportsman and lover of nature might then enjoy the same sports and studies that made the remembrance of their former homes so dear . . . [The country would be] rendered more enjoyable, tables will be better supplied, and new industries fostered'.[23]

The introduction of birds was usually the first order of the day. Birds survived the journey from England more readily than game animals, and most were first introduced by the end of the 1860s. Songbirds such as blackbirds and thrushes were introduced by both individual immigrants and acclimatisation societies for sentimental reasons as well as for their role in controlling insect pests, and game birds such as pheasants and quail were introduced for sport as soon as the societies were formed. Not all the introductions were successful, and even pheasants had a patchy history. For some years after their introduction into various regions their population increased rapidly, but then declined for the same reasons as those of native birds: the introduction of mustelids (stoats, ferrets and weasels) from the mid-1880s and the loss of habitat through forest and scrub fires. Bruce Ferguson, who was born at Pakawau in the Nelson region in 1917, recounted that when his father was a boy 'there were pheasants digging up and down the potato rows', but by the time Bruce himself was old enough to shoot birds, they had completely disappeared from the area, so he shot ducks and godwits.[24] Various acclimatisation societies around the country continued periodic releases of pheasants until the 1960s and 1970s, by which time they were regarded as no longer 'worth pursuing as a game bird'.[25]

Quail, particularly California quail, on the other hand, were marvellously successful. Shooting seasons on quail began in the late 1860s and their numbers increased sufficiently to enable the Nelson Acclimatisation Society to supply live birds to Australian colonies, and for New Zealand to export frozen and canned quail to Britain. In the 1890s tens of thousands of tinned quail were sent to London. The successful acclimatisation of these birds is reflected in records kept by bird hunters. A Nelson sportsman, George Elliott, shot 28,666 quail in a 70-year shooting career starting in 1900, including annual totals of 1077 in 1915, 1118 in 1935 and a daily record of 95 birds in 1915.[26]

Mallard ducks were late starters. Introduced in fits and starts from the late 1860s by both acclimatisation societies and private individuals, many flocks did poorly in the wild. Because they were not vigorous, they were not specifically hunted for most of the nineteenth century. More concerted efforts to establish mallards began in the 1890s, but mallards were not included on shooting licences until 1931, and the development of sizeable mallard populations occurred only with the importation of American mallards in 1937. These birds adapted quickly and began to interbreed with the native grey duck, and are now the most abundant wetland bird in New Zealand.[27]

The introduction of red deer began in the 1860s and continued into the early years of the twentieth century. The first introductions were fine animals from the elite herds of England and Scotland. Introducing deer was a piecemeal and risky affair. The journey was long and, if animals did arrive safely and in good health, their success in New Zealand was far from certain. Overall, there were at least 220 separate liberations of deer, each involving just three or four animals.[28] Once established, however, deer were phenomenally successful in New Zealand and, as we shall see, mobs of hundreds of them became common by the 1920s. Seven other species of deer were also introduced into New Zealand from Asia, Europe and the United States; all but one was successful, but none reached the population levels of red deer.

Acclimatisation societies introduced deer mainly for 'sport' hunting and tourism, and for the character-building effects of hunting on the colonial population. Hundreds of years of British tradition had instilled in colonists the notion that deer-stalking was ennobling, and that the colony would prosper

Opposite: California quail were the most successful of the game birds introduced in the nineteenth century. New Zealand native quail became extinct soon after European settlement through loss of habitat, predation by rats, cats and dogs, and hunting.

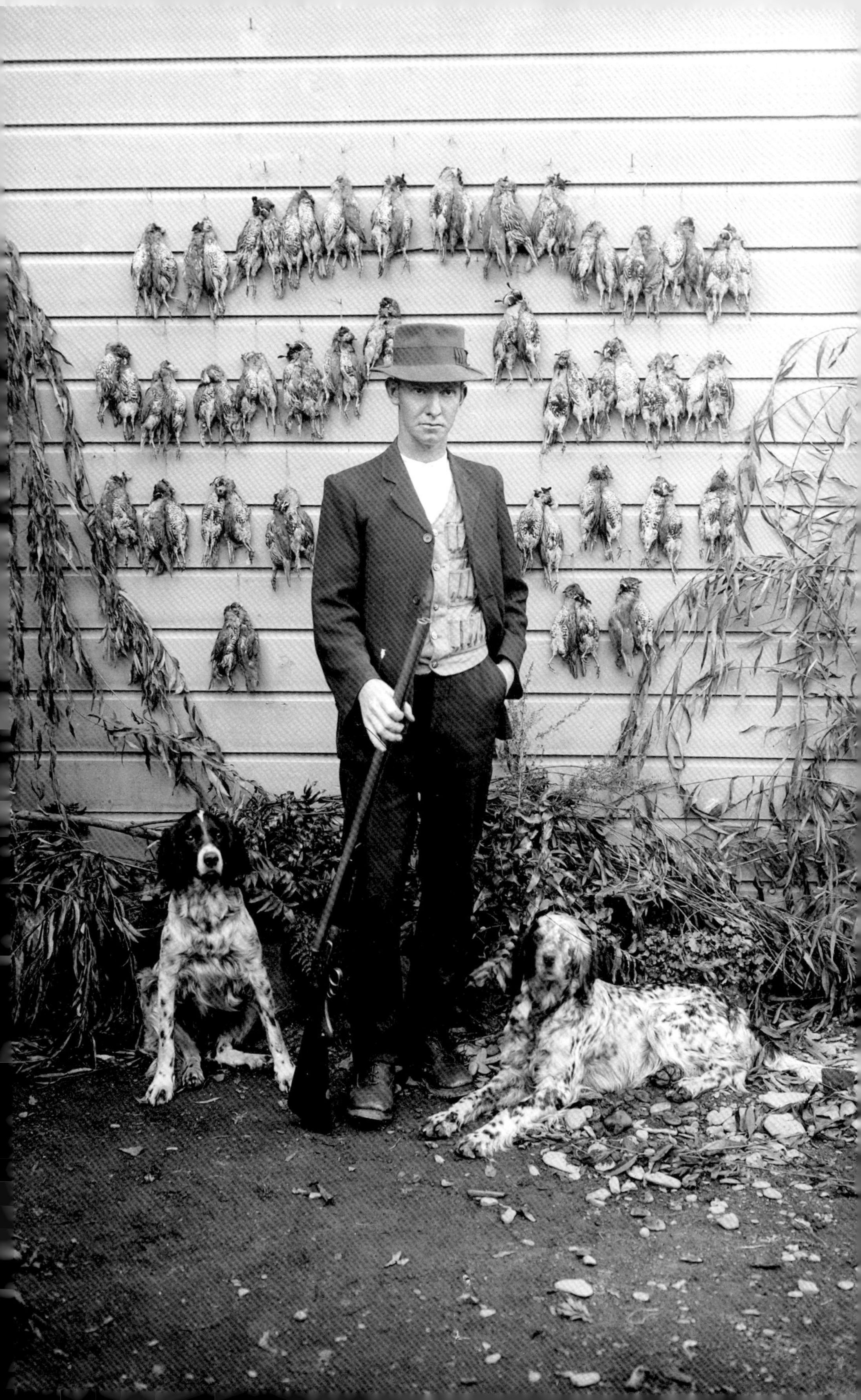

through the introduction of deer-stalking. Charles Hursthouse made what is now a well-known remark, writing that the young man of the colony should rather take his recreation 'in rural sports, "chasing the red deer and following the roe", than he should relax himself in city dissipations and the laps of ballet girls'. Hursthouse went further, too. It was not just the nerves of young men that concerned him, but the very character of the colony. 'We don't go to New Zealand, as we do to Victoria [Australia],' he noted,

> with pick and pan, to dig for dear-won nuggets, to gulp gallons of rum, and then, rich or ragged, hurry home. We go to the Britain of the South to create an estate — to raise a home wherein to anchor fast and plant our household gods; and all we do to make this home a glad and happy home tends to increase both our profits and our pleasures.[29]

Here then was not a vision of the bachelor sportsman's paradise, but a vision of homes, 'estates', complete with wife and children and 'household gods'. The introduction of game animals and birds was integral to this vision.

There were those who saw in hunting the means to improve the moral character of the country — the creation of such homes and estates would 'improve' New Zealand. And there were those who, for political reasons, depicted the New Zealand bush as a wasteland in need of improvement. In his report for the Waitangi Tribunal, Brad Coombes has argued that 'Urewera country was depicted arbitrarily as untouched wilderness . . . [and] as an inviolable wilderness'.[30] This depiction made it easier to introduce exotic species to forests and to deceive the local Tuhoe population about the purpose of various liberations. Maori Member of Parliament James Carroll, for example, led Tuhoe to believe that exotic game animals would be available for them to hunt, thereby alleviating their food shortages in the early 1890s, but this was not the case because the game was protected. A Forest Service report of 1965 demonstrated the range of species introduced to the Ureweras in the nineteenth century, including 'rats, weasels, polecats [ferrets], mice, feral cattle, feral pigs, feral goats, feral sheep, opposums [sic], red deer, javan rusa deer, sambar deer and Japanese [sika] deer'.[31]

The desire to improve the character of the country was linked to romantic ideals of the countryside, which was especially important where that countryside had been the site of wars, as in some parts of the North Island. Coombes suggests that acclimatisation was, in fact, an 'antidote to colonial history'.[32] For example, a reporter on the *Bay of Plenty Times* extolled the virtues of the peaceful, English-style environment created by the introduction of the game birds by Tauranga Acclimatisation Society in an area marred by war in the early 1860s:

> Neat verandah cottages and bright gardens surrounded by plantations of trees in a few years only assume giant proportions in this climate; and every now and then the pheasant whirring out from the hedges or the quail running under the roadside weeds, and the lark carolling away everywhere, give an air of civilisation and Old Country reminiscences to the scene. And all this peace and gentle comfort and plenty for man and beast beautifies the ground that was dangerous and hideous and blood-stained only a few years ago![33]

Acclimatisation, while a powerful force in colonial New Zealand, was not entirely unopposed. By the 1870s there was already considerable opposition from segments of the British scientific community to the introduction of exotic species to New Zealand because of the impact it was having on native birds. In the scientific journal *Nature*, acclimatisation was described in 1872 as a 'silly mania' which had introduced animals and birds 'of extremely doubtful advantage' which were 'in a few years . . . found, not only to be ousting the kinds which are less specialised, and therefore less able to meet them on an equal footing, but unaccompanied by any of those checks, which keep the whole of natural fauna balanced'. It concluded that 'the importations will inevitably become the greatest of nuisances'. A letter from 'Pakeha' in the English magazine *The Field* expressed similar sentiments: 'Well may the local naturalist exclaim, "Who will save our indigenous birds!" But the rage for acclimatising . . . will go on with unabated zeal so long as Englishmen have a voice in the matter.'[34]

Not all exotic species were introduced by acclimatisation societies. Captain James Cook is credited as beginning the acclimatisation of European species in New Zealand when he and his crews released animals intended as food sources for later expeditions. The crew of the *Resolution*, anchored for six weeks in Dusky Sound in Fiordland in 1773, not only ate their way through thousands of birds, but also liberated five geese from the Cape of Good Hope.[35] The crew of the *Adventure*, anchored in Queen Charlotte Sound, liberated chickens, goats and pigs. Pigs were also released at Cape Kidnappers on the east coast of the North Island. Whalers, too, while they came to New Zealand to hunt in the sea, introduced food plants and animals to the land. Pigs, cattle and goats were all brought to New Zealand for purposes other than sport, chiefly as food for later visitors and shipwrecked sailors. There are many reports of liberations of pigs by sailors, whalers, missionaries, miners and settlers.

Pigs spread both through natural increase and Maori breeding and trading of them. By the 1820s they were plentiful even in the remote Ureweras, and by the 1840s many visitors described various disparate parts of New Zealand as 'thick with pigs'.[36]

Overall numbers of feral pigs are very difficult to gauge, but they were the most numerous wild mammal in New Zealand for most of the nineteenth century. Some historical records give a sense of the density of the pig population. An early settler in the Otago region, Robert Gillies, wrote that in 1848 wild pigs were 'very common' in the Dunedin area. In 1854 he and a group of friends killed 70 pigs in two days near Flagstaff Hill. Gillies noted that 'the long, pointed snout, long legs and nondescript colours of the true wild pigs showed them to be quite a different breed from the settlers' imported pigs. Their flesh tasted quite different from [domestic] pork, being more like venison than anything else'.[37] On the high-country South Island runs owned by Charles Tripp and John Acland — although over what part of their 46,500 hectares is not recorded — 1000 pigs were killed each year between 1856 and 1861. In the 1860s in the Nelson region, 25,000 pigs were killed in two years on an area of 400 hectares.[38] Pigs were so numerous on the Mount Peel station in Canterbury in the mid-nineteenth century that they were shot by the dray-load.

> *Wherever the Spaniard [plant] was plentiful, there were always numbers of wild pigs ... When we went pig-hunting, we had nothing as a rule but a dog or two. We fixed shear-blades on the end of rickers [saplings] from eight to ten feet long, then when the dogs baled [sic] up the pigs, we speared them, took out their insides, and carted the pigs home in a bullock dray. On arriving home we skinned the pigs and salted them down. The places where the largest number of pigs were was in the swamps at Longbeach, Coldstream, Mt Peel, Anama and Pudding Hill. It was easy, if one had a couple of good dogs, to kill as many pigs as would load a bullock dray in a day.*[39]

The damage pigs caused was also recorded. While travelling through the Nelson Province in 1860, Dr Ferdinand von Hochstetter 'saw several miles ploughed by pigs'.[40] Travellers through the South Island high country commented on the 'honeycombing' of pasture and the killing of lambs by pigs. Station workers and musterers were expected to carry rifles and many station owners provided their workers with ammunition.[41] Settlers built walls around houses and gardens to keep pigs out. George Baker's grandfather built his house in Kaiapoi in 1856, complete with a 'four foot thick sod wall as protection against wild pigs which, at the time, proved quite a menace'.[42]

Pig populations were encouraged by the farming methods of the day. The practice of sowing cleared land with turnips, grass, mustard and cress to break up the soil and provide fodder for cattle and sheep created a magnet for pigs. While not usually thought of as predators, pigs are, however, omnivores — they eat almost anything — and they are opportunists. While it is impossible to measure the damage they caused to populations of native invertebrates and birds, it is safe to assume that they would 'certainly never pass up the opportunity to crunch up a nest full of eggs or a large native snail'.[43]

> *Pigs were integrated into Maori culture and traditions and became an important currency of trade. In some areas pigs were regarded as 'belonging' to Maori, and William Cullen wrote home from Nelson to his family in 1842 that while the settlers could catch their own fish and eels, and shoot 'weka, kereru, kaka and kakapo . . . Wild pigs were very numerous but were explicitly claimed as property by Maori'.[44] In other areas however, pigs were hunted freely by pakeha.*

Above: Hunting is depicted in many early sketches and paintings of New Zealand. Artists travelling with explorers and surveyors used hunting scenes to enliven their landscapes. People in the foreground shooting birds or pursuing game made alien landscapes seem familiar to European viewers, and gave a park-like character to what was being depicted. This view of Wairoa Creek painted in 1862 was inscribed 'Pheasant shooting on the estate of Alexander Kennedy Esquire'.

Goats, like pigs, were introduced to New Zealand by seafarers, including Cook, as food for sailors to come. Later in the nineteenth century, angora goats were imported for their fibre and for their usefulness in controlling blackberry. Feral goats were very often hunted simply because they were so prolific. Benign conditions in New Zealand meant that goats could breed almost continuously throughout the year, and twinning was common, so their rate of increase was (and still is) exponential. Over a million goats were shot in government control operations between 1931 and 1970.[45]

Cattle were also introduced as domestic livestock, but many became feral and were hunted. Records of their introduction to the colony are difficult to find, but the first cattle beasts were brought by whalers and missionaries. By 1839 there were herds of wild cattle on the fringes of settlements: Edward Jerningham Wakefield saw wild cattle on the hills at Pelorus Sound; in 1840 wild cattle were reported as being 'abundant' on Kapiti Island; and early Canterbury settlers were troubled by wild herds.[46] These animals were described as 'shy and wild, scudding off like buffaloes, and dangerous to approach when wounded'.[47] James Ashworth, who worked on a Canterbury station as a boy in the 1860s, described how the presence of wild cattle made any trip eventful:

> Frequently I used to go from Purau over to Kaituna for cattle . . . We used to get a good many scares through wild cattle and from large wild pigs charging across the track. The bush and undergrowth were so thick and tall that it joined overhead all the way, and when one heard wild cattle crashing about and could not see where they were going to, one was apt to take a real interest in the proceedings.[48]

The feral cattle population was reinforced by the practice of releasing cattle to graze in the bush for the winter. Chris Maclean writes of the Tararua Ranges that as a result of this grazing technique, 'the hills soon became infested with wild cattle . . . [and] it was not until the 1930s that wild cattle were finally exterminated'.[49] The names of Cow Saddle and Cattle Ridge recall the presence of feral cattle in the Tararua Ranges, long after their eradication in the 1930s.

Of the species deliberately introduced to New Zealand as game animals, deer were the most important. They were associated with nobility, royalty and aristocracy, both literally and figuratively. The red deer imported into New Zealand came from the elite game parks of England and Scotland, including the royal herd at Windsor Great Park. Introductions began privately in the 1850s, then by acclimatisation societies through the remainder of the nineteenth century. The Department of Tourist and Health Resorts was responsible for liberations in the early twentieth century, including those on Stewart Island and in Tongariro National Park and Fiordland. Apart from the very early transportation and liberations, which were dogged by animal deaths, deer were a wildfire success in New Zealand. Precise data on the early increase of the species is limited but biologists describe a general population pattern for browsing mammals in New Zealand: Northern hemisphere winters are characterised by a shortage of feed for browsing mammals, but in New Zealand the dominance of evergreens and the relatively mild climate mean that population numbers can increase steadily with no marked slow-down or decline in the winter. Left unchecked, herds can increase for up to 30 years from the time of their release. By the time their populations peak, they are eating their least preferred vegetation. From there, condition is lost and so

Opposite: Rolled penguin skins collected for trade by early sealers are a reminder of the hunting that first brought traders to New Zealand waters. These skins, probably harvested during the eighteenth or early nineteenth century but never collected, were photographed on the Antipodes Islands in 2004.

52 Hunting

their numbers begin to decline over a five- to 10-year period until populations reach a balance with the feed available. Rates of increase among deer were also described in State Forest Service reports in the 1920s and 1930s, in which the annual rate of increase of deer herds was estimated to be 25 per cent.[50]

Between 1850 and the early 1900s there were more than 200 separate liberations of a handful of deer each. Assuming adequate feed and favourable climate conditions, it would take only 15 years for a small release of four deer to become a herd of more than 100 animals, and only another five years for that herd to number over 300. Red deer ranged very widely, and by the 1920s the many small herds had coalesced into larger groups, adapting to the different feed offered by sub-alpine and alpine environments. The grasslands created for farming were also conducive to a healthy deer population and in the spring and summer months provided grass feed on the edges of the forest.

Tahr and chamois were both introduced by the Department of Tourist and Health Resorts in the early 1900s, also for sport. Julius von Haast had agitated for the introduction of these alpine ungulates in the 1880s, envisaging 'shy animals keeping to the mountain-heights, hard to stalk and affording sport to the hardy mountaineer'. Six tahr were released at Mount Cook's Hermitage in 1904, followed by another three in 1913. Eight chamois, a gift from Austrian emperor Franz Josef, were also introduced to the region in 1907 and another pair in 1913. In the early 1920s guides at Mount Cook estimated there were 100 chamois and by 1940 their range extended north through the alps to the Nelson Lakes area.[51] Like deer, the breeding of tahr and chamois was boosted by evergreen vegetation, and while they are not prolific breeders like goats, their rate of increase was nonetheless probably faster than in their natural

Opposite top: Austrian Emperor Franz Josef, pictured here in his hunting garb, made a gift of chamois to New Zealand in 1907. Released in the Mount Cook area, the chamois were exchanged for several kiwi and tuatara, which failed to thrive in Vienna while the chamois adapted well to New Zealand.
Opposite lower: Only nine Himalayan tahr were released in the Mount Cook region at the turn of the twentieth century. They thrived in the mild winters, with constant feed and no predators. Because botanical knowledge of alpine plants was very limited in the nineteenth century it is difficult to know exactly how plant communities were changed through their introduction, but as with bush habitats, it is safe to assume that the balance of palatable and unpalatable species was altered significantly.

## Trophies inside

*The nineteenth-century fashion for decorating interiors with trophy heads was part of the aristocratic hunting cult, an attempt to invoke the grandeur of the Middle Ages. British architects designed great stairwells, billiard rooms and smoking rooms in the style of the medieval hall, and New Zealand architecture reflected this trend. Trophy heads adorned these spaces. Stag heads were most common, but in an age where most aristocratic British families had sons serving in India and Africa, elephant tusks, horns of all sorts and the skins of big cats complemented the domestic trophies. By the end of the 1800s, hunting tourism reinforced the idea that trophies reflected the spread of the empire. The trade in trophy heads meant that British middle-class householders could, without hunting themselves, have a stag's head hanging in the entranceway of their homes.*

*In New Zealand, however, middle- and working-class homes were adorned by trophies hunted, not bought. Stuffed birds in glass cases were also very popular*

Above and opposite: From the modest to the elaborate, trophy heads and skins were used to decorate all sorts of rooms in late nineteenth and twentieth century New Zealand.

during this period, but have not survived in such numbers. Through their own efforts, even farmers' sons such as Manawatu lad William Dawbin could have trophies decorating his bedroom; in Dawbin's case a display containing a huia he had shot, a kingfisher, a banded rail and a tui.[52]

When high-country runholder Lady Mary-Anne Barker described her own home in a letter to her sister, the hunting equipment used as decoration reflected the imperial world in which she lived. She noted, 'the prints you know so well [hang] on the walls, and a trophy of Indian swords and hunting spears over the fireplace.' Commenting on the drawings on the walls of a shepherd's hut on her station, she wrote, 'This man is quite an artist and the walls of his hut were covered with bold pen and ink sketches chiefly of reminiscences of the hunting-field in England, or his own adventures "getting out" wild cattle on the Black Hills.' At another 'charming little station' in the district, 'the only thing to remind me that I was not in an English cottage was the opossum rug with which the neat little bed was covered'.[53]

**Swarming with game** 55

habitat. Reports from government shooters in the 1940s and 1950s recorded large, healthy mobs of tahr and chamois in the Southern Alps.

## Native game

The introduction of these kinds of exotic game animals and birds led to the creation of a frequently changing legal framework to manage and protect them, with acclimatisation societies setting the rules and regulations around seasons, bag limits and the issuing of licences. Deer, tahr and chamois were all protected as game animals, as were possums, because of their valuable fur. But what of game already here? 'Native game' — that is, native birds — had an uncertain legal status and the need to manage native bird populations as 'game' brought local acclimatisation societies and the government into conflict with Maori.

As in other settler nations in the British Empire — Canada, Australia and South Africa — as well as in America, the new laws and policies surrounding game affected indigenous people, usually detrimentally. Maori were no exception. Along with other native species, kereru, the native wood pigeon, was included in game laws from 1864, with a season set down as April to July. This was the first law to potentially affect Maori access to kereru, although the impact of the designation of a season on the bird's population in these early years is not known. There were recorded complaints of hunters taking

Above: One of the most famous topographical paintings of New Zealand, Thomas Allom's depiction of Palliser Bay, was based on sketches by Surveyor General Samuel Brees. Pig-hunting was an activity often depicted in Brees's drawings, and this lively example appeared in Edward Jerningham Wakefield's *Adventure in New Zealand* in 1845.

kereru 'out of season' over the decades to 1922, when seasons were abolished and the bird became entirely protected. Records of prosecutions, however, suggest that pakeha were as likely as Maori to do this. These complaints reveal a resentment of poachers by pakeha 'sportsmen', a self-assuredness on the part of Maori that the Treaty of Waitangi guaranteed their rights to pigeons, and a sense of just how difficult it was to enforce the laws over large areas of bush.

Tension between hunting for food and for sport was a constant source of conflict between pakeha — as represented by the acclimatisation societies — and Maori. Kereru were a major food source for some iwi and the timing of hunts was dictated by the birds' plumpness and suitability for the pot. The birds were best to eat when they were fat after eating miro berries, usually between July and September. This kind of traditional regulation, or rahui, was explained to Parliament many times over the 50 years to 1922. The Colonial Secretary, however, was under pressure to set the seasons at a time when the kereru were more lean and swift, so as to provide the best sport for pakeha hunters, hence the season was usually set for between April and June.

The question of whether or not Maori needed a licence to hunt native birds also illuminated wider tensions about Maori rights generally. The Protection of Certain Animals Amendment Act of 1866 extended the game-licensing system to include kereru; a licence cost £5, and there was a fine of up to £20 for hunting kereru without one. This licence fee was revoked after only one year, however, when the distinction was made between introduced game — which had been brought to New Zealand at some considerable expense and was defined as the property of the acclimatisation societies — and native game, which was essentially defined as 'free'. Nonetheless, as James Feldman argues, the 1867 Act 'set an important precedent by establishing Government-granted property rights to wildlife'.[54] The government of the 1860s had designated native game, in effect, government property, which meant that Parliament, not acclimatisation societies, had control over its hunting and therefore responsibility for its protection.

There were attempts by individual acclimatisation societies to impose native game licence fees but never successfully. For example, in 1887 the Hawke's Bay Acclimatisation Society introduced a licence fee for the shooting of native game (at that time defined as including kereru and kaka but not tui, which were added to the list later). The confusion arising from the acclimatisation district boundary running through the middle of the Ureweras, the difficulty for Tuhoe Maori of acquiring a licence from Wairoa, many days' travel away, and a lack of enforcement by rangers meant Maori were probably poachers in the eyes of the acclimatisation society but were also beyond the reach of prosecution.[55]

The question of licences for Maori hunting continued to come up at acclimatisation society meetings. In July 1904 it was cause for debate at the New Zealand Acclimatisation Societies' Association meeting in Wellington. 'Eventually, the motion was amended to read: "That provisions be made for the issuing of licences to take or kill native game at a fee of five shillings each, and that Natives be exempted from the operation of this provision".'[56]

The extent of Maori hunting rights under the Treaty of Waitangi was a question the government and the judiciary never really answered, especially not to the satisfaction of the acclimatisation societies. Maori certainly asserted their rights under Article Two of the treaty, and in some cases hunting kereru was a deliberate act of anti-colonial defiance. In 1898, Hone Toia and 15 other Maori appeared in court charged after the so-called 'dog tax war' in the Hokianga. The defendants were defiant, declaring 'they would not pay the dog tax and would not stop shooting pigeons'.[57] Many pakeha assumed Maori rights to kereru were guaranteed by the treaty; in 1904, the owner of the New Criterion Hotel in Wanganui was forced to plead guilty to a charge of possessing native game more than seven days after the end of the season due to confusion over these rights:

*Defendant pleaded guilty, but stated that he knew nothing about the pigeons being there. They had been given to his son by a Maori, together with some quail and ducks, and nothing had been said to him (defendant) about them. His son reckoned the Maoris were permitted to kill whatever native game they liked. Sergeant Norwood stated that on the date in question he visited the hotel for the purpose of inspecting the premises in connection with the Licensing Committee meeting, and had found a servant cleaning*

LOOK OUT!

*the pigeons and quail. Defendant had made much the same statement to him as he had made in Court. A fine of 40s, with costs 9s, was inflicted.*[58]

Similar views were expressed in a 1908 newspaper column appealing for the protection of kereru. James Drummond wrote, 'Bird-lovers regret to know that any killing takes place, but as sentiment must give way to utility, the Maoris' rights in this direction are admitted'.[59]

The lack of clarity surrounding Maori rights frustrated acclimatisation societies. Lengthy discussions were held at a meeting of the Auckland society in 1907 about the ownership of two kerosene tins of pigeons preserved in fat, sent by train to Otorohanga:

*Constable Fraser ... met the train at Otorohanga and saw two tins, each of which contained about forty pigeons, preserved in fat. A half-caste Maori claimed the tins, and said he was going to forward them to Huntly. He also stated that the birds had been shot during last year's shooting season. He said he would admit being in possession of the pigeons, but claimed that he was entitled to have them, as it had been the custom*

Above: Pigs were hunted frequently throughout colonial New Zealand. Travellers' and settlers' sketchbooks, letters and reminiscences described pig-hunting to those at home as high adventure and as a great freedom of the new colony. This sketch appeared in *Crusts or A Settler's Fare Due South* published in 1874.

of the Maoris to take and preserve the birds so that they could have them for food at big Maori gatherings. He also stated he had two other tins of preserved birds at Piopio, near Otorohanga. A letter was read from Inspector Cullen asking whether the society desired the police to institute proceedings in the matter. He did not think a magistrate who was well versed in Maori lore would convict. The secretary (Mr. T. F. Cheeseman) said the Maori was liable to be convicted for having the birds in his possession, if the Treaty of Waitangi did not over-ride the Act. Mr. E. Anderson said it seemed according to the Treaty of Waitangi that Maoris could shoot pigeons all the year round. The question of whether the birds were shot last season or not did not come in, as in any case a person was liable under the Act for having pigeons in his possession more than seven days after the closing of the season. The question was whether Maoris could shoot at any time and preserve the birds. It was resolved that a full statement of the case, together with copies of the correspondence, be forwarded to the Colonial Secretary for his opinion.[60]

The Colonial Secretary had been asked for his opinion many times: John Solomon Pohio asked Joseph Ward for clarification in 1901 and while the Colonial Secretary's office replied that 'native game cannot be taken or killed by any person except as provided by "The Animals Protection Act 1880"', this did not constitute a definitive ruling on the status of the treaty.[61] In 1908 it was still the impression of the Bay of Plenty Member of Parliament that 'It was . . . doubtful whether Maoris could be prevented from shooting the pigeon for food, close[d] season or not, as in the Treaty of Waitangi they were guaranteed that right'.[62] Henare Kaihau, MP for Western Maori, certainly upheld that view in 1910: 'The Maori people . . . are under the impression that they still possess the right conferred by — and held by them since — the Treaty of Waitangi to kill and take for the purposes of food, native game and fish throughout the Dominion'.[63] And in 1912, in answer to the very direct question 'Have Maoris right under Treaty of Waitangi to shoot native pigeons?', Wanganui ranger Thomas James received this rather unhelpful reply from the Department of Internal Affairs: 'Question you raise re pigeons is a legal one which this Department is not prepared to answer'. James, in frustration, suspended all prosecutions of poachers, be they Maori or pakeha, because 'it is such a rotten state of affairs and manifestly unfair . . .'[64]

In many ways, the conservation movement saved the government from having to wrangle with the question of Maori rights to game under the Treaty of Waitangi. From the 1890s, clearly declining numbers of pigeons as well as pressure from conservationists led to various measures to protect them. The most common of these was a closed season sometimes combined with a ban on the sale of game. In 1896, several other species of birds were added to the native game list and hence came under government protection: korimako (bellbird), kokako, kakapo, kiwi, tieke (saddleback) and hihi (stitchbird).[65]

Maori rights to hunt native birds were caught up in other tensions between them and the government. Maori MPs continued to argue that Parliament had no rights to exclude Maori from hunting on their own lands. Hone Heke, the MP for Northern Maori, argued in 1899, 'I think the restriction imposed upon native birds ought to be removed, as far as the Natives are concerned who have Native properties belonging to themselves. It can be fairly applied to all bush country owned by the Crown.'[66] This highlighted the divisions between Maori who continued to reside on their own lands and those who did not. As Feldman has pointed out, for Maori whose lands had been confiscated by the Crown or where pre-1865 purchases had taken place, 'the policy suggested by Heke would have excluded many Maori from access to kereru. Large portions of the South Island provided one example of such a region'.[67] There were also no allowances for the fact that some iwi were more heavily reliant than others on bird harvests because they lacked access to coastal resources.

While clauses in the Animals Protection Act 1895 allowed for the granting of permission to some native districts to hunt kereru, some iwi were favoured by the government over others when it came to these privileges — and not necessarily on the grounds of need. At the beginning of the closed season of 1901, notices were printed in English and Maori, and mention was made in the *New Zealand Gazette*, the government's official newspaper, of an exemption to the closed season for Maori and 'half-caste Maori' in districts around Rotorua and Taupo. These exemptions were granted on an ad hoc basis, however. Despite an explicit request from Te Heuheu Tukino for an exemption for Ngati Tuwharetoa in the Tongariro and Matatua districts, and despite specific mention in the legislation of exemptions for Tuhoe (in the Ureweras), in none of these districts were Maori granted permission to hunt.[68]

By 1908 a further argument was being posited against Maori rights to shoot kereru: that of modernisation and progress. Harry Ell, MP for Christchurch South and a promoter of protection for native birds, argued that there was no longer any need for hunting of kereru for subsistence in New Zealand, where 'there is an abundance of food'. He was, however, swayed by arguments to the contrary on this occasion, becoming convinced that 'in certain parts of the North Island it was necessary that these birds should be killed for the food-supply of the Natives'.[69]

The Ureweras rated specific mention in the Animals Protection Act of 1895 because of negotiations for the 1896 Urewera District Native Reserve Act, which contained the double-edged provisions of securing government rights to release exotic game animals to foster tourism at Waikaremoana while also guaranteeing Tuhoe rights to 'maintain traditional use of forest and bird resources'.[70] Heke had been wary of the government's intentions towards Tuhoe during the passing of the Urewera reserve act, and had attempted, unsuccessfully, to shore up the tribe's access to natural resources with a proposed amendment: 'I would like to see added . . . rights, as conferred upon them by the Treaty of Waitangi'. He was very specific in the wording of his amendment: 'for the preserving to the Native owners the full enjoyment of their rights to the lands within the said district, and to the forests, fisheries, and other properties which they may collectively or individually possess, as provided by the second article of the Treaty of Waitangi'.[71]

The government was attempting to use hunting rights as a bargaining chip with Tuhoe. It was Premier Richard Seddon himself who included the specific mention of Urewera district in the Animals Protection Act. Brad Coombes has argued that Seddon was attempting to reduce points of conflict between Tuhoe and the government at this time because of clashes over road surveying in the district. Seddon's promotion of Urewera in this case was also a rare intervention in acclimatisation matters and possibly reflected the depth of his involvement with Tuhoe. The previous year, in 1894, he had travelled to the area with Maori MP James Carroll, who drove the Urewera reserve act. Coombes' final argument for Seddon's manoeuvring is that while other iwi were more vociferous in their demands for the cultural harvesting of kereru, they were ignored in favour of Tuhoe in the Animals Protection Act.[72]

The extent to which closed seasons on kereru were observed and were enforceable in the 'native districts' is difficult to gauge. Newspaper reports give some indications that Maori continued to exercise what they saw as their right to hunt native game in spite of prescribed seasons. The Hawke's Bay Acclimatisation Society complained in 1901 of the 'slaughter' of birds by

Opposite: Maori access to hunting kereru became increasingly restricted from the 1870s onwards. Native game had become the province of the government and tensions increased between Maori and 'sportsmen'. By the mid-1890s, conservationists had become a third player in the battle over native birds, their preservation and their harvest. By 1922 kereru were totally protected. This 1872 painting by Charles Barraud is of Makawhai Stream in the Lower Rangitikei.

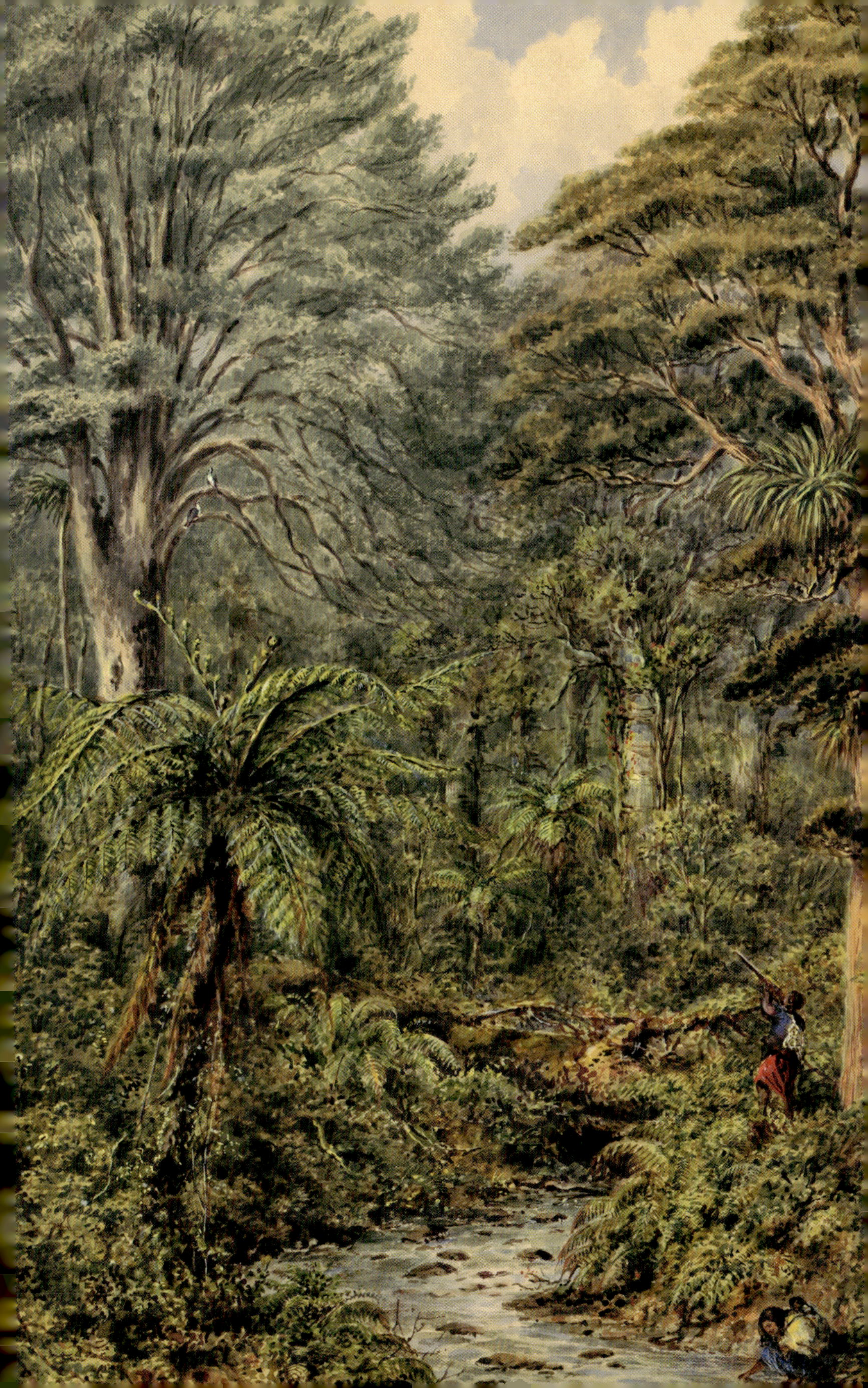

Maori, and a suggestion was made that the newly formed Maori Councils be requested to supervise the observance of a closed season.[73] In 1912 *The Evening Post* reported that:

> The sophisticated Maori still affects one belief of his grandfather who lived in the unsophisticated days of 1840 when all the game laws of the colony were contained in the Treaty of Waitangi, which gave the Maori the freedom of the rivers and all that in or on them was. This belief is combined with an instinct which guides the native unerringly to hidden breeding-places of fowl and fish in the swamps and shallow waters, and the Auckland Acclimatisation Society has been perturbed by reports that natives in some parts of the district carry off the eggs of wild ducks and swans in great quantities during the nesting season. The society intends obtaining advice as to the legality of this action by the natives and taking measures to have it stopped.[74]

The Auckland society's complaints echoed the decades-old conflict between food-gathering and sport.

Above: Even though the government assumed ownership of native game, Maori continued to assert their rights under the Treaty of Waitangi to hunt all year round. A great number of pakeha also assumed Maori had rights to shoot birds, and several hoteliers used this as a defence in court when being prosecuted for buying birds out of season from Maori.

At the August 1912 meeting of the New Zealand Acclimatisation Societies' Association, members complained that 'the Maoris are in the habit of collecting vast quantities of duck and swan eggs — for eating — to the detriment of the sport'. In discussions about the fines that should apply to egg-stealing 12 years later, the 1924 delegates, 'replying to questions said the eggs were not taken so much by schoolboys as by the Natives'.[75] Coombes goes so far as to argue that these concerns about Maori poaching 'initiated a theme which would predominate in the twentieth century history of conservation management: condemnation of Maori for acts of "poaching" on the basis of little evidence, and the attendant targeting of enforcement to Maori communities'.[76] By and large, however, newspaper reports of poaching referred to the prosecution of pakeha; and where Maori activity was reported upon, it was usually in connection with illegal fishing.

Complaints about Maori shooting pigeons were common even if the number of prosecutions was low, and are perhaps more illuminating because of this lack of legal action. As early as 1884, correspondents to newspapers were referring to 'unrighteous slaughter' of pigeons by Maori out of the imposed season, although some wrote of the 'unseasonable slaughter' by poachers generally, and did not specify Maori. 'Ramrod' defined these men as the antithesis of 'true sportsmen' who adhered to the seasons.[77] But it was the conservationists who pointed out that kereru were endangered by both Maori and pakeha. In 1908, James Drummond wrote in his preservation-minded column that:

*The present protection, apparently, is often ignored. The bird is shot in season and out of season. In the Ohakune district, in Wellington province, last season no fewer than 5000 pigeons were shot and forwarded by train to Wellington city. Most of the slaughter took place on the Raetihi Block, which is Maori land, but some of the birds were shot on lands occupied by Crown tenants. It was stated in the House that pigeons were killed in hundreds by sawmill 'hands' and men employed on the construction of the North Island Main Trunk railway line.*[78]

The question of the legality of snaring as a hunting technique also impacted upon Maori practices, highlighting again the ambivalent relationship between the government and Maori. There was a brief ban on snaring between 1865 and 1867, opposed by MP and later Prime Minister Harry Atkinson, who asked specifically how the ban would affect Maori. He argued that they would become poachers simply for following customary practices and that their sources of food would be threatened: 'In some parts of the country the Natives live on wild ducks, which were invariably taken by snares. To prohibit it would only give rise to much difficulty'.[79] Snaring was legal under the Animals Protection Act until 1907 when Parliament, on the advice of the acclimatisation societies, outlawed the practice. Heke was again the vocal opponent of this amendment in Parliament: 'Before the gun came into the country the Natives caught pigeons and other birds by snaring, not for the purposes of sport, but for food. And here is an attempt to prevent the Natives from securing these birds'.[80] (Once again, Heke was unsuccessful.[81]) However, based on newspaper reporting, Maori did not seem to be suddenly criminalised if, indeed, they continued their snaring practices after the introduction of the 1907 act.

By the end of the nineteenth century it was clear that, despite the long debates and law changes, native game were declining rapidly. In 1922 laws were introduced to fully protect most of New Zealand's birds. Even if the protection measures for kereru had been strictly obeyed, the loss of lowland forest through fire and felling had reduced the bird's habitat dramatically, and the introduction of predators and browsing mammals continued to pressure bird populations.

## Changing the environment

By the 1920s, the growing conservation movement that brought about a national shift in attitudes towards hunting native birds began campaigning for the protection of native flora from damage caused by browsing mammals. While kereru were being protected from hunters, calls to lift protection on deer were getting stronger.

The cultural and legal environment in nineteenth-century New Zealand encouraged particular types of hunting and protected game animals and birds. Hunting for sport was prioritised over hunting for food, especially as the colony became more prosperous and the idea of subsistence hunting became less desirable. During the same period, due largely to the development of agriculture, the physical environment of New Zealand was altered rapidly and dramatically. While tens of new animal species and hundreds of new plant species were introduced to New Zealand, the largest environmental change of the nineteenth century and beyond was the clearance of forest by humans. Between 1882 and 1909 almost 40 per cent of the 11.4 million hectares of New Zealand forest that existed at the time of European arrival was destroyed.[82] The changes caused by introduced game mammals were significant, but it is important to put these consequences into perspective. Ecologists generally agree that, 'compared with the changes wrought by 2.8 million people, 8.6 million cattle and 60 million sheep, the damage done by wild animals has been quite trivial'.[83]

The clearing of the bush had implications for both native and introduced game — through the destruction of habitat — as well as for hunters when the preservation/conservation movement gained a footing. The amount of forest cleared for agriculture and forestry made the conservationists' desire to

Above: More than 200 separate liberations of deer took place in the nineteenth and early twentieth centuries. Only a handful were released each time but mild temperatures and abundant feed meant that mobs of hundreds of deer were found over much of the country by the 1930s.

maintain what native bush was left even more fervent, which played a large part in shaping official antipathy towards deer by the 1930s (see Chapter 5).

It is difficult to know how vegetation has been changed through the introduction of browsing mammals into New Zealand. The first obstacle is that we do not know exactly what the environment was like before cattle, deer, goats, tahr, chamois, possums and pigs were introduced. Early impressions of the bush in the writings of European travellers and explorers emphasised its lushness. Early accounts 'suggested that the land was covered in a luxuriant, green, tropical-like vegetation that was largely either forest or fernland. The various reports also claimed that the vegetation was of enormous size and profile when compared with British vegetation . . . [and] that the luxuriant vegetation was common throughout New Zealand and extended from hilltop to water's edge'.[84] These descriptions were usually very generalised and did not distinguish between types of vegetation, let alone species. Images of such verdant forest were taken as a sign of the fertility of the soil, and often focused on the large trees. Descriptions of the undergrowth were rare, but one pamphlet did state that because of the favourable growing conditions, the forests were thick with undergrowth that was 'almost impassable render[ing] travelling exceedingly fatiguing'.[85] Inland hill country and alpine vegetation were undocumented for much of the nineteenth century, but botanists assume that the constitution of the understory 'was certainly much more varied' than is the case today.[86] It is very difficult to reconstruct the character of these plant communities before the invasion by browsing mammals, but various studies show that preferred species almost certainly comprised a far higher proportion of overall vegetative cover than was the case by the 1950s. The depletion of these plant communities had far-reaching and complex consequences for birds, invertebrates and soils which are still as yet little understood.

The impact of browsing mammals on New Zealand's plants varied. Browsers are selective feeders and so alter the balance between palatable and unpalatable species; tasty species are reduced, leaving room for not-so-tasty species to flourish. Less fussy animals eat a wider range of vegetation, therefore areas with high populations of indiscriminate browsers such as goats and sika deer are more severely affected. Even where browsers were greatly reduced, relationships between plants were altered. Data collected where deer were reduced significantly through commercial hunting have demonstrated that palatable species can and do recover, but the extent of that recovery and whether it is sufficiently sustained is debatable.[87]

Nineteenth- and twentieth-century observers — generally amateur naturalists and trampers or bushmen — recorded changes to both the general structure of the forest and to specific species. In 1892, amateur naturalist the Reverend Philip Walsh delivered a paper to the New Zealand Institute that represents one of the earliest attempts to describe damage to the forest as a system — what we would call its ecology — caused by browsers. While Walsh's argument appears naive to the modern reader, he did understand the broad principle that changing part of the bush changed the whole. Walsh wrote that as first cattle then deer browsed the colonies of small and tender forest-floor plants:

> *The larger trees, deprived of the shelter at their feet, gradually grow thin and open at the top. The cathedral gloom and the damp solitude in which flourished the palm-like nikau and the stately fern tree are penetrated by the burning sun, and invaded by fierce and parching winds. All the magic profusion of grace and beauty begins to shrivel and die; and as further desiccation takes place the unprotected roots can no longer support the strain they have to bear, and every here and there some hoary patriarch falls crashing amid an acre of ruin. And thus the game goes on . . .* [88]

Sixty years later, describing changes in the Tararuas, Norman Elder contrasted the bush of his boyhood at the turn of the century with the vegetation of 1955 saying, 'the bush was no longer a dark green carpet, but moth-eaten and tattered with scrub and tussock showing pale in the gaps'. Looking into the head of South Mitre Creek, he lamented that while it was 'a cherished axiom that Tararua leatherwood, like Tararua weather, is unique and changeless . . . whole belts of leatherwood were dead, dead stems stripped of foliage on bare peat trampled like a stockyard'.[89] From the 1930s, deer-cullers, too, reported vast damage to the bush done by deer. On his way through a regenerating gully, culler Bert Barra reported seeing 'more sign of deer in a few minutes than what I saw in my five or six hours trip through the gorge . . . I was amazed to see all these [second-growth] gullies are well tracked and thousands of young trees destroyed'.[90] (Deer favour second-growth forest because a high proportion of colonising species are palatable to them, and because more of the foliage is accessible, unlike the lofty canopies of mature forests.)

Professional biologists and botanists of the early twentieth century attempted to measure the changes caused by browsing animals. Papers delivered to the New Zealand Institute detailed the demise of several species such as tainui (*Pomaderris apetala*) and species of *Panax* (now *Pseudopanax*) before 1912, all the victims of goat-browsing.[91] Biologist and keen tramper

Mavis Davidson wrote that one of the joys of her first crossing of the southern Tararuas in 1935 was the 'luxuriant Prince of Wales feather fern (*Todea* [now *Leptopteris*] *superba*) [which] bordered the zigzag on the way from the saddle to the top of Hell's Gate' but that in 1945 this area was so badly browsed 'it was feared that this slope would become a scree slide'.[92] Another tramper and botanist, Victor Zotov, in a 14-year study of vegetation on Mount Matthews in the Rimutakas, found that goats appeared to eat 'everything within reach', and that there had been 'wholesale destruction' of the tender and presumably tasty bryophytes (mosses and liverworts).[93] By 1942 apiarists in the North Island were reporting a sharp decline in the numbers of flowering native

Above: The shift from a legalistic towards a scientific approach to managing game animals led to the advent of research into the effects of browsing mammals on forests. Methods commonly used to measure change include exclosures and photo-points. This deer-proof exclosure fence was built in 1952 near Tuatapere, where deer had multiplied steadily since their release in 1901. An exclosure is used to compare the composition of the forest inside the fence, where browsers are absent, with a control plot outside. Jocelyn Danderson and Margaret Stevens were photographed in 1953 recording seedlings on a plot at the Orongorongo Opossum [sic] Research Station, three years before protection for possums was finally lifted. The variety and frequency of species and their size would have been recorded.

**70 Hunting**

species, most likely the victims of possums. These observations were part of the impetus in the 1950s to study the impact of possums on forests.[94] Studies of islands, however, give us the clearest picture of the extent of damage done by introduced mammals. Reports on the vegetation on Great Island in the Three Kings group before the liberation of goats there in 1890, and in the decades that followed, documented the extinction of almost half of the island's plant species.[95] Similarly, on Macauley Island in the Kermadecs, where goats had been introduced before 1836, the vegetation and birdlife had been transformed by the late 1880s: 'the indigenous scrubland [was now] close-cropped, eroding grassland. In 1966 the goats were exterminated, but by that time virtually no woody vegetation or forest birds remained'.[96]

While deer were introduced into the Tararua foothills in the 1860s, records of the damage they caused to the environment are rare until the 1930s, when tramping became more popular. (Even in the 1920s, tramping in the Tararuas 'constituted an expedition, unlike the fast 1½ day trips of later years, and only casual reports [of deer] could be made'.[97]) It was clear from even those casual reports that deer were everywhere in the Tararua ranges in the 1920s, and by the 1930s they were reported to be in herds of tens and hundreds. Even non-scientific observers regarded them as a menace to the vegetation.

Botanists continued to demonstrate the damage deer were doing to the forests and tussock grasslands. Zotov argued that deer were 'the most destructive animal' in the Tararuas, and 1930s Department of Internal Affairs reports on deer damage in various places, including the Abel Tasman National Park, pointed to damage caused by browsing, ring-barking from antler-rubbing, the prevention of regrowth, compacting of the soil by trampling and the muddying of tarns through wallowing. The high altitude scrub zone suffered most, leading to the replacement of minor leafy species and alpine shrubs with less palatable tussock. Davidson writes that in order to assess the damage deer have done in the mountains, 'one must know what plants should be there, the palatable species that have been swept away; a jungle of pepperwood (*Pseudowintera colorata*), rohutu (*Neomyrtus pendunculatus*), or crown fern (*Blechnum discolor*) [all non-palatable species] does not represent regeneration of the original forest but marks areas of extreme modification'.[98]

Reverend Philip Walsh had made an appeal to protect native forests from deer as early as 1892; however, their value to New Zealand as sporting and tourist assets at that time was considered to outweigh the value of conserving the bush. By 1922 the red deer population had grown to such an extent, and the consequent damage to the bush was so severe, however, that forestry scientist Allan Perham declared 'It is a matter of deer or forests'. After 30 years of conservationist lobbying, Perham's bald assessment fell on more sympathetic ears. Perham clearly knew how to push the government's buttons and he outlined the damage that deer were causing to the state's exotic forest plantations as well as to native flora. He also argued that 'the effect of deer on agriculture was considered to be as great as that on silviculture [forestry], to which should be added the depletion of mountain pastures. The destruction of the latter would lead to severe erosion and would influence the supply of water for hydroelectric works'.[99]

Added to this was the voice of New Zealand's most respected botanist, Leonard Cockayne, who wrote in his *Monograph on the New Zealand Beech Forest* that deer were the most destructive of all the animals introduced to New Zealand:

> The New Zealand high-mountain forests are the finest in the temperate zones as protection forests [protecting against erosion], on account of their undergrowth and the thick water-holding bryophyte carpet, or cushions, of the floor, but these features can be entirely destroyed by deer, and with it the main value of these forests is gone.[100]

Perham, too, had written that where the herds were large 'and food in short

### The guts of the problem

*Ruth Mason graduated with an MSc in botany from Auckland University College in 1938. She took up a position with the Department of Scientific and Industrial Research, where she became a pioneer in seed research. As part of this, she examined the gut contents of hundreds of feral animals, providing key data on their eating habits. Mason examined the gut contents of 130 possums collected in the Orongorongo bush (near Wellington) in 1946–7, finding the leaves and flowers of konini, northern rata, titoki, kamahi, fivefinger, clover, rangiora and manuka, as well as the fruits and seeds of pigeonwood, tutu, hinau, kawakawa, poroporo and some sedges. She found tahr ate puharetaiko (mountain daisy), hebe species, koromiko, snow and silver tussocks, Mount Cook lily and speargrass. Goats were the least fussy eaters. In a study of the stomach contents of three goats shot in Egmont National Park in 1947, Mason found leaves of wineberry, kamahi, putaputaweta, haumakoroa, karamu, raurekau and other comprosmas and broadleaf plants, as well as twigs and scraps of native broom, lichen, flaxes and ferns.*[101]

supply, all undergrowth is eaten out as high as the animal can reach'.[102]

By the 1930s botanists had also identified tahr and chamois as threats to a wide range of plants. These species had not remained confined to the high altitudes, but ranged down into the valleys where they 'lay bare not only the sub-alpine scrub and shrubs, but also the lower lying ranunculi, celmisias, and flowering plants at the foot of the mountain'.[103] Because tahr and chamois were selective feeders, those plants not being grazed by them began to dominate the alpine and sub-alpine environments by the mid-1930s. By 1932 sheep farmers were also calling for action to be taken to reduce the numbers of tahr and chamois, because they were competing with livestock.[104]

## Swarming with game

Between 1850 and 1930 the New Zealand environment was altered radically. Regarding it as empty and needing improvement, acclimatisation societies and enthusiastic individuals had filled it with animals, birds and plants. It was then necessary to create a legal environment to protect and regulate those animals and birds introduced for hunting, and then finally to protect native species.

Maori were in an unenviable position in this environment, their traditional lands and foods diminished by fire, war, agricultural development, European settlement and introduced predators. Their customary hunting was denied them (at least in theory). Then, as happened in Canada and the United States, the forces of conservation acted to restrict their access to birds as food even where some iwi retained their own lands. The colonists' voracious need for agricultural land and timber also meant that, by the 1920s, calls were very loud to protect the remnant forests and mountain pastures left in New Zealand. Botanists and naturalists demonstrated the changes to vegetation and laid the blame for these changes squarely at the hoofs of browsing animals.

Interwoven with these physical and cultural changes, hunting became a widespread and common part of New Zealand life. In spite of Hursthouse's vision for the country as a vast game park, for much of the nineteenth century provision of food was the main motivation for hunting. It was not deer and pheasants that formed the basis of the hunting tradition, but pigs and native birds. Pork filled the larders; tui and kereru hung in butchers' shop windows. That the provision of food, cooking and eating should have dominated the relatively unrestricted hunting culture in the colony is not surprising: the hearth and table are as central to the hunter's world as the bush.

# Hunting for the pot

2

One of the many factors tying the New Zealand hunting experience to that of the wider British Empire is the extent to which hunting kept colonists from starving in their new home. In the early years of settlement, before agriculture was well established and while introduced livestock were almost too precious to eat, the plentiful supply of birds and pigs in the bush kept settlers, explorers, surveyors, bush workers and prospectors fed. As in other colonies, local indigenous people also played a crucial role in providing food to settlers. Without such local assistance, European settlers in New Zealand would have had a very difficult time surviving in what was to them a strange land.

Even as settlements became established and the luxury of butchers' shops appeared in larger towns, hunting continued to play an important role in provisioning. Game was cheaper and often easier to procure than farmed meat, even from a butcher's. Purchased meat was seen by many as a luxury — something for special occasions and to break the monotony of the colonial diet. For a lot of people, of course, butchered meat was simply not available and settlers in more remote areas, bush and railway workers and many Maori communities continued to eat game as their staple protein. For many families this is a tradition that has continued to this day.

## Learning from the locals

In all parts of the British Empire, explorers and settlers were very interested in indigenous methods of hunting and provisioning. Many records detailed

Maori methods of hunting birds, including snaring methods for weka and pigeon and the killing of waterfowl. The extent to which different Maori groups depended on hunting was largely governed by climate and suitability of conditions for agriculture; hence the small groups of Maori who lived in the south of the South Island were more heavily dependent on hunting, fishing and gathering of wild plants than those of the north.[1] At the Shag River mouth site in Otago, archaeologists have uncovered thousands of small bird bones and have identified the remains of 49 bird species or sub-species, leading them to conclude that 'the magnitude of fowling at Shag Mouth . . . represents food enough for between 40 and 65 people to have one average sized bird each per week for 20 years'.[2]

Many explorers found their daily travelling contingent on their guides' hunting schedule; for Maori, an opportunity to capture a large number of

Above: Early explorers, surveyors and settlers relied on Maori guides and local game for food. Long expeditions could be mounted only because of the food that hunting provided. In the records of these travels Maori methods of snaring, trapping and hunting were often documented. This 1846 watercolour by William Fox shows a Maori guide snaring a weka.

birds could not be passed up. In 1844 Bishop Augustus Selwyn, travelling near Timaru, recorded ducks being caught by hand by his guides. The party came across a flock of paradise ducks in moult:

> *The natives immediately threw off their blankets and rushed into the water, which was shallow and about a furlong in length. After an animated chase of two hours . . . they captured eighteen, which formed a seasonable supply of food in this thinly inhabited country.*[3]

Edward Shortland's notes, written in 1844 while exploring the east coast of the South Island, revealed an almost daily hunt. Ducks were the main quarry but sometimes other birds were shot. His guides' dedication to hunting was sometimes a cause for frustration; he wrote on 16 January 1844, 'bad walking: plenty of ducks which caused delay — so shy we could not get near enough to kill. Gave up after several attempts.'[4]

Maori methods of managing waterfowl were also recorded by early colonists. As with kereru-snaring (as described in the previous chapter), the condition of waterfowl was checked before harvesting began. Travelling through Cloudy Bay in Marlborough in 1911, surveyor WH Skinner noted that Maori drove ducks from the lagoons into canals so they could assess the birds' overall condition before killing them. The process was carefully managed:

> *During the moulting season . . . the birds being unable to fly were easily taken by hand in the narrow water lanes and cross drives. When in this condition they were known as Maumi, or 'flappers'. The parera or grey duck moulted in April and May and were dealt with in the same way as the Paradise ducks. They were slowly herded up and driven into the catchments and there quietly sorted out. Each duck as it was caught was carefully felt-over, and if in good condition was appropriated for the larder, if in poor condition it was passed over and released.*[5]

Large catches of birds were preserved in their own fat: 'The birds were roasted on a spit over a fire and the fat was collected in a trough below. It was kept liquid by means of hot stones. The hot fat was then poured over the birds in the container.'[6]

According to ethnographer Elsdon Best, Pacific rats were also preserved in this way. In his book *Forest Lore of the Maori*, first published more than 10 years after his death in 1931, Best described Maori methods of trapping kiore (Polynesian rat) and bats, as well as snaring birds. A reviewer of the book noted that ornithologists would find 'fascinating accounts of habits, folk beliefs, and ingenious snaring techniques'. Traps for rats were varied:

> The native [sic] rats played an important role in [the] Maori economy, providing a staple food supply in the absence of other land mammals. Large numbers were trapped, cooked and potted in their own grease for future consumption. The excellent descriptions and illustrations of Maori rat traps will interest mammal collectors. The usual trap consists of a looped cord passed between two firmly anchored parallel sticks

and attached to a bent stick spring, which is released by a treadle or by tugging at the bait. In a clever portable variation, the rat releases the spring by gnawing through a string barring access to the bait . . . Bats were likewise eaten, large colonies sometimes being smoked out of hollow roosting trees.[7]

## 'Necessary and profitable'

Before the start of organised settlement, many pakeha relied on game for food, documenting their sometimes clumsy efforts to adapt to a hunting way of life. In 1823 missionary the Reverend William White wrote to his mentor and friend the Reverend John Butler in the Bay of Islands that keeping his staff fed at his mission at Whangaroa necessitated the acquisition of skills not usual for a man of the cloth. He reported, 'I begin to feel my ability in shooting. It would appear strange to some people for a missionary to have to make a boast of this; but in New Zealand it is necessary and profitable'.[8]

Whalers and sealers, too, relied on New Zealand's game for food. John Boultbee wrote in 1826 that

*Milford Haven [Sound] is a wild romantic looking place, abounding in high mountains, and intermediate deep vallies [sic], the woods are abundantly supplied with game, as woodhens, green birds, emus [wekas, kakapo, kiwi] etc — these birds are of large size, they lay their eggs in holes in the ground and in hollow trees and as they cannot fly, they are easily overtaken with dogs.*[9]

Whalers from semi-permanent stations hunted, not so much to survive, but to break the monotony of a coastal diet. Surgeon and politician Dr David Munro, travelling through Otago in 1844, noted 'There is a famous cover for pigs, too, between the upper part of the [Taieri] Valley and the sea. The whalers come up the river in their boats and kill great numbers of pigs here'.[10] Missionaries, too, longed for a more varied diet. At Samuel Marsden's mission at Rangihoua in the Bay of Islands the cows ran wild and 'for years the only beef or mutton to be had was from the occasional hunt for these creatures which roamed wild in the bush. Goats were easier to keep, but for many years the staple meat diet was pork, varied with wild pigeon, duck and fish'.[11]

Like the earlier sailors and missionaries, the bush workers, miners and

Opposite: Working away from towns and farms meant that bush, railway and roading workers had to hunt regularly to supplement their diets. This man on the Central Otago Railway is shooting rabbits ca. 1900.

**Hunting for the pot**

railway workers of nineteenth-century New Zealand ate a fairly monotonous diet based largely on bread cooked in camp ovens. The bush provided the opportunity for variety. Timber workers, musterers and prospectors often kept dogs and/or guns nearby while they worked in order to take advantage of any opportunity for free meat. Otago settler Elizabeth McDiarmid, who wrote her reminiscences in 1916 when she was 61 years old, recalled that when her parents moved to West Taieri in the late 1840s, pigs were a standard part of many Europeans' diets. 'Nearly all of the sawyers kept a pig dog and as butcher meat was expensive in those days, they went pig-hunting at intervals, and provided for themselves a supply of wild pork. My father, Mr Francis McDiarmid, also at times went pig-shooting'.[12] John Bethell, who worked with his brother on their father's land in the Waitakere Ranges in the 1870s, lived in a nikau whare and 'killed hundreds of pigs and pork was the only meat we had, salt and fresh'.[13] Sawyers' huts were typically made with wide chimneys for smoking fish and game.[14] Wild pig and pigeons continued to be the main source of meat for many colonists living in the bush even into the late nineteenth century when sheep and cattle numbers had grown substantially. Pigeon fat was often used as a substitute for butter until a dairy herd could be established.[15]

Virtually every record left by explorers and surveyors of New Zealand during the nineteenth century demonstrated the importance of game to these ventures. Explorer Charles Heaphy wrote at length about the different kinds of New Zealand birds, commenting, 'they are of great service as an article of food, to the settler on his clearing, where he is often in but little communication with the town. While on exploring and surveying expeditions in the interior of the country, I have often had occasion to appreciate their existence'.[16] The Bannister brothers, Charles and John, spent their annual holidays away from their family's Wairarapa farm exploring the Tararua Ranges, usually relying on game to keep them going. One fortuitous encounter with wild cattle on a trip up the Waingawa River in 1881 meant they ate well that night and 'salted, rolled and stashed in a stream' the remaining meat.[17]

Charlie Douglas, legendary explorer of South Westland, ate a great many native birds in his time but also commented on their scarcity where he felt

Opposite: In the twentieth century, deer-cullers were public servants who supplemented their government-issued rations by hunting. At this hut in the Hurunui, North Canterbury in 1950, the firewood had been cut long to feed into the fire as it burns, a rack for drying deer skins is visible behind the trees at right, and the meat safe is hoisted high into a tree where the breeze, cooler air and smoke from the fire would discourage flies.

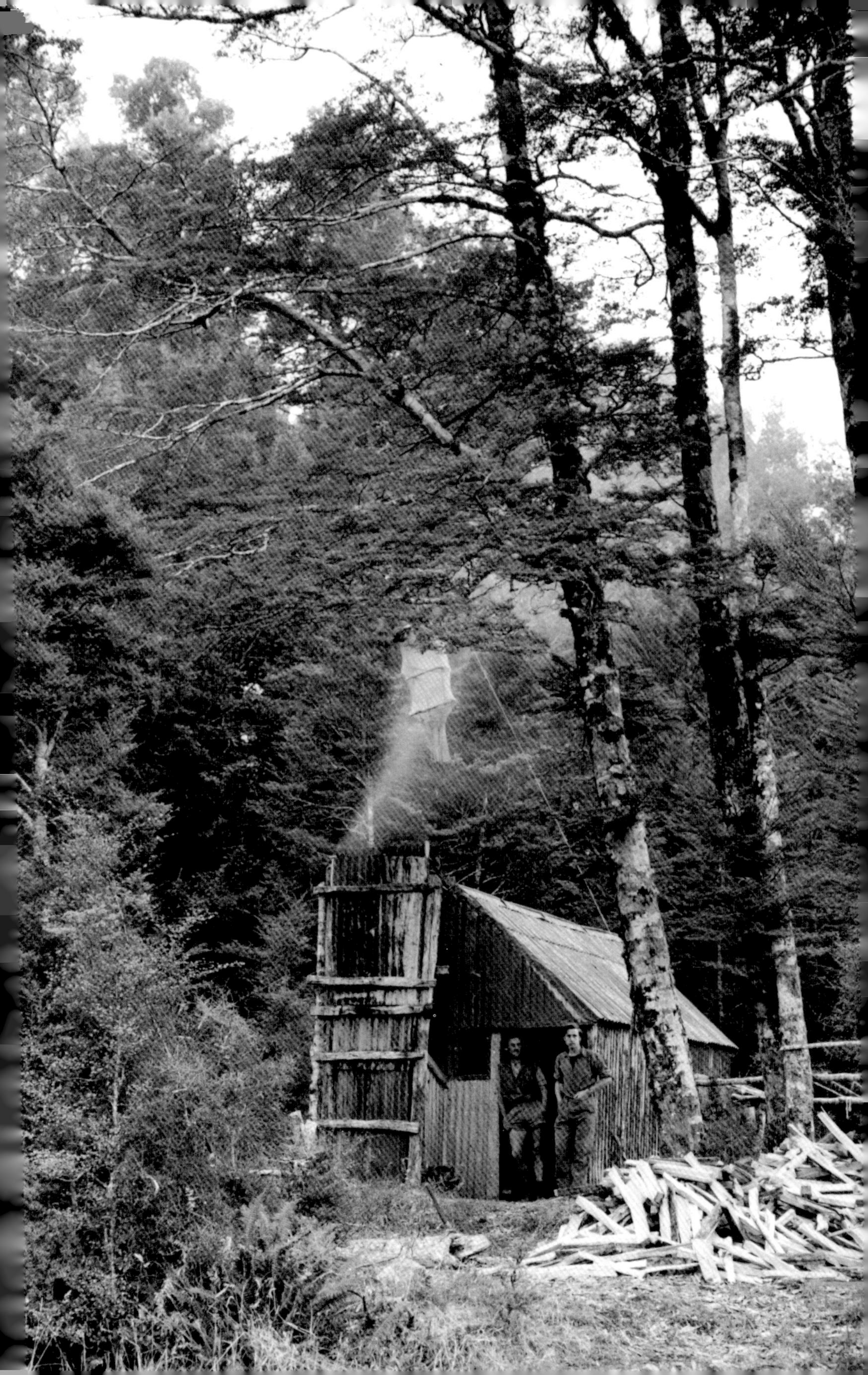

## Survival in the bush

*In March 1885, when the harvest was finished on the family's Wairarapa farm, young Charles Bannister decided upon an unusual summer holiday. The government had recently purchased from local Maori a large block in the Tararua Ranges, with the exception of a 1000 acre (405 hectare) reserve with a lake known as Hapuakorari at the centre. Government surveyors had been unable to locate the lake and were offering a £200 reward for its discovery. Charles and two Maori friends, Mundy and Akitu, decided to try their luck. Akitu was older than the other two boys and Charles asked him to go along not only because he was 'a really good bushman' but because he had been a gold prospector, and 'in the event of our finding a reef on the western side of the range, he would know what to do'. The party planned to provision themselves with game, taking a single-barrelled shotgun, 'some cartridges loaded with shot for birds and some loaded with bullets for cattle or pigs'. They carried large scones instead of bread, and also took 'a certain amount of pepper and salt, a splendid piece of home-cured fat bacon, tea, sugar, two pounds of rice and a dozen shallots. I preferred these,' noted Bannister, 'as one shallot equals two large onions for flavouring purposes'. As they were leaving, Bannister's girlfriend, Repeka, gave him a package containing extra scones, made from pounded fern root, dried crayfish tails and pork dripping, saying, 'Taari, here is some kai for you. Grandmother showed me how to make them. They are made the same way as she used to make them for Grandfather when he went hunting.'*

*After a few days working their way up streams, doing a little prospecting and getting up onto the main range, Bannister had a fall in a gorge. He was not badly hurt, but having had 'a nasty shaking', the party continued on. The next day, they climbed to the summit of what is now known as Arete (described by Akitu as Hanga Ohia Tangata) and then down to the Waingawa River. Camping beside the river that night, they shot blue ducks for their dinner, but during that shoot Bannister slipped on a loose rock, badly wrenching his knee. To add insult to injury, the blue ducks were found to be so tough — Mundy claiming one of them was 'Adam's pet duck from the Garden of Eden' — that* they had to be returned to the pot and stewed for several hours before they were edible!

Now deep in the Tararuas and considerably slowed by Bannister's injuries, the party decided to head home. The formidable face of Mitre Peak stood in their way and Bannister decided to try to cross the spur between North Mitre Creek and the Waingawa River. It was going to be slow going. That night the last of their provisions were used up in a stew of moreporks and speargrass roots, and Akitu made a poultice from horopito leaves for Bannister's knee. Eels from the Waingawa provided breakfast and their fat a liniment for Bannister's knee; a mid-morning expedition saw Akitu return with a bag full of fresh-water crayfish. Mundy meanwhile returned to camp with two kaka and a pigeon, and weka caught later that evening were cooked as provisions for the next day.

The party entered familiar territory the next day, following 'the Miki Miki down the north side. We knew this part well as we had often been pig-hunting there'. Getting closer to home there was an unexpected surprise.

'We had not gone far when we heard the shrill whistle of a huia. I put my fingers in my mouth and answered it. Mundy put a cartridge in the gun . . . Two huias came into sight, hopping from tree to tree, a male and a female. I told Jackie [Akitu] to shoot the female bird first as the male would stop to look for his mate. He shot both of them. We skinned them, being very careful of the tail feathers. These skins were for Repeka['s] Granny.'

When their adventures were over, Bannister cured the huia skins. 'It did one good to see the smile on the old Maori lady's tattooed face when I handed her the skins. It came from the bottom of her heart.'[18]

they had been hunted out.[19] At the beginning of a trip to Waiatoto in 1891, he longed to be away from 'the blighting bird destroying influence of the Special Settler' so as to have more to eat than bread and eels. During this miserable expedition, Douglas scratched in his diary 'one comfort I am among the birds again, pigeons and Kakapos are fat, and tomorrow I [will] be among the hens [weka], it makes a wonderfull difference in the Flour, having birds'.[20] 'Laying in a stock of birds' was a common activity on Douglas's expeditions. He was always mindful that at any point food could become scarce or that the weather could close in for days at a time. Because of this precaution, although other supplies could run short, he usually had enough to eat. Pinned down by a storm, he wrote, 'Hope to get away tomorrow, as I am on quarter rations Flour, no Tea or Sugar but fortunately plenty of Birds & Tobacco'.[21] This was

Above: Fish, kereru, duck, eels and a deer skin speak to the great bounty available in the bush and to the highly varied diet of this group camping in the 1890s.

not to say that a steady diet of birds was not monotonous. Douglas complained in his journals, 'Splendid weather but . . . not high enough up for hens and am sick of Pigeon stew'.[22] He was often hungry, as were most explorers and surveyors, but sometimes put up with eating nothing but bread because he did not want to kill the birds around him which had young. That is not to say that his conservation ethos was not sometimes overridden by his stomach. He once ate two rare 'mountain kiwis', admitting 'being pushed with hunger, I ate the pair of them, under the circumstances I would have eaten the last of the Dodos'.[23]

Settlers' dependence on Maori for food in the early period of pakeha settlement is especially clear from their recollections. William Swainson, writing about Auckland in the 1850s, recorded the remarkable hospitality of local Maori, writing, 'pigs, potatoes, fish, vegetables and pigeons abound here, and the necessities of life can be had for a trifle; if you lend your gun to a chief he will return in the evening laden with game'.[24] Elizabeth McDiarmid's parents, among the first colonists at Woodside in West Taieri in Otago in the early 1850s, were also reliant on their Maori neighbours. On more than one occasion when their food ran out, the newly married couple had to walk to 'the Maori Kaike where they were hospitably received by the Maori chief, who supplied them with mutton birds'.[25] Ernst Dieffenbach's party, while exploring the Taupo region in 1841, relied enormously on the hospitality of local iwi, but came across the occasional problem where Christian teachings had reached the region before the explorers:

> A slight disagreement arose on the following day, which was Sunday. They refused us food, saying they had become missionaries of late and had been told it was the greatest sin to kill a pig or to cook on Sunday. That we demanded it on that day was not our fault, as we had solicited it the day before. Titipa [their guide] started off to a neighbouring Heathen pa, although the rain fell in torrents, and came back in the afternoon with a pig.[26]

In the early twentieth century, latter-day explorers also relied on bush food. The former chief engineer of the New Zealand Telegraph Services told a reporter of his bush experiences in the early 1900s 'when he was exploring a telephone line route in the south-west of Southland, to link up Preservation Inlet with the outside world. He had a small rifle, which enabled him to obtain some extra fare for his party, in the way of pigeons, ducks and weka, in the wild country beyond the Waiau River'.[27] Many trampers and hunters relied on bush food when they'd been caught out. Lifelong tramper and hunter Viv Collings recalled that in the late 1940s, she, her fiancé and another hunter were caught in a storm on Mount Luna southeast of Karamea:

> The river came up, the storm came up and we couldn't get back for about three days. So we had to eat our venison and, what did we shoot? A Paradise Duck, which was ghastly! We wasted a lot of energy chewing it![28]

## Perks of the job

Hunting for the pot also formed a vital part of an informal economy. In what has become a long tradition of making up the difference between poor wages and the cost of living, bush workers took full advantage of the perks of their location. Tree-felling and road-building were hard labouring jobs and sometimes poorly paid. In the late nineteenth century, men working on the Cameron family's station in the Wairarapa felling bush, scrub-cutting and road-making went hunting for recreation and to improve their diets. Robert Cameron wrote:

> Often these men and my elder brothers who were getting to be very good shots with both gun and rifle would go pig-hunting and then, as there were plenty of pigs about, there would be plenty of free pork for all. Often in the evenings we could see wild pigs out feeding in a valley above some bush near the house. These pigs were hard to stalk and generally disappeared before anyone could get a shot at them.[29]

At the same time, in the Wairarapa bush camps of Scandinavian settlers, hunting wild cattle provided protein for these hard-working men.

> The best gang of bushmen I have ever had to do with were New Zealand born young fellows from a Danish settlement. They would work mightily all the week, and instead of resting the seventh day, they would be off [wild] cattle hunting miles away among the precipitous ranges, and after a whole day's rough and most arduous bush clambering, would come gaily up the long track to camp, 'humping' on their backs the most surprising loads of good beef.[30]

Opposite: These pheasants were destined to hang on the back of the kitchen door. Isobel Broad, in her 1889 New Zealand Exhibition Cookery Book, instructed that 'pheasants should be kept, and hung for some time, before roasting; a fresh pheasant is flavourless. On the other hand it should not be high, but just getting so.' She instructed that the birds be roasted 'before a clear fire' for about 45 minutes and served with bread sauce.

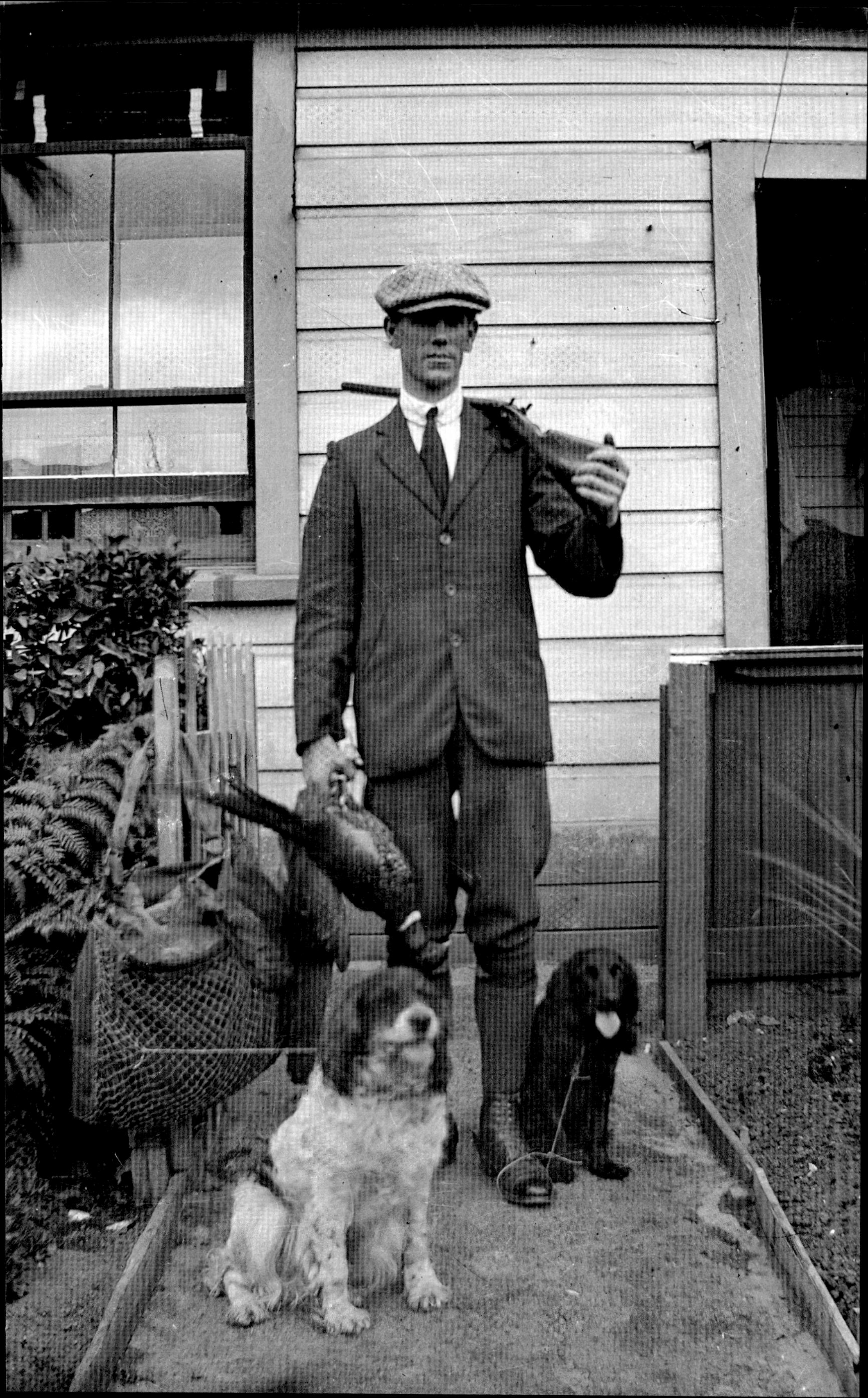

There was even more advantage for workers if stealth rather than ammunition was used. One of the roading contractors who worked near the Camerons' property made the most of the pigs living near his camp:

*On one job, Charlie had his camp near the edge of some bush in which there were numerous wild pigs. At the edge of this bush there was a large tree with the base at one side rotted away leaving a large hollow under the tree trunk. In the hollow a mother pig chose to make a home for herself and young family. From his camp, Charlie could keep a close watch on the incomings and outgoings of the mother pig. When mother pig went out for a feed and stroll, he occasionally went up to see how the baby pigs were growing. Patiently he waited until they had grown into nice little suckling pigs. When they had got to this stage he would watch until mother went out for her evening meal and stroll. After he thought she had time to get a fair distance away he would go up, taking with him his faithful companion, a pet dog. This he would do in case mother pig unexpectedly returned. Charlie would then select a nice young suckling pig for his larder and off back to his camp he would go with it. When the supply of suckling pig in his larder was getting low again he would make his observations of mother pig's movements again and when he reckoned she was safely out of the way, Charlie would go up and acquire another suckling pig. By repeating his raids, Charlie was able to keep himself provided with delicious young suckling pig for a long time, and so making up for some of the sweat and money he had lost toiling in swamps and on roads.*[31]

Solicitor Hubert Ostler (later Sir Hubert, a Supreme Court judge) spent six years in the 1890s, between finishing school in England and beginning his law degree at Victoria College in Wellington, clearing bush on his mother's property near Levin. He enjoyed the outdoor, physical work and loved the ready-made opportunity for pig-hunting, often for the pot. Writing his reminiscences in the 1930s, he recalled:

*We always took our lunch into the bush, and also the dogs, including old Rob ... the best pig dog I have ever seen. He had a marvellous nose, and could smell a pig half a mile off. Often as we chopped away we could hear the dogs barking away in the bush. Rob had found a pig. Then one of us would run off, for that would be our meat for the week.*[32]

The perks of bush work ensured that many British immigrants could enjoy a much higher standard of living than their counterparts who had stayed behind. Letters home frequently extolled New Zealand's plentiful wild-food supplies and described the settlers' diet to their families. In a letter to a friend in England in 1851, Canterbury settler Dr Alfred Barker described the fauna of New Zealand — birds, rats and lizards — always with an eye to the best eating. He noted during his description of 'the birds of the plains' that there were 'four or five species of ducks of which the best eating is the grey duck about the size of a mallard with very unpretending grey plumage and a bright shot of green on the wing'.[33]

Settler Henry Woulden described his situation to his father in 1841:

> . . . *it is a pleasant country: we can see the tops of the mountains is covered with snow: the ground is covered with Geranuems [sic] and myrtles and Fuccer Trees 40 foot*

Above: Hunting for the pot cemented family and community ties. Going hunting together as well as eating meals, offering hospitality and sharing game among family and friends have long been important to community prosperity and wellbeing.

**Hunting for the pot**

hie; we have non of any kind of frutt, no orinages, nor coconuts; our frutts is wild Hogs and fish and birds . . . I shall never think of coming to England whiist I can git plenty of Pork, For you are wost of then our convicts, for they doant work half so hard as you do [sic].³⁴

In 1875, Joseph Brocklesby, a 38-year-old farm labourer, wrote home from the Waikato:

It is a beautiful country, there are all kinds of fruit grows wild; you can go out and gather as much as you like . . . The peaches are as big as a good-sized apple, and grown by tons. There are scores of pheasants, and you can go and shoot one when you think well, and no-one to interfere.³⁵

James Randall came to New Zealand in 1872, with his wife and four children joining him the following year. He wrote to them in 1872 from Picton:

I am very comfortable here; like all colonials, we make a hut and live in it, but have got to cook our own food . . . We can go out and catch a pig any time we like two or three *miles out in the bush. My brother was talking about coming; I wish he would, he could not do a better thing. Tis better to be living here like a gentleman than to be in England starving . . .* [36]

It was not only labourers who had the opportunity to hunt on the job. A school teacher at Aoroa, Northland in the 1890s, Joe Elliott, took advantage of the school's proximity to the bush to occasionally acquire his dinner. George Campbell, a boy in Elliott's class, described him as 'a splendid sportsman' who 'always kept a double-barrelled gun standing in the classroom and, when the class was quiet, he would stand at the window and watch for pheasants. Suddenly he would snatch up the gun and have a couple of shots through the partly opened window, and then hurry to the fallen trees about fifty yards from the school and return with a cock pheasant or two'.[37]

In the twentieth century, hunting continued to provide a variety of diet and much needed recreation for men working in remote areas. Lineman Bill Hiku started work when he was 16 years old on electricity transmission lines in a remote area of the Waikato in the mid-1960s. The linemen were paid fortnightly and he recalls that on the weekends between paydays they would go pig-hunting. His boss wouldn't let the men use a company Land Rover for hunting trips, but he allowed them to come back to camp to get a vehicle to pick up what they'd killed — usually three or four pigs. 'Because it was used as food for the camp, it reduced our board and all the married people would share in it as well.' Pigs were so common near the camp that it was 18 months before Hiku went out and did not get a pig.

At around the same time, Pat Toi worked at Newton Flat putting electricity lines into the Buller Gorge. The linemen hunted a lot from the camp, for both pigs and deer, taking all the meat back to the cookhouse and selling the skins to the local Forest Service office. When he moved to the camp on Rainbow Station near Nelson, venison was on the menu regularly, as was wild duck.[38]

Perhaps more than any other group of rural workers, government shooters, who were employed from 1930 in the deer destruction campaigns, lived off game. In the 1930s, the supplies provided by the Department of Internal Affairs to deer-cullers were constrained enormously by difficulties of transportation. Bread was rarely supplied, although it was acknowledged

Opposite: This group of waterfowl hunters includes shooters young and old, men and women. No doubt many of the non-shooters of the party would have been involved in processing the birds. The occasion was clearly a social outing and probably included a picnic. Christchurch district, ca. 1915.

that it saved the men a great deal of time if they did not have to bake their own bread. Potatoes and other fresh vegetables very quickly ran out. Dripping was supplied only early in the season while the deer fattened up sufficiently to provide it, and the men were provided with only enough fresh meat to last until the first venison was shot. An Internal Affairs memo about food supplies in 1936 stated:

> As in the past, a very few tins only of preserved meat will be supplied to each camp for use only in cases of emergency . . . With the above exceptions, no meat will be provided as venison, obtained by the men themselves, only will be used.[39]

Bush workers were not always single men, and large numbers of families fed themselves by hunting during the early years of clearing bush, before farms became established. That immigrants enjoyed a standard of living higher than their counterparts at home is clear from many letters and reminiscences, and game was central to that abundance. Isobel Kemp, who grew up in the 1890s on the East Coast of the North Island, described her family's diet:

Above: Difficult terrain made hunting in some areas more challenging than others. Boats were a common and logical form of transport for those living on rivers. These hunters' horses are towing them upstream on the Hokianga River.

**94 Hunting**

*We used to use 150lbs of flour and 70 of sugar in 28 days, all bread and cakes being made at home. Food to burn, game unlimited, wild pork, fish, paua, mussels and — say it with bated breath — pigeons cooked whole while feeding on miro and hinau berries . . . the birds were simmered gently with rice and watercress added, and with boiled kumuras [sic] made a feast fit for a king.*[40]

Elizabeth McDiarmid's father Francis frequently went pig-hunting from their home at Woodside in West Taieri. Family stories were passed down about these expeditions and the anxiety created by what was a reasonably dangerous activity, where the death or injury of a husband could be disastrous for a young bride and mother:

*On one occasion, shortly after he was married, he went up the mountain alone on a pig hunt and shot several pigs (I think 3) which he opened and cleaned, and then put what he could not carry under a running stream. The operation took rather long and as night was coming on Mrs McDiarmid got anxious about him, and went up the mountain to try and find him 'cooeeing' repeatedly as [she] went until she heard a response, and then she knew all was well.*[41]

Jean Boswell grew up on a newly broken-in Dargaville farm in the 1890s and recalled that when her father and older brothers were bush-felling, her family was 'dependent on the gun'.

*Two or three times a week, my father would take the gun with them on their tramp to the felling, always returning at night with several wild pigeons. They might have brought hundreds for the bush was alive with them, but powder and shot were expensive and had to be strictly conserved.*[42]

The family's diet was restricted because of poverty and remoteness. Generally, they ate oatmeal porridge with treacle but without milk for breakfast; lunch was usually bread (a couple of days old — their mother would not let them eat it fresh because it went too quickly) with pigeon fat or lard. At dinner they ate pigeons or salt pork with potatoes or rice. As more children were born and times got tougher, hunting became more important, but it was not without cost. Every Sunday had to be spent digging for kauri gum to exchange for powder and shot, as well as for essential foods. But for the children, there was still romance in this life:

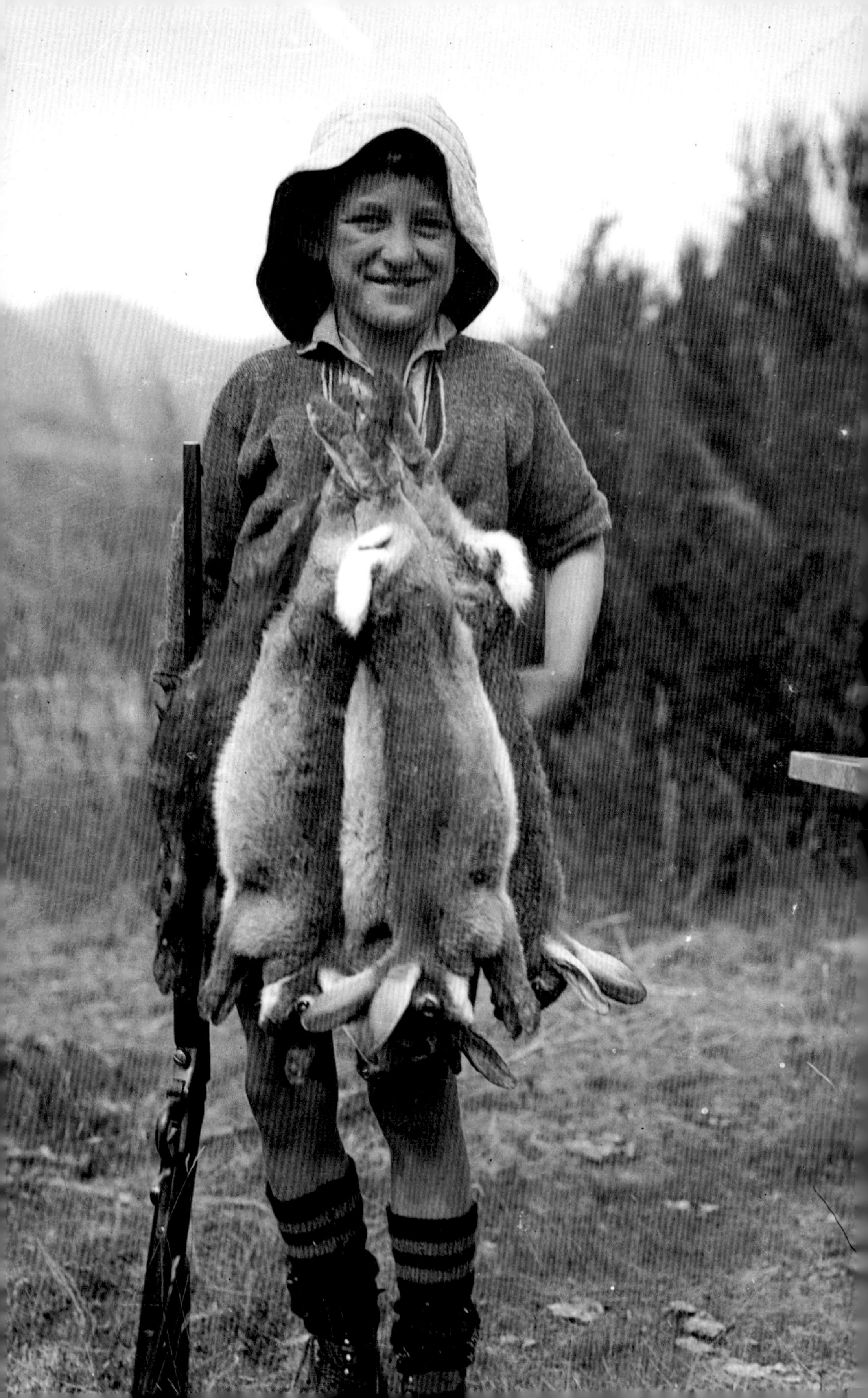

*I can see my father and the boys now in my mind's eye returning home in the evenings with their pikaus of gum on their backs, several birds, pigeons and kakas, hanging from their shouldered guns, each carrying in his free hand a great bunch of tawharas or, in autumn, patungatungas (flower and fruit of the kiekie vine) or the scarlet-berried fingers of the wharawhara.*[43]

Further north at about the same time, 14-year-old May Brown was housekeeping for her father and brother on the family's new bush section outside Dargaville.

*Fresh [butchered] meat was a luxury, but we always had plenty of game. When I first went into the Avoca [to the new bush section] the pheasants were that tame they used to come right up to our shanty door. They used to wake us up crowing in the mornings and Father or Jack would shoot one just when we wanted one and to get a meal of wild pigeons, they only had to sit under a tree for a while and shoot three or four . . .*[44]

Remoteness rather than poverty made Kathleen Bourke's married life one where hunting was important. She married 'fresh from an office in Napier' in the late 1910s and she and her husband Harry, along with her brother Koi, took up a back-country Hawke's Bay farm. 'There were quite a number of wild pigs in the bush and Koi went pig hunting with [neighbour] old Walter every Sunday; they nearly always "brought home the bacon"; the wild pork made a welcome addition to our diet and Koi enjoyed the sport.' In 1924 the family's home burnt down and Harry and Koi decided to try bush contracting. They won a contract to produce 10,000 totara posts for the East Coast Railway, and planned to split and stack them, then float them down the Mohaka River. They employed local Maori because they were the experts on the river.

*At last the great day came. The Maoris arrived at mid-day in two Model T trucks, with their gear, fourteen of them, all as happy as kings without a care in the world. The afternoon was spent pig hunting to ensure a good supply of food for the first stage of the trip. The meat was boiled and packed in its own fat in kerosene tins. It will keep for quite a while in this way.*

Kathleen and Harry's children grew up in a very practical house. Their eldest daughter, Rita, became a land girl when she finished high school during World War Two and lived and worked on the family's farm while she waited to turn

Opposite: Children contributed to household provisioning and earned pocket money by selling meat to local butchers and skins to fur traders.

21 so she could become a herd tester (testing milk samples for fat content). Once, when Harry was ill with bronchitis, he lay in bed bemoaning the lack of 'dog tucker'. Rita disappeared for a while; 'I thought she was probably doing some necessary chore about the place. After an hour or so, in she walked, proudly carrying a large sinister looking Billy goat's head, with tremendous horns, a horrible gory looking object, dripping blood. It was her first kill; she had quietly taken Harry's .22 rifle, stalked the old goat and had scored a bull's eye.'[45] It was an event the whole family remembered for many years to come.

There is no doubt that having access to game helped families get through difficult times. Sarah Higgins's family was caught up in the fallout from the clash between Maori and pakeha settlers in 1843 at Wairau in Marlborough, making provisioning difficult. 'There was no food and no money. There were no shops to get anything . . . We had to build our houses again. There were plenty of wild birds — those who had their own ammunition could shoot them . . .' Even once hostilities ceased, the Higgins family, like many others, endured separation while fathers and brothers found work. Her father found employment on the farm of a fellow Kentishman, 'so he was away all week from me, he went Monday and came back Saturday nights so I had to be by myself. We had no meat to cook for him and I used to take the gun and shoot a pigeon, a caw-caw [kaka] or a tui to cook when he came home, and docks, thistles and potatoes, if he brought any home.' Sarah's brother 'had a dog and ammunition and he used to get a wild pig occasionally', and she saved the fat from any pork they had.[46]

Into the twentieth century, rural people with their own cows and poultry and access to the bush often managed tough economic times better than their urban or labouring counterparts. Jack Bull's family moved from Wellington to the Wairarapa in the early 1930s after Jack's father's employment was reduced to one week in four. The family paid £5 per year in rent on 2 hectares of land on which they grew onions and from which Jack and his brothers had access to the bush for hunting. 'We'd get five or six deer, miles of meat, you know, that we'd give away. It was there for the taking if you had the ability to get there. So while the Depression was terrible for some, we were free and easy.'[47]

**Meat was not the only household item obtained by hunting game animals. In early twentieth-century Nelson, Newton McConochie's mother made tallow candles from deer fat. One yearling stag was in such good condition that his mother made 11 pounds (almost 5 kg) of candles from its fat.**[48]

Men were not the only hunters in colonial families. Shanghais, 'pea rifles' and traps were all used by children to gather food. George Campbell, a schoolboy in the 1890s in Aoroa in Northland, was caught by his teacher using a shanghai to kill a bird in a tree. He was ordered inside the classroom but instead of the expected reprimand, the teacher quizzed him about his accuracy and the areas in which he hunted. 'As I could see he was interested, I invited him to come to my place the next Saturday and go with me into the bush. Sure enough Mr Elliott arrived on Saturday morning and we went deep into the bush and returned with a bag of pigeons and kaka.'[49]

Opposite: These dogs are showing great interest in a live pig being taken home for fattening. Boosting domestic herds by adding wild piglets or weaners was common right up to the mid-twentieth century and continues today.

As a child, Ngati Porou activist and clergyman Reweti Tuhorouta Kohere frequently accompanied his father on pigeon-shooting expeditions in the 1880s. 'Pigeon-snaring and piercing [a form of spearing] was an art in the old days, but in these days of guns, shot and powder, pigeon-shooting is downright business.' He recalled that the characteristic beat of kereru wings was 'nothing compared to the thunderous noise made by hundreds of birds on the wing after a shot had been fired, and the sky darkened with them'.[50]

Pigeons were also targeted by Lavinia Mair and her siblings in their travels from the Manawatu to Northland during the 1880s, but sometimes they got more than they bargained for:

Above: The provisioning ethic was instilled in many hunters from when they were children. Up until the late 1960s, when prices for wild venison made selling the meat more economical than eating it, a great number of hunters and their families ate only wild meat. This young red stag in the back of Brian Woodley's car was destined for the freezer.

*In the good old days, when the wood pigeon was so numerous, my sister and I would go out shooting them. With our brothers, we would make an early start on horseback, reaching the feeding ground about sunrise. The birds sleep in the middle of the day. One day as we were having our lunch there was movement in the trees overhead and some ripe berries fell. My sister fired into the foliage and down came a pair of fine blue wattled crows [kokako]. Then towards sunset, the pigeons began their evening meal, and we would have great sport with our four guns, muzzleloaders at that. With a heavily laden packhorse we would reach home soon after dark.*[51]

Lavinia's bag of pigeons often numbered in the twenties.

Growing up on the family's farm in the Nelson region at the turn of the century, the McConochie boys found their efforts at hunting for the family were not always appreciated. When Newton McConochie was only eight years old and his brother just five, they snared a wild pig using flax, as they'd seen local Maori do. Their mother was furious, probably more because of that mix of relief and anger that comes when your children have avoided injury or death only through sheer good luck. They promised never to do it again.

When Newton was 12 and the family was going through a difficult time, he shot a deer out of season and without a licence. 'When my confession was made, a good, sharp reprimand was handed out by my parent. As he said, it put him in a most invidious position for he was a great advocate for everything being straight and above-board in sport. I, his son, had broken an age-old rule of Scottish tradition, and by my action I'd become a common poacher.'[52]

Children's food-gathering continued into the twentieth century, judging by a report of the Manawatu Acclimatisation Society in the 1950s that large-scale poaching was being carried out by school children. Mr Beattie reported that 'he had heard of one party being apprehended with a sack of 22 ducks, 8 of which were dead. Their method being to drive the ducks up small streams and drains into waiting nets'.[53]

The provisioning of families also saw the blurring of the lines between 'game' and 'livestock'. The Manawatu children poaching ducks might have been going to sell their catch, but could equally have been going to domesticate them for future eating. In the 1880s George Campbell and his band of 13 siblings capitalised on wild cattle getting bogged in Northland's swamps by rescuing them and domesticating them for family use.[54] It was common practice in the timber settlement where they lived when out pig-hunting to scoop up piglets and bring them home. Although the pigs ravaged the family's vegetable garden, Campbell contended that they 'were not considered a menace' (his mother might have disagreed!). Pigs were 'a rich food, and when caught young and housed, soon became domesticated and fattened quickly on skim milk'. Despite this 'we preferred the meat of wild pigs to those we raised, and mill hands and Maoris from the pa hunted every week with the dogs and guns. Our nearest neighbours used a boat to cross the river to Harding's property where the wild pigs were more plentiful. I often accompanied them, and we never failed to get pigs'.[55]

Not only pigs were caught for domestication. Nelson settler J Downie wrote of a goat hunt in 1887:

> After following this spur for about half a mile we sent the dogs away and presently, to our astonishment, we heard them bark, not a hundred yards away to our right down a small valley, and after a little while we heard a kid . . . Then we commenced jumping logs, sliding down small precipices &c till we got down to the bottom of the valley here we seen a billy-goat facing one of our dogs. Immediately one of our party caught the billy and tied him up to a sapling and went in pursuit of the mob. About half a mile from the place where we caught the billy the dog caught a fine nanny which father caught and tied a rope round its horns and fetched it to the billy then the four of us had to take the two goats down the creek for about two miles, the best way we could.[56]

In the 1940s, David Marino's family in Te Horo near Wellington also raised pigs captured in the wild. Marino's father and uncles were keen pig-hunters and often brought home 'young suckers and we'd feed them up, give them a bit of milk for a while . . . any young ones, we'd catch them and put them in a sack — they didn't weigh much, two–three pounds, not much. Oh we had pigs all the time, you know from one winter to another, we'd catch them in the spring.' Pigs were part of a wide variety of foods this family gathered in the wild; the fare also included puha, poroporo berries, blackberries and watercress. These supplemented the milk and butter from their own cows.[57]

Similarly, in the 1930s, Sonny Te Ahuru and his brothers and cousins caught wild young cattle to sell to neighbouring farmers near Te Rena, the central North Island mill town where they lived, and larger beasts to kill for the family. The method sounds simple enough, but could be very dangerous.

> We had ropes prepared when we leave here all ready with loops, you put a couple of ropes around my shoulder, go out with our team of dogs . . . When the dogs got onto any wild cattle, sometimes a mob of five or six, or there might be a mob of twenty, eh.

*I notice with wild cattle, when the dogs get onto a mob, you walk straight in while the dogs are rounding, if you walk straight in they don't take any notice of you, that's my experience, they're more concerned about the dogs, eh. Then you're right there amongst them and you walk in with a rope and slip it over their horns — they're all horned cattle — you've got all the loops ready, you slip it all over the horns and tie it up to the nearest tree. Before they know what's going on it's tied up to a tree. But after a while, if you play around too long, then they get to know who you are, then you've got to be careful . . .*[58]

Getting the cattle out of the forest also required skill and a certain amount of daring. 'We used to carry a bundle of sacks in front of our saddle, and we take it off and cut it up and put it round their horns, that'll stop them hurting your horse.' A rope was tied around the horse's tail and the horse backed up to the cow. The cow was tied on and the rope around the tree released 'and that's how we'd lead them out. But after a while you could take the rope off your horse's tail and lead them by hand and that cow'll just follow you right out.'

Above: Before the wide availability of household freezers, game often had to be shared out among family and friends, preserved in some way or stored in the local butcher's freezing chamber. Sharing game was encouraged by acclimatisation society regulations that forbade the storing or freezing of game more than seven days after the close of the season.

**Hunting for the pot   103**

The only problem was stopping the cattle drinking at creeks: 'If you let 'em drink they'll just lay down and you won't be able to get them up'.[59]

Born in 1938, Fred Richards grew up in Owhango in the central North Island, where his father worked for the Dominion Timber Company. He described a great range of childhood pursuits in the bush including eeling, catching freshwater crayfish and hunting goats with his friends. When Richards and his mates were around nine or 10 and too young for rifles, they would 'run the goat down, we'd do it in relays'. They would find a mob of goats, single out a young nanny and 'then we'd take off':

Above: Cyril Rutland and Nob Goile (on launch) loading a wild pig on to a launch on the Mokau River after a successful hunt in 1930.
Opposite: Well-established camps were central to many hunting expeditions. More than a staging post, they were a base for day hunting or from which to launch lightweight overnight trips. Cooking, eating, resting, planning and exchanging information all went on at camp. Such camps were frequently described in writings, diaries and letters; they were sometimes photographed and, in the case of the Spooner Brothers (see pages 200–1), drawn.

OUR CAMP AT FOOT OF BALDY, BUILT MARCH 1937.

> One joker'd chase it so far and we'd meet up on a ridge somewhere, then another'd take over and chase it so far, then we'd try and herd it back in the direction where the third fella was and he'd chase it back and we used to catch 'em, we'd come home with a goat... we'd jump on it and cut its throat, gut it, skin it and fetch it home, cut the hindquarters off and that was meat that we were fetching home.[60]

This was providing to be proud of. 'Mum'd cook the hindquarters up, a roast, we used to take it in our lunch to school and we used to tell all the children at school that this was a goat that we caught, the meat on our lunch. We thought we were quite neat.'

Richards's father instilled in him an ethic of providing. 'We *never* bought meat, I was raised on wild meat and even to this day luxury to me is a piece of mutton. The first twelve years me and Beth were married [from 1962] we had wild pork and venison, that's all we lived on.' These lessons started when Richards was very young; his father began taking him hunting when he was about seven years old.

> My dad had an ancient .303... and he had three big pig dogs and they'd get onto a pig or [cattle] beast, and he used to leave me by a tree and threaten me with my life if I moved, and I'd have to sit there, the dogs'd be barking and there'd be all this commotion, then all of a sudden the .303'd BOOM out and then there'd be dead silence and I'd be sitting there shaking wondering what to do if a beast walked round the corner... I'd be really worried, then all of a sudden this 'FRE-ED' would come through the bush and in the bush... you'd get a lot of echo and it was hard to tell where the voice was coming from. I'd get 'Fre-ed' three or four times and after a quarter of an hour or half an hour I'd finally track my way through to where my father was. By the time I got there, nine times out of ten, he had the beast down, bled it... and then it was a matter of cutting it all up and I'd wind up with a front shoulder or a piece of back leg and we had to carry it out. This is the reason, I tell my boys, why I never grew tall cos I spent all my life carrying meat out of the bush.

### Keeping meat fresh

*Before the development of home refrigeration, a variety of cellars, cool stores, meat safes and preservation techniques were used to keep meat fresh. The 1883* Brett's Colonists' Guide *instructed settlers on keeping game meat fresh using coffee sprinkled over the animal or bird.*

GAME — TO KEEP — Newly ground coffee sprinkled over game will keep it sweet and fresh for several days. Clean the game (that is, wipe off the blood); cover the wounded parts with absorbent paper, wrap up the heads, and then sprinkle coffee over and amongst the feathers or fur, as the case may be; pack up carefully and the game will be preserved fresh and sweet in the most unfavourable weather. Game sent open and loose of course, cannot be treated in this manner; but all game packed in boxes or hampers may be deodorised as described. A teaspoon of coffee is enough for a brace of birds, and in this proportion for larger game. Pound charcoal will serve the same purpose. The taint may be removed from meat or poultry by washing with chloride of soda.[61]

*Surprisingly similar advice was still being dispensed in 1950, in* Tui's Third Book of Commonsense Cookery. *Under 'Venison — How to Keep', Tui advised 'Hang it, wipe it with a clean cloth daily, sprinkle with ground ginger or pepper. When required, wash and dry well, rub with butter or good dripping, cover with a paste of flour and water.'*[62]

## The pot versus sport

Acclimatisation societies had a great deal to say about eating game, and the tension between sport-hunting and pot-hunting was a constant feature of their management activities. For example, the selling of game to hotels and boarding houses was a practice widely condemned by societies. Selling meat to such establishments was a common income-earning strategy for hunters (see Chapter 3) but it was considered antithetical to 'sporting' interests.

## Hunting deaths

*While hunting sustained many, it caused the deaths of others. In a society awash with firearms, as colonial New Zealand was, it was inevitable that guns would be involved in accidental deaths, deliberate woundings and murders, as well as suicides.*

*Deaths while hunting were not common, but like contemporary hunting deaths, most occurred when hunters were shot by their companions. A survey party in the north Rakaia in July 1865 who were sustained almost entirely by duck-shooting were terribly shocked when one of their number shot another. Alfred Newberry described what happened in a letter to his brother:*

> Another man was firing at some wild ducks close to the tent, we were all in fact close together, and the man with the gun stumbled over the tent rope and in falling the Gun went off the muzzle being close to poor Trounce's leg close to his groin and shattered the bone for 4 or 5 inches all to pieces. We immediately made a hammock and strung it on a pole and carried him to the nearest station about 5 miles ... The road was something awful to walk over with nothing but uphill and down dale snow and boulders we got him there at last.

*It was too late for Trounce, however, who died from blood loss and shock during the night. Newberry remarked, 'He left a wife, but no children'.*[63]

*In 1875 The Timaru Herald reported the death of William Hens at the hands of his friend John Ritter. The two, 'Germans who resided together in the Waimate bush', were out shooting ducks in mid-July.*

> While the men were walking along endeavouring to get a shot at some ducks, Ritter, who had had his gun at full cock, tried to lay the hammer down carefully. While trying to do this, however, the hammer slipped through his finger, and discharged the gun, the contents entering the head of Hens who was close by, killing him instantly.

*When the police and the doctor arrived on the scene 'they found Ritter in a sad state of anguish, embracing the body of his dead comrade'.*[64]

Another terrible accident occurred in 1899, when 19-year-old Ernest Hunt killed his 18-year-old friend, Cuthbert Walker. Planning a few days' shooting on the Wainono Lagoon near Waimate, Hunt and Walker had made camp on the shore. After a reasonably successful day on the Saturday, they got up at 2.45am the next day and took the boat out onto the lagoon. A little after 7am they pulled up their decoys and left to go back to camp for breakfast. Hunt told the story in the Coroner's Court:

Walker was rowing and over came some swans. He stopped the boat and said give me my gun, and get your gun ready, and we'll have a shot — I handed him his gun. He turned around to take it, afterwards turning to his front. While lifting up my own gun and pulling up the hammer the right barrel went off — the shot struck Walker on the left hand side of his head and he fell into the bottom of the boat dead — I saw a quantity of blood. The gun was loaded with shot . . . I didn't know what to do then, I couldn't row. I paddled across out of the deep water as far as I could so that I could walk. I then got out and pushed the boat to shore as far as I could out of the water. I then went and harnessed up the horse and fetched the horse and cart to the boat. I tied the wheel of the trap and tried to put Walker's body into the trap, it took one a long time, but I got the body in at last and covered up the body when I got to where the tent was . . .[65]

Despite asking many people for help along the way, poor Hunt took the body all the way to the Junction Hotel at Studholme — nearly a full day's travel — before anyone would alert the police or send a message to Walker's father. Once again, a verdict of accidental death was entered and no blame was attached to Hunt.

In each case, the coroner and the jury had to determine whether there was a case for criminal prosecution and hence there was an emphasis in many of these inquests on the friendship between the men. It makes for poignant reading, as in the case of 19-year-old Percy Stephenson, who was shot dead by his companion Harold Warren while they were pig-hunting near Gisborne in 1902.[66] The men were part of a group staying and working together on a station. The pair went out shooting one afternoon and, after getting one *pig and two pigeons, Warren was handing the pigeons to Stephenson when his shotgun went off, catching Stephenson in the side of the head. Another man, Harry Green, who was working nearby, heard two shots and 'about half an hour after, I saw Warren on opposite side of the Wharekopae [Creek]. He threw up his hands and said "I have shot Percy. What shall I do" and he fell on the ground and started crying'. In his evidence, Warren made a statement — possibly in response to a question — about his friendship with Stephenson: 'I had no quarrel with the deceased, we were very good friends. I helped to bring the body here. I knew him about 10 years. When we left McCutcheon's we were both in the best of spirits, and we had arranged to carry on a lot of work and were packing in stores.' Green also noted, 'When Warren came to me he was very much distressed. I have no doubt it was an accident.' Another witness, Michael Collins, declared, 'Deceased and Warren were on the best of terms. They were mates.'[67]*

*Elizabeth McDiarmid's parents told her of a shooting accident in the West Taieri community where they lived in the 1860s, and the long-term effects on the people involved.*

Mr John Curral was the name of the young man who had just come over from Australia. Either 2 or 3 men were shooting at a target that was fixed on a tree in Mr Lee's bush. Mr Curral had, as I understand shot at and wounded a kaka on the roadside and went down into the bush to get it, and so, poor fellow, caught a bullet that was intended for the target. Mr Edward Lee, it was said, had forbidden trespassers on his property so the men who were shooting might conclude that no-one was near. I can barely remember the circumstances, only seeing Mrs Abel [for whom Curral worked] in our own little home on that evening weeping about him. Dr Cockeril (not a duly qualified doctor, we understood, but a medical student) was one of the men who was shooting at the target and he must have thought, or perhaps known that it was his bullet that had caught the unfortunate young fellow, for I was told he fainted when he heard there was an accident. He left Woodside not long after, and lived almost a hermit life until he died on Ram Island (lower Waipori).[68]

The most obvious difference between nineteenth- and twentieth-century hunting deaths is that as gun technology improved, the numbers of deaths from accidental discharge of weapons dropped dramatically.

Another change in technology brought a sudden rise in hunting deaths, however. In the 1960s and '70s there were a number of deaths associated with helicopters working in the venison recovery industry. The flying itself was dangerous: the mountain environment was unpredictable, flying had to be low, and flying at night was disorienting. High altitudes, snow and ice meant that the helicopters' skids didn't always have much purchase. Hunters were not familiar with helicopters in the early days and several terrible accidents and fatalities occurred while dragging deer down to the helicopter or tightening the strop under the chopper. Using Civil Aviation Authority records, Graeme Caughley calculated that almost every helicopter working in New Zealand in the late 1970s had been involved in an accident of some sort. In 1977 there were 85 helicopters at work and 32 reported accidents. Of these, 23 occurred when the helicopter was working either in meat recovery or live animal capture. In these accidents, 11 of the machines were totally destroyed and 12 badly damaged (there was no record in CAA notes of men injured or killed). Caughley argues that the ratio of reported to non-reported accidents was 1:3, and that most of the helicopters working in venison recovery had probably had an accident that year.[69]

Pilots, while agreeing with Caughley that accidents were massively under-reported, reject the suggestion that most pilots were involved in an accident at some stage. A few operators had several accidents and that could account for the figures. Most pilots were skilled and professional fliers who took few risks with their expensive machines.[70] Pilots and hunters agree, however, that several of their number were killed in helicopter accidents during this period. It was known as a dangerous business.

In the late twentieth century, shooting deaths of hunters remained rare. In a 2003 report, police inspector Joe Green calculated that approximately 40,000 hunters spent 260,000 hunting days in the bush each year in New Zealand, putting into statistical perspective the 36 deaths between 1979 and 2002 in which one hunter shot another.[71] The emotional scale of these events however, remains enormous for everyone affected.

Acclimatisation societies could not resolve how to discourage the practice, however. Motions to ban the serving of game in hotels outright always failed — in part because some society members enjoyed having their freshly shot duck cooked by the accommodation house where they were staying. It was beyond the remit of acclimatisation societies to ban the sale of game to hotels and would have been impossible to police.

Developments in refrigeration also caused problems for the ability of acclimatisation societies to regulate the taking of game and its consumption. The ability to freeze game increased the difficulty of regulating poaching — how could a ranger tell if a duck had been shot in season and frozen for later consumption, or shot out of season and sold illegally to a hotel after the close of the season? Up until household freezers became widely available in the 1950s, the general rule was that game could not be served in a restaurant, hotel or boarding house more than seven days after the close of the season.

Even in the 1950s, some societies continued to control not just when and how much game could be killed, but when people were to eat it. The Manawatu Acclimatisation Society went into committee in October 1953 to discuss a report 'from Mr Boness that ducks shot in season are still being held in cool store in Fielding (more than three months after the conclusion of the shooting season)'. The delegate to the acclimatisation societies' council (the national body that succeeded the association) took the problem higher up and returned to the November meeting with the verdict that 'the Council does not wish to see ducks held in cool store for commercial purposes but are inclined to turn a blind eye where they are held for private consumption'. Nonetheless, at the December meeting the society resolved that a ranger needed to take action if the ducks were still in the cool store.[72]

By and large, society members were mystified by the desire to keep game. In 1928 'Mr C. Baker (Otago) asked if it were necessary at all to allow birds to be kept in the freezer after the end of the season. He would rather be inclined to give his friends a treat'.[73]

The theft of eggs was also a problem that was considered by the societies. 'Schoolboys' and 'natives' were the culprits according to society members, and in 1924 there was a proposal to raise the minimum fine for stealing eggs to £5 for the offence plus five shillings per egg. But many times before this, the collection of eggs for food was railed against. At the meeting of the New Zealand Acclimatisation Societies' Association in 1912, the Auckland member wanted a harder line against the Maori 'habit of collecting vast quantities of duck and swan eggs — for eating — to the detriment of the sport', requesting that the association 'make representations to the Government against such a practice'.[74]

## Cooking and eating

Despite their importance to hunting, those who have cooked and eaten game have not been much talked about in histories of hunting. As has been discussed earlier, many early pakeha surveyors and explorers would have gone hungry but for the hunting and cooking skills of their Maori guides and companions.

The sharing and eating of game has been a constant feature of New Zealand's hunting history. During Charles Carter's travels through the Wairarapa during the 1850s, he spent a night at Mr Matthews's station, then stayed on because of rain the next day. He and Matthews went for 'a gallop': 'still through swamps and streams we go, splashing and frightening the wild pigs on the adjoining fern-ridges, and the goats on the near hills, and the wild ducks on the reedy waters . . .' Carter was then thrown from his horse, so,

> we returned to the house by the shortest route. Here another change of clothes and a seat by the side of a large talking and laughing fire . . . and tea with rashers of bacon (wild pig), potatoes, bread and butter placed before us — of which we partook with a keen appetite . . . We passed the evening away in telling stories, as they say in England, sitting round by the common hearth; Mr M's two assistants at shepherding and tilling the ground told stories about the natives and about the wild cattle they had seen in the bush, the pigs they had killed, the boars they had fought and slain, and the great eels they had caught — all of which was then new and strange to me.[75]

The importance of hospitality to greasing the wheels of politics was also recognised in the colonial period. In 1882, various newspapers reported that Maori King Tawhiao was hosting a large 'Kingite meeting' and that the Native Minister, John Bryce, had 'sent Tawhiao a present of sporting powder etc which the latter accepted, and stated he would use it to shoot pigeons for the meeting'. A few days later the papers reported that Tawhiao had shot 180 kereru.[76]

Family visits were important occasions for hospitality too. In the 1880s, a special effort was made to treat Robert Cameron to a special dish even though he was only a boy visiting his cousin on his family's Wairarapa bush block:

> Knowing how much I liked pigeon stew cousin John soon got out his gun and ammunition. We were soon out round the bush looking for pigeons. As they were very

## Hunting on the subantarctic Islands

During World War Two, New Zealand participated in a Pacific-wide coast-watching operation. Some men were stationed on the Chatham Islands and Norfolk Island, while others served on New Zealand's subantarctic islands. Three camps were established on these islands: two on the Auckland Islands and one on Campbell Island. Most participants were civilians — meteorologists and biologists among them — and most were trampers, hunters or climbers. One of the men was a hunter who was a qualified butcher, and one of the wireless operators was described as a West Coaster 'quite used to knocking around in the bush and doing a lot of shooting'.[77]

Their isolation meant that the camps had to be very well equipped: 'egg-beaters to tobacco, rifles to hair clippers'.[78] Rations were plentiful and included luxuries such as chocolate and rum, but by mid-year the menu became very monotonous. Fresh food was very limited because the climate was not conducive to vegetable gardening, so the coast-watchers became a bit more adventurous in their diets. Fish were not an option because of concerns about parasites, but wild ducks — if they could be shot — and shags were occasionally on the menu. Wild pigs, sheep and cattle were also hunted, their presence the result of seafarers' releases and animals abandoned after a failed attempt at farming on the islands. These animals were not ideal fare, however. Rowland Lopdell commented that the pigs and cattle grazed on kelp, which made their flesh very bitter.[79]

Once a month, some of the men at the Auckland Island camp went

Above: During World War Two, groups of coast-watchers were stationed on New Zealand's subantarctic islands. Populations of wild sheep and cattle lived on many such islands, their ancestors released by eighteenth-century seafarers or abandoned after failed farming attempts. They provided the men stationed on the islands with some variation in diet.

*to nearby Enderby Island for what was known as 'the butcher's picnic', to shoot a cattle beast. 'We could never shoot one handy. They were always a long way off. It had to be skinned, usually in the rain and a cattle beast seems to roll away down into a wet hollow always. We'd have to skin it and cart the meat out and it was a very difficult job.'[80] Sometimes a leg of beef was strung up in the rigging of their ship, in the salt spray and breeze, but to make the meat tender enough to eat it had to be chopped up finely and made into patties.*

*Shooting sheep on Campbell Island was easier than hunting cattle, but because there was no cover they had to be stalked. On a windy day, coast-watcher Alistair Duthie found he could get right up behind them and either catch them by hand or shoot them with a .22. They were 'miserable little sheep', however.*

*The rabbits on Enderby Island also provided a good supply of fur. George Bish recalled that while the cattle, sheep and pigs were hunted steadily, 'we didn't decimate the local population', but 'the rabbits on Enderby got a bit of a hiding; everybody got a fur coat out of that for their girlfriends or wives'.[81]*

*At the end of Lopdell's service as a coast-watcher, he went to Dunedin, where his wife had moved for war-time work. They had three weeks' leave together. 'We just loafed about, then she went back to work and I went deer-shooting.'[82]*

*numerous cousin John soon shot a good number whilst I carried the swag. Soon we had plenty so we returned and I being used to the job helped to pluck the feathers off them. Cousin John soon cleaned and cut them up, prepared some vegetables, and soon one of the iron pots was put to good use cooking them.[83]*

Jean Boswell remembered her mother as a wonderful cook with a reputation throughout the timber community near Dargaville in which they lived in the late nineteenth century. She was a talented pastry cook once butter became more available — pigeon fat not being ideal for making puff pastry! She 'made the best toheroa soup in the district', and excellent bread. Jean, however, considered her mother's greatest achievement to be 'the tinning of wild pigeons'.

*She preserved dozens of them every season, and once we tasted the tinned we always preferred them to the fresh. They had the most marvellous flavour. She used treacle tins, sterilizing them in her old boiler and sealing the lids with beeswax. Each tin held a pigeon and a half, and in the summer time or during a closed season we were the envy of the settlement with our wonderful tinned pigeon.[84]*

**Hunting for the pot**

Game-cooking methods were the subject of serious attention. In his book *Red Deer Stalking in New Zealand*, published in 1924, Thomas Donne included an entire appendix on 'camp cooking'. While most overseas stalkers were accompanied by a guide, it was an added expense to also engage a cook and camp-hand. Donne clearly thought it important to inform potential stalkers of the range of delicacies that could be produced in camp. Although stating that stalkers must prepare themselves for 'a menu that is restricted in its variety if not in quantity', he then listed recipes for deer brains (sprinkle with

Above and opposite: Making good camp-oven bread was an acquired skill. To government shooters reliant on their own cooking for months at a time, a decent loaf of bread and a pot of venison stew were a man's best friends in the bush. Colin Turnbull (above), taking pride in his loaf baked over the fire in a Forest Service hut, even donned an apron for its presentation in the 1970s, while HJ Ollerenshaw (opposite) taught young hunters at the Golden Downs Training Camp the basics of bread-making in the 1950s.

a handful of salt, rinse then fry in butter before serving on toast) and 'angels on horseback' (made with canned oysters sprinkled with a few drops of lemon essence, wrapped in a strip of bacon and fastened 'with thread or small pin of pinewood, fry until nice and crisp, serve on toast'), as well as a long list of rabbit, pork and bird recipes. A savoury roll could be made with any game meat wrapped in suet pastry; game pancakes and soup with meatballs were equally versatile. If a stalker had a bottle of anchovy sauce and a can of salmon, a passable salmon mould could be created in camp. One wonders how many stalkers attempted Donne's deer's head recipe, however:

> *A common method of cooking a deer's head in Northern America is to cover it entirely with a thick coating of stiff clay. Place it in a hot hole in the Maori manner [hangi], cover with a wet sack and then with earth. Leave for eight or nine hours. The clay bakes hard; it is then easily removed, and brings off all the hairs. The meat is well cooked, and very appetizing to hungry hunters.*[85]

New Zealand cookery books and columns give us another window onto how game was prepared. While some published cookbooks were sponsored by the food industry and so contained no recipes for game, community cookbooks — compilations of contributions from various amateur cooks — usually did. These cookbooks contained recipes contributed by local people (church and school communities predominantly), readers (in the case of newspapers and magazines) and listeners (in the case of radio), and featured the type of recipes cooked in ordinary kitchens.

Isobel Broad's 1889 *New Zealand Exhibition Cookery Book* contained 30 recipes for game, including suggestions for hare, rabbit, venison and a range of native and introduced game birds. Broad's cookbook instructed cooks how to cook 'N.Z. Pigeon' — baked, roasted or stewed — and how to roast pukeko. The Nelson Club had donated their recipe for braised quail, and there were two recipes for quail pie, one for curried quail, and one for quail made into an entrée. *Colonial Everyday Cookery*, published in 1901, continued instructing New Zealand cooks on stewing wild ducks and pukeko (usually referred to as pukaki), roasting a haunch of venison and jugging hare, rabbits and pigeons.[86]

### Mrs Broad's '(N.Z.) Pigeon Stewed'

*Thoroughly wash the bird inside and out, and dry it. Rub the outside with a compound of pepper, cinnamon, nutmeg and grated lemon peel. Put into the stewpan one teacupful of lemon juice and one of port, four or five sprigs of parsley and a little thyme. Let this commence to boil, then put in the bird, and allow it to stew very slowly for fully half an hour. Keep the pan closed the whole time, and send to the table as hot as possible, garnished with slices of lemon and red-currant jelly.*[87]

The evidence from New Zealand cookery books also indicates that more difficult economic times saw a return to cooking with game. While the numbers of game recipes in published recipe books declined steadily after 1909, there was a resurgence in the 1930s. Similarly, in the years immediately following World War Two, game recipes appeared more frequently in cookbooks, with recipes for rabbit and duck abounding.

> "N.Z. Truth," Wednesday, May 17, 1950—Page 31
>
> ## Making Good Wives Better
> # A TASTY DUCK CASSEROLE
>
> WITH the game season now in full swing, many housewives will be confronted with ducks as a weekly offering. For those who are short of ideas of how to cook them, this week's first prize-winner of duck with a difference will prove helpful. Those whose husbands do not indulge in game shooting should also keep this recipe on hand in case kind friends present them with part of the "bag." The apples will enhance the flavor of the duck and casseroled dishes are always popular. With tomatoes in full supply, tomato hot cakes, which gain second place, will make an appetising and satisfying change. This dish, which combines a tomato filling with flat batter cakes, is excellent for the main meal on meatless days.

*Aunt Daisy's New Cookery No. 6*, published in 1947, contained recipes for roast quail alongside the perennial 'stewed pukaki [or pukeko]', roast wild duck and many rabbit recipes. Listeners to radio station 3YA in Christchurch in 1947 could tune in to 'Cooking with New Zealand Game'. Recipes for rabbit dominated the game section of Katrine Mackay's 1929 *Practical Cookery Chats and Recipes* compilation and Kathleen Johnstone's 1932 *Self-Help Recipes and Household Hints*, although one could count the 'mock game-steak' recipe if pushed. The community *Waiau Cookery Book*, published in Christchurch in 1933, indicated a wider range of game meats being consumed: recipes for roast venison (stuffed or haunch), venison pie made from shoulder meat, and 'fricassed [sic] rabbit' were presented along with the more adventurous game soufflé and rabbit mould. Jugged hare appeared in the game section of nearly every cookery book in the inter-war period, along with recipes for pukeko and swan.[88]

Hunting and cooking came together at the sometimes extravagant, annual dinners of acclimatisation societies and deer-stalkers' associations around the country. The menu for the Invercargill Deer Stalkers' Dinner in 1931 was 'rather elaborate' — and rather tongue-in-cheek — so much so that it was published in the *New Zealand Fishing and Shooting Gazette*:

> *Soup:* Manuka Broth, Consomme of Fern Root. *Fish:* Poached Trout; Eel in Season. *Entrees:* Pigeon Pie, Braised Hawk, Bittern Stew, Kaka Cutlets, Wild Sow Sweetbreads. *Hot Joints:* Roast Venison a la Monowai, Roast Leg of Wapiti a la Glaisnock; Roast Paradise or Teal Duck (mostly out of season), Wild Pork ex Tuatapere. *Cold Joints:* Hamilton Donkey a la Bray, Spikey Stag a la Alton. *Sweets:* Home Sweet Home (75 miles away), Jellied Red Pine Sap, Miro Berry Pie with Doe Cream. *Refreshments:* Buck Juice and Home Supply while it lasts. *Savoury:* Sapleby's Piston Ring Seal, Pig Tails on Toast.[89]

Clearly some licence was taken with the titles of the dishes, but venison, pork, duck and wapiti would all have been included in this meal. Likewise, the fiftieth anniversary history of the Taupo branch of the New Zealand Deerstalkers' Association made particular mention of the Deerstalkers' Ball as 'an event everyone looked forward to . . . Saturday was hall decoration day (ferns, deer and pig heads, etc), tables and chairs set out, band set-up, supper brought in. Lots of pork, venison, trout, plus all the other goodies that the wives cooked to make a memorable night . . . Generally home by 3 or 4am'.[90]

*The knife is a hunter's essential tool. In early descriptions of bushmen, knives were ever present. In Edward Jerningham Wakefield's diary, he contrasted himself with the 'suite of young gentlemen' who arrived in Wellington on the Brougham in 1842. He had been in New Zealand for some years and to his eye, the neatness of these young men and the fineness of their clothes spoke of their inexperience — 'Everything about them was so evidently new; their guns just out of their cases, fastened across tight-fitting shooting jackets by patent leather belts' — while he, on the other hand, was entirely appropriately kitted out. 'They considered me as one of the curiosities of the interior, turning up their noses with evident contempt at my rough red woollen smock, belted over a coarse cotton check shirt, without neck-cloth . . . They appeared, too, to view with some distrust a sheath knife, about eighteen inches long in the blade, which I had made my constant companion'.[91] In the Reverend James Millar Thomson's adventure story* Bush Boys of New Zealand, *published in London in 1905, the bushmen carried similar knives. The boys found themselves lost in the bush; 'suddenly, however, help appeared from a quarter altogether unexpected. Along one of the narrow tracks . . . came a motley crew of stalwart, sun-burnt men. Each carried his "swag" on his back . . . At the belt of each hung a billy, a tin pannikin, and a sheath carrying a large pig knife'.[92]*

*Department of Internal Affairs equipment lists for government shooters from the 1930s insisted upon two sheath knives, along with a sharpening stone or steel. 'At least two are necessary owing to the danger of loss and the fact that a man is useless without a knife.'*[93]

*Rifles were almost redundant without a knife. What would be done with any animal killed if no meat or skin could be retrieved from it? Occasionally knives were put to unorthodox purposes, as in the case of hunter Jon Knight in the late 1960s. After jumping from a helicopter onto the side of a mountain to retrieve a tahr, Knight realised too late that he was jumping onto ice. As he began to slide down the slope, he managed to get his knife out of its sheath and drive it into the ice until he slowed to a stop. Astonishing flying by his pilot meant that the helicopter could be manoeuvred close enough to pick him up by sliding the helicopter skid between his legs and lifting him off the precipice.*[94]

*More usually knives were used for dispatching pigs, skinning, cutting up meat and breasting ducks. They sliced onions and deer liver at the hut for a fry-up, diced meat for stews, carved camp-oven bread and spread jam. Government shooter Ken Francis noted that for many weeks after cullers returned to 'civilisation' after a season, when they sat down to a meal they could be seen reaching around their back for their knives.*[95]

## Surviving and providing

Hunters provided for their families and communities for a range of reasons. Geographical remoteness and the need to save money were constant motivations, but even as those drivers diminished, hunting could provide a family or a camp with far more — and better quality — meat than was available through other avenues.

Eating together and hospitality were also socially important. The sharing of meat or birds and the sharing of meals bound communities together. But hunting for the pot could also have more economic motives. As will be seen in the next chapter, the selling of game to hotels, butchers and boarding houses was one of the most common ways an income could be made from hunting, and this hunting for other people's pots had its most extreme manifestation in the commercial venison industry of the 1960s and '70s.

# 3

# Bringing home the bacon

When times were tough, very little could be allowed to stand between a hunter and a bit of extra cash. In the 1970s, living in Wanaka, Brian Burdon matched his modest Pest Board wages by selling venison — he was paid $37 per week by the board and made about another $35 from each deer shot on the weekend. His wages paid the mortgage and a few bills, but the family generally relied on credit for their groceries, and on venison sales to keep out of real financial trouble. Brian's wife, Carol, sent him into Wanaka one morning to buy $5 worth of groceries out of a $10 note. With the remaining fiver in his pocket, he popped into the pub for a jug of beer and 'a yarn for a quarter of an hour'. Running into two old friends led to a few more drinks and then an invitation to a party at another friend's place. At 9pm, Burdon arrived home 'to a very frosty welcome' and quickly fell into a 'deeply drunken sleep after telling Carol that the hunt I'd planned for tomorrow morning was off'. At 4am Carol woke him, 'offering a hot cup of tea in one hand and a smack in the ear with the other if I didn't get the hell out of bed that minute'. This was the beginning of a truly awful day: Burdon was badly hungover, he fell asleep during the day and got badly sunburnt, he spooked every deer he saw until, finally, at about 6pm he managed to shoot a very big stag. This, of course, meant carrying about 60kg of meat for two hours to the road end. 'That must have been about the hardest day I ever had on the hill, and it served me right. At least that's what Carol kept telling me every time I mentioned it.'[1]

For thousands of New Zealanders, hunting has long been a means of earning an income. Usually hunting was one of many activities cobbled together

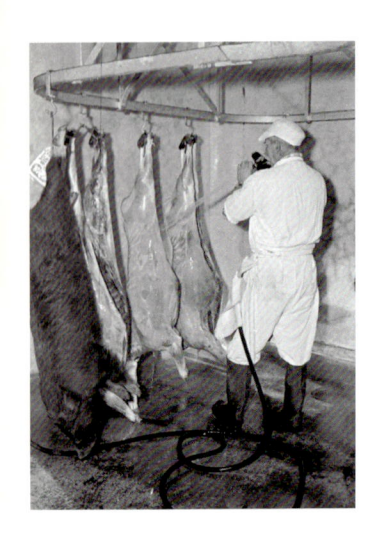

126  **Hunting**

over a season or a year or a lifetime through which ends were made to meet.

There was a surprising number of ways money could be made from hunting, the most obvious of which was selling the meat. Game animals and birds were sold to hotels, restaurants and butchers in the nineteenth and early twentieth centuries, and from the late 1950s, when export markets for game meat were developed, to meat-processing plants. Bounties paid on various pest animals were another source of income, as were the commercial industries dealing in skins, fur and feathers. Furriers, milliners and others in the fashion industry paid handsomely for fur and feathers, and skins were desired by a great many industries. Other parts of deer, such as velvet from antlers and scent glands, were highly sought after by Chinese herbalists and others. There were also many adjunct industries or avenues for earning an income from hunting without actually hunting. Taxidermists, gunsmiths, guides, horse-handlers, pilots and dealers in birds could all make part of their income through their association with hunting and hunters. By far the most famous of New Zealand's hunting-income earners, however, were government deer-cullers.

## The business of selling meat — hotels to helicopters

Possibly the first income earned by pakeha from hunting in New Zealand involved selling braces of ducks to the local hotel. Selling game was very common and quickly became seen as a problem by acclimatisation societies when it involved game under their control (see Chapter 1). Hunters sold meat to hotels, boarding houses and butchers, and Henry Cox, an apprentice butcher at Port Chalmers, wrote to his parents in the 1870s that they hunted wild pigs and cattle for the crews of ship in port.[2] As various animal protection acts were passed, butchers in some districts needed licences to buy and sell deer meat, leaving some records of the amount of game that passed through their shops. For example, in the first deer season defined by law in New Zealand in 1882, the Nelson Acclimatisation Society issued a licence to butcher

Opposite: Commercial game-meat sellers ranged from those who supplied local butchers, hotels and guesthouses to large export operations. In the 1890s Kirkpatrick & Co exported tinned quail to Britain, but when the price of quail climbed to ten pence per brace the trade became uneconomic. Rabbits, however, remained cheap and plentiful. Several attempts to establish an export game-meat industry were thwarted by the distances between hunting areas and processing plants. It was not until the 1960s that the use of aircraft to retrieve game and improved freezing technology enabled the industry to thrive.

Frank Trask to trade in deer meat. His shop processed 14 red deer stags and a fallow buck during the month-long season (keeping in mind that hinds could not be shot, and the bag limit for each licence was six deer), and probably held many more private carcasses in his freezing chamber. Trask wasn't above using these carcasses for advertising; when local hunter John Oldham shot a six-year-old stag Trask hung it in the window of his shop. Dressed (gutted and head and feet removed), it weighed 292 pounds (about 132 kg).[3]

Earning money by selling game, especially native game, to butchers and hotels was such a common occurrence that most of the surviving records of the trade describe breaches of various regulations and tensions between sport hunters and those hunting to earn an income. In 1908, the *Taranaki Herald* reported, as part of an appeal to protect kereru, that during the previous shooting season 'no fewer than 5000 pigeons were shot and forwarded by train to Wellington city'.[4] In 1884, a letter to the editor of *The Evening Post* complained that butchers were getting in ahead of the season. 'When passing a butcher's shop today [April 2], I noticed a large number of native pigeons exposed for sale. A Gazette notice . . . informs sportsmen that they may shoot native game between the 11th April and 31st July . . . I am rather curious to learn how it is that butchers are privileged thus to take "first cut" and make wholesale slaughter of the young birds before the season officially opens.'[5] The answer could have been that the butcher either bought from poachers or from Maori. As described in Chapter 1, there was substantial confusion about Maori rights to hunt native birds and clear evidence that Maori earned an income selling game to butchers and hotels.

People earning an income from selling game rubbed against the grain of the sportsmen's ethic of many acclimatisation societies. Their meetings often discussed the shooting and poaching of game for sale and the freezing of game by hotels and butchers for sale outside of the season. The Hawera society complained in 1912 that some licence-holders, 'particularly Natives', were shooting for hotels and were being given ammunition as well as payment to do so.[6] In 1925 a resolution was put up:

> that hotels and restaurants be prohibited from serving game, on account of the fact that many shootists shoot game for sale and supply hotels and restaurants and also clubs; further, on the ground that sale of cooked game encourages the sale of game birds for purpose of such supply. Members of this Society know of cases where men have shot over 200 birds in the season, and have sent all of them to Auckland, apparently sold, but it is difficult to procure convictions. It was stated that ducks were often sent in sacks to hotels.[7]

## Quick recovery

*The boom in venison recovery brought out many innovators. Deer carcasses were recovered from the bush using the relatively conventional means of light aircraft and helicopters, but also by jet boat, raft, modified Land Rover and motorbike. Bringing carcasses in to a central collection point also tested ground hunters: they used rickshaws, wheelbarrows and tractors that had been flown piecemeal into the bush and reassembled.*

*The aerial hunting industry involved a range of pilots and aircraft. Aeroplanes supported government shooters from 1948, dropping in their supplies, hut-building materials and other requirements. 'Hunter-pilots' were private meat shooters who had aircraft and could fly (usually as a result of agricultural work). They flew into remote locations, hunted and flew out with their deer. Other pilots did not hunt themselves but transported ground hunters and collected the carcasses from pre-arranged assembly points. Helicopter pilots were hunters of sorts, even if they didn't fire a shot, often having to track deer through mountainous or heavily forested terrain. They then herded groups of deer to more accessible locations where they could be shot and the carcasses recovered.*

Left: Shooting from helicopters required great skill: the machine was moving and vibrating and the small target of the head of a bounding deer or tahr zig-zagged and bounced all over the rough terrain. Shooting from helicopters, or 'gunshipping', streamlined meat-recovery operations enormously. It greatly reduced the time taken to find and shoot animals and enabled commercial hunting in remote and inaccessible places where animal numbers were highest. This picture shows Ken Smith shooting in the Tasman Valley, 1967.

In 1932 there were still complaints from some societies about 'professional men who went round providing the hotels'. There was also acknowledgement that there was a black market in game: in 1906 the national association agreed to a proposal to ban the display of stuffed game in the windows of game-dealers' shops because 'these stuffed birds were used as an advertisement to notify that ducks could be bought at the shops out of season'.[8]

Legitimate commercial meat-selling operations were also in existence in the nineteenth century. In a court case in 1891, the workings of some of these businesses were revealed — but only because they had overstepped the law. Several defendants were charged with selling game without a licence: William Conrad sold a sack of pigeons, James Hastie was charged with selling 15 pairs of kereru and George Tilbury was charged similarly for selling ducks. In the testimonies in these cases, game-selling was revealed as being very common indeed: the defence put up for each man was that they were doing nothing unusual.

William Stewart, a fishmonger, had bought the pigeons from Hastie and had noted it in his register, as he was required to do by law. At one stage the defence counsel remarked that if the acclimatisation society ranger had examined the register of local hoteliers he would have found another 'fifty cases marked in their registers'.

Tilbury had sold to Hugh Ross, a poulterer, who gave evidence that 'a number of his country customers . . . brought a little game' for him to sell on. Tilbury was a carrier who bought goods from country suppliers and distributed them in the city. Hastie was an 'expressman' — a similar occupation, but it included a 'pigeon run' around a series of butchers, fishmongers, poulterers and hotels. Everything presented in these cases indicated that a wide range of colonial men were involved in selling wild game in some capacity.[9]

Exporting game meat was tried in New Zealand several times. At the turn of the century, S Kirkpatrick & Co, a Nelson cannery, exported tinned quail and rabbits. A substantial attempt to establish an export business was made between 1924 and 1929 by a Wellington butcher, R Philp. He applied to the Department of Internal Affairs for an exclusive licence to export venison, arguing that unless he could be guaranteed a monopoly it was not worth his while trying to establish the trade. The national president of the New Zealand Acclimatisation Societies' Association and Philp's local MP made representation to the department on his behalf. There were administrative difficulties to be overcome, especially because levels of protection on deer varied across acclimatisation society districts. The other problem from the department's perspective was that there did not seem to be a market for the meat.

In November 1924, the food section manager of Harrods reported to the New Zealand High Commissioner in London that during the English season for venison (August to February) 'we sell approximately 40 carcasses. In our opinion customers merely have this meat as a change, and perhaps not more than once or twice during the season'. There seemed to be too small a demand, and certainly no market for frozen venison. However, Philp was persistent and insisted that a market could be found, and in April 1925 he received a licence for three years provided he exported 500 deer in the first year.

The muddled jurisdiction over deer proved to be a problem. Unable to get cooperation from the Wellington Acclimatisation Society, he approached the Forest Department to be told that 'as far as the Forest Department was concerned Mr Philp could kill all the deer in the Dominion but that the Forestry Service was not the statutory authority'; permission was required from the Minister of Internal Affairs to shoot deer in government-owned forests. Needless to say, Philp had trouble filling his annual quota in 1925–26, but the government was prepared to let him carry on. In 1927 Philp wrote to the minister saying he had orders for 2000 hindquarters per month, but the distances to the freezing works were making the operation difficult and expensive. His men would be encouraged to keep working hard if they could get a five shilling tail bonus (paid for each deer killed, based on the tail being presented as evidence of each kill) from the government instead of the one shilling they were currently getting. 'So Sir, I will leave it to you to put it before Cabinet to get the increase for my men otherwise I will have to drop this new industry.' Cabinet approved a rise to three shillings, but there was an increasing awareness within the department that Philp's trade was conflicting with another new export possibility, that of skins (to keep the meat clean during transportation, the skins were left on, and this meant cutting the skin if only hindquarters were being taken). Enquiries about deer skins had been made from California, and given that Philp had only filled half his quota in the first two years of operation, the export of skins began to look more attractive to some in the department. In 1929, defeated by the difficulties, expense and bureaucracy, Philp gave up the venison export trade.[10]

It was not until 1959 that the effort of recovering game meat for export proved commercially worthwhile. Two West Coasters, Henry Buchanan and

Opposite: Meat-hunting could provide a respectable living. In the mid-1960s, when the price of venison was a modest 32 cents per pound, a medium-sized hind was still worth an average week's wages. In the early 1970s the price reached an astronomical $1 per pound. It is little wonder that so many men tried their hand at meat-hunting at one time or another.

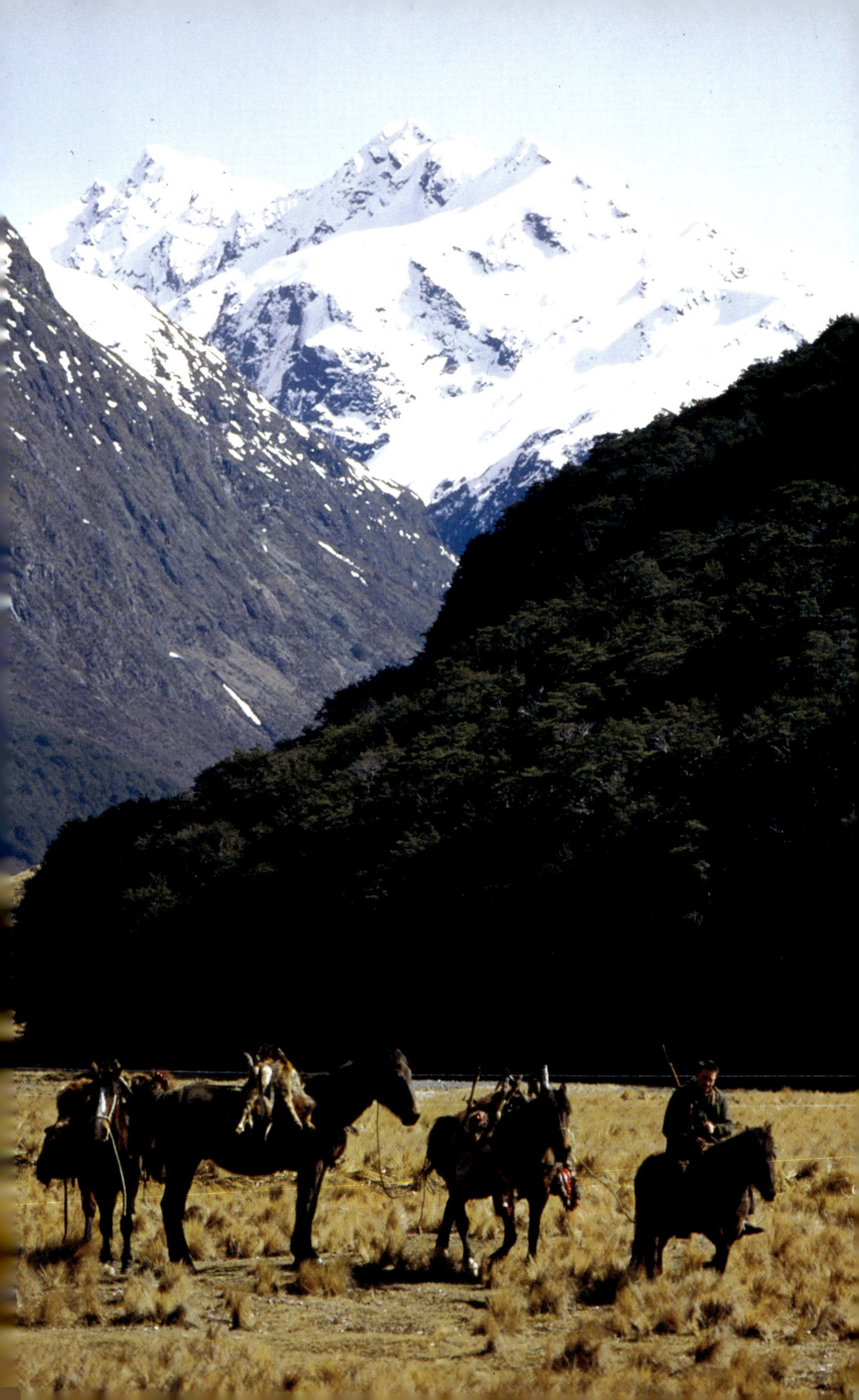

Malcolm Forsyth, managed to secure a market in the United States and by 1963 the number of meat-recovery businesses was growing rapidly. Over the next 10 years the commercial game-recovery industry exploded, but then suffered a slump that put many game processors and exporters out of business. The boom resulted in a huge increase in the numbers of meat-hunters as well as jobs processing venison, supplying the hunters, running packhorses to carry in supplies and carry out carcasses and, most famously, flying small planes and helicopters.

Buchanan, born 1917, had grown up in a sawmilling community in Okuru, Haast, where kereru was a staple food (even though technically they were protected from 1922). He did a great deal of deer hunting and 'whenever we had time off we'd go away deer hunting. Deer were pretty thick here in those days . . . Every weekend the weather was good we were off'. He worked as a roadman and a fencer when he left school, and many of his mates were skin-hunters as well. Buchanan had an eye for easier money and first 'got into planes' to fly whitebait from the more remote parts of the West Coast to Greymouth for sale to the city markets. He began doing the same with venison in the late 1950s because 'it seemed an awful waste, them lying around the flats when they were shot, it was a hungry world, must be some use for it. Skins were valuable too, we used to get 10 shillings a skin . . .' Shooting locally, he could get between 12 and 15 deer a night 'up the Haast with the Land Rover'.[11]

The first processing plant was simply a freezer at the Greymouth aerodrome, then Buchanan and Forsyth took over a building in town where they processed venison and fish for export. When Ministry of Agriculture and Fisheries regulations required separation of the products, Buchanan expanded to the factory next door and continued running two separate operations.

The first export market Buchanan and Forsyth tapped into was the United States, but they were 'too finnicky' (in 1958 the United States government began requiring a certificate of animal heath for all meat brought into the country[12]). The German market was 'a lot less particular' and came to dominate the export trade. At its peak, the company bought meat from 150 shooters, many of whom moved into the area for the work. They had three planes and 'agents everywhere . . . In the finish it was colossal really'. When two other companies set up, the competition 'cut us back', but it was helicopter hunting that spelled the end of Buchanan's involvement in the venison-export industry. 'I never thought the deer'd be silly enough to stand there and let the helicopters shoot them or I'd have had one. Instead of buying the Apache [plane] I'd have bought a helicopter and I'd have been right amongst it then'.[13]

This page: New Zealand hunter-pilots went to Mexico, Alaska, Canada and Africa. While pilots in those countries were usually excellent flyers they often had little experience of hunting or managing wild animals from the air. New Zealand pilots, on the other hand, were highly valued for these skills. Pilot John Fogden worked in the North Island, firstly in venison recovery and then in the capture of live deer for deer farms. In 1980, when he felt the peak of the industry had passed, he wrote to helicopter operators in Canada and South Africa seeking work. By coincidence one of the South African operators had just won a contract to capture and relocate game in game parks in the eastern and northern Transvaal. Flying in the lightly wooded Transvaal was very different to flying in the North Island's heavy bush country, and working with African species very different to working with red deer. The game capture season was winter when the trees had lost their leaves (improving visibility), the ground was dry enough to drive on and the game had no young. Tranquilliser darting was the usual method of capture. The pilot would fly close to the animal so the shooter could fire a dart, then back off while the tranquilliser took effect, leaving men on the ground to watch the slowing animal. Fogden spent 13 years working in South Africa and now works for the Civil Aviation Authority in Wellington.

Hunters working for commercial meat companies worked in remote areas of the country. The isolated back country of the Haast, where many South Island ground hunters worked, was largely unexplored apart from initial forays by Charlie Douglas in the 1890s and a visit from an adventurous party from the Tararua Tramping Club in 1951. Some infrastructure was the first order of the day for men wanting to hunt in the region, including a bush airstrip to service their camps and then shelters and huts in which one or two men would live for the eight- or nine-month season. This was hard work in one of the wettest parts of New Zealand.

Mike Bennett, one of Buchanan and Forsyth's ground hunters in the Haast region, tells the story of one hunter who had gone into the bush to build the airstrip. His rifle was with the first load of gear to be dropped in when the strip was complete. The weather was terrible, the plane could not get in for weeks and, to make things worse, there were 200 deer that grazed the flats nearby. As the hunter's rations ran out he was reduced to 'black re-stewed tea, keas knocked out of trees with sticks, and balls of soggy flour disguised as dumplings'. When the weather finally broke and the plane came in, the hunter complained bitterly that if he had 'eaten any more of the bastards [keas] I'd have sprouted wings and flown down the bloody gorge myself'.[14]

Venison hunting was hard work and hunters often worked for nothing up front; they were paid by the pound for meat. It was a gamble. Bennett describes the money being offered in the early 1960s as enough to make a reasonable living — he was making 24 cents per pound in these early days of the industry. When Buchanan's company stopped operating, Southern Scenic Air (using Cessnas and Austers) serviced most of the hunters in Bennett's area. 'Plane-day' meant meat going out and supplies, special requests and mail coming in from Cromwell, but these rendezvous were often delayed by poor weather. Once planes were flying, speed was important; there were lots of hunters to relieve of deer carcasses that had been hanging in meat safes near the strips and the mountain weather was fickle.

Meat-hunting could be a lonely business, and many men were separated from their families. Mike Bennett's letters to his wife, sent out of the bush with the pilots, showed that the weather dominated the lives of these hunters.

At the end of winter, when Bennett's season began, the deer could be relatively scarce and his letters acted as the conversation he was missing:

*Not much doing on the flats at all. Bit of night-sign. Everything else [I am getting] out of the bush. Must try for one more in the morning for the hundred quid, an absolutely ridiculous price for a Cessna load if you come to think about it . . . . There is so much to do in here . . . Two urgencies clamour for fulfilment — a long haired cook and a hut, in any order. The hut if anything is possibly of more importance at this stage of the game, I've only been in a week after all. This tenting with the present climate is somewhat unhealthy, apart from proximity to the riverbank, everything stays sodden as I fear this old tentage has had it. All the wood is still half-frozen and I eke out the kindling like an old miser with a dozen on Sunday. Could you spare me a working alarm-clock? . . . Even my bloody watch keeps stopping. Just had the tea, as usual enough for two. I somehow managed to scoff the lot and drank the silver-beet water. Tiger for me vitamins like. Or is it perhaps I drink anything? Must admit it is a bit of a shock to the system drowning in gallons of tea, but no doubt we will survive. This first week is always the worst . . . I hope.*[15]

Other letters asked for newspapers, tobacco, envelopes and tools — a power-saw file in one and in another 'four D.16 spark-plugs from the garage . . . also four gallons of white spirits. Also the very large Crescent spanner hanging up in the tool-shed, have to do the wheel bearings on the tractor'. The planes also brought hunters diesel generators and tractor engines to power freezers as the weather warmed up, lighting set-ups, baths (cut in half to fit in the plane then soldered back together at the camp), washing machines (run by the tractor motors), radios and record players. Some camps had extensive vegetable gardens. Sometimes wives and children joined the hunters; Bennett's wife Lorraine usually flew in with their young children in the height of the summer to spend time with him.

With the end of light-aircraft hunting and the ascendancy of helicopter hunting, ground hunters lost the need for many of these comforts, as their forays could be shorter, even though they were into much more remote country. What they lost in the bush lifestyle was more than made up for by increased wages and the comforts of doing a day's shooting in the back country then having a beer at the pub at the end of the day.

Even though there had been experiments with helicopter recovery in the early 1960s, a running cost of £60 per hour meant the price of venison was not high enough to warrant more than a few hours of use, and then only if you had a lot of meat to recover. By the mid-1960s however, venison prices had risen sufficiently that it was worthwhile using helicopters if more than nine deer could be recovered per hour.

The remote back-country basins of both islands were alive with deer and helicopters made them easily accessible to groups of ground hunters. Winter shooting also became a possibility.

Mike Bennett and Les Kemp worked for Graham Stewart & Co in Christchurch, and one winter week in the late 1960s they made more money than either of them had ever seen in their lives. In the head of the Te Naihi River near Haast, Bennett and Kemp shot enough deer to secure £800 *each* that week (the equivalent of $25,500 today). However, there was a great deal of ambivalence about this kind of work for hunters. Of this week, Bennett wrote 'it wasn't hunting, we never thought about it as that, we were killers and it was our job'.[16]

Helicopter hunting became even more efficient with the development of 'gunshipping', the shooting of deer from helicopters rather than by ground hunters. By 1968 this technique was being used widely and had been pared

Above: A chance encounter with a stag gave these high-country musterers a trophy head as well as meat for their camp and a skin to sell. Rural workers were in a position to add a little to their wages through skin- and meat-hunting, as well as through collecting bounties on birds and pigs.

## Too valuable to eat

*One of the ironies of the venison trade was that, with rising prices, recreational hunters and those who hunted meat to supplement their incomes could no longer afford to eat the meat they shot. Hunter Brian Burdon worked for the Pest Board in Cardrona, near Wanaka, in the early 1970s, trying to support his wife and baby twins on $37 per week. Before moving south, Burdon had been making up to $100 per week as a private meat-shooter, but in 1971 the price of venison had plunged to 24 cents per pound and the family had opted for steadier work in a beautiful part of the country. They were often in arrears to the grocer, 'but he knew we were decent folk and would pay the bill when we could'. Hunting — trespassing on private land in the process — became the way this family made ends meet.*

Carol and I evolved a plan whereby she would place our twins in their bassinet in the back seat of our old Victor and drive me up the valley to that nice new concrete bridge. I would retrieve my packframe and rifle from the boot, and very quietly slide under the bridge and into no-man's-land. Carol, in the meantime would drive back down the valley in the 5am chill to replace the offspring in their respective cots, and maybe catch a couple more hours of sleep herself. The latter part of the plan was that she would again put the kids in the rear seat on dusk and arrive at that bridge, parking well out of sight among the scrub an hour after dark, when I should appear, hunch-backed and exhausted with a week's wages on my packframe.[17]

*Burdon could get 32 cents per pound for venison and a 120 pound (54 kg) hind would double his wages for the week. Other Pest Board workers had variations on this practice, such as taking higher calibre rifles than the .22 they used for rabbits and goats with them on their rounds towards the end of the year; getting on towards Christmas, the boss turned a blind eye to the possibility of 'a deer for beer money'.*[18]

down to an incredibly efficient meat-hunting system. Very specialised skills were required. While flying in extremely demanding mountain environments with unpredictable winds, pilots had to hunt for and herd deer, then shooters had to shoot accurately out the door of a juddering, thundering machine while being buffeted by rotor wash, as well as memorise where the deer fell over a wide area of broken country — all without shooting the helicopter or its rotors. Added to this, for a right-handed shooter the easiest side of the helicopter to shoot out of is the left, but this is where the pilot sits. Some shooters taught themselves to shoot left-handed to overcome this difficulty. Most just put up with the discomfort and adapted.

The venison-recovery business reached a heady peak in the early 1970s when venison prices broke the 'dollar per pound' ceiling. Suddenly, venison was very big business. By the late 1960s, super-charged helicopters that could fly above 2500 metres were being brought into the country, extending the range of helicopter hunting. When the Los Angeles Police Department sold eight of their Hughes 300 helicopters in 1971, all eight were bought by New Zealand venison hunters, for $20,000 each. By 1977, most of the 85 helicopters at work in New Zealand were involved to some degree in venison recovery.

The record number of deer shot and retrieved in one day by one helicopter team (of pilot, shooter and gutter) was 212, by shooter Peter Campbell and pilot Russell Gutschlag in 1972. At approximately $50 per deer, this day earned them $10,600. Even subtracting the $1200 cost of running the helicopter for 10 hours, this was enough money in 1972 to buy a house.

It couldn't last, of course. Between 1971 and 1975, New Zealand exported 4200 tonnes of game meat each year, then in 1974 the international price for venison dropped suddenly from $2.20 to 65 cents per kg. This was still respectable, but it took the heat out of the industry. At the same time Inland Revenue finally caught up with this rather informal economy, introducing a withholding tax of 25 per cent, meaning the hunter could only be paid in full when he submitted a tax return and his receipts. The Civil Aviation Authority also brought in new regulations in 1973, attempting to control the numbers of bush pilots and light aircraft involved in the venison business, and the Ministry of Agriculture and Fisheries introduced increasingly stringent regulations regarding the handling of wild meat for sale. The requirement to bring out the carcass with the heart, lungs, liver and kidneys attached increased the carry-out weight of deer by 15 per cent; requirements that the carcasses had to be cooled to -6°C within 12 hours of being shot further complicated the process, and put an end to any part-time or recreational ground hunters legally selling game to local hotels. Deer had become so valuable that Lincoln University began running experiments with farming them, sparking the live-animal recovery business. By the late 1970s deer were worth more alive than dead, with hinds selling for $3000–4000 and stags for over $4000 (almost $23,000 today).[19]

The commercial venison industry continued at a more sedate pace through the 1980s. It was still earning New Zealand valuable export dollars until new European Union regulations required separation of processing premises for farmed and wild venison by 1993. Farmed venison was much cheaper to get to market and therefore took over the market. Between 1989 and 1991, the three remaining wild venison packing houses halved the number of deer they processed from 30,000 to fewer than 13,000 per year.[20]

The death knell for many hunters earning private incomes from hunting, however, was the 1977 Wild Animal Control Act, that for the first time in New Zealand's history effectively vested the ownership of wild animals killed on private land in the landowner. Poaching had finally become a crime in New Zealand.

### The Ranginui

*The Ranginui was one of two boats converted to mobile game-processing plants by aviation entrepreneur Tim Wallis. The boats were moored in the Fiordland sounds, but a great deal of the processing went on in the mountains, as helicopter pilot Bill Black explains:*

So the general thing was full tanks, which would last for two hours. We'd come across a couple of deer, let the gutter out and it was his job to gut them. We'd leave him there and carry on with the shooter so you'd be nice and light, and go and shoot probably 20 or 30 deer. Then pick them up and take them to the gutter . . . By the time that two hours was up you'd have roughly 30 deer on the gut heap, and he'd have a load ready for you to take down to the boat. So you'd . . . take them down when you were light on fuel . . . It was hard work, it was long hours . . . The biggest day was 14 hours flying. We had 185 deer that were found, shot, picked up, gutted and ferried back onto the boat. So the gutters and the shooters really worked hard, cos that's a lot of animals to process.[21]

# Bounties, skins, fur and feathers

Meat was not the only game product sold by hunters. Some took the opportunities of bounties offered by acclimatisation societies on animals and birds considered to be pests to earn a shilling, and others supplied the fur industry. Feathers, too, were in demand by milliners and clothing makers for much of the nineteenth century and into the twentieth. Game shot or trapped in New Zealand — native and introduced — could end up gracing women in London and New York. It could also end up on World War Two bomber planes: the government encouraged the development of a skin market as part of deer-destruction campaigns from the 1930s, and one of the end-users was the aviation industry. This was one of the many and varied uses for skins, fur and feathers once hunters had brought them into depots or trading houses and been rewarded for their effort.

Above: The fur trade provided work for thousands of shooters and trappers, as well as for the many tailors and furriers who produced the garments. Furs were part of almost every middle- and upper-class woman's wardrobe in the late nineteenth and early twentieth centuries. In 1918, when this family were photographed, rabbit was the mainstay of the New Zealand fur industry. Twelve million rabbit skins were exported each year during World War One and in the 1920s there were furriers in all the major cities and towns in New Zealand. These fashionable garments belie the difficult and dirty work of animal trapping and skin preparation that was involved in the industry.

Top: Which one is the pest? For decades acclimatisation societies paid bounties on the legs or beaks of native birds of prey. Keas, shags, moreporks, falcons and harriers were all targeted because they were believed to attack or eat sheep, trout, pheasants and hares. Many New Zealanders earned their income destroying thousands of native birds.
Above: Petone schoolboys earning holiday money drying rabbit skins in the early 1930s.

**Bringing home the bacon 143**

Many hunters made part or all of their income from bounties (in the case of private hunters) and bonuses (in the case of government shooters). Various organisations paid bounties on a wide variety of birds and animals well into the twentieth century. Several native birds were hunted for bounties, usually to promote protection of other, introduced species; for example, in the Wanaka area from the 1870s, shepherds were paid a shilling a head for kea. Naturalist Thomas Potts estimated that more than 1000 were killed in this area in 1881–82, and 20 years later Walter Buller was quoted as describing the 'kea-menace' as so extensive that 'run-holders have been fairly driven off the country'.[22]

Hunters continued to earn kea bounties well into the twentieth century. In 1946–47 the Department of Agriculture paid out £368 to claimants from Westland, which represented the killing of 1472 kea in a district with no sheep. Forest and Bird Protection Society president AP (Arthur) Harper wrote

*Above:* From the turn of the century until 1956 possums were protected by a system of seasons and licensing. Many poached possum skins, however, were exported among bales of rabbit pelts. After protection was lifted in 1956 possum-trapping became a source of income for many more people until the 1980s, when the European fur market contracted sharply.

**144 Hunting**

in 1949 that this was 'just "blood money" paid for an unfortunate bird, which was doing no harm'.[23] Other native birds were identified as 'menaces': the shag was the enemy of trout, hawks the enemy of quail and pheasants, seagulls were sometimes regarded as vermin, weka were accused of eating pheasant eggs and the morepork was said to steal game-bird chicks.[24]

Jack Bull and his mother earned money during the early 1930s shooting shags for the Wellington Acclimatisation Society:

> While I was in Wellington there was a chap, Wiffin, he'd been to the Boer War with Dad and was secretary to the acclimatisation society in Wellington ... I went and saw him and I said there are shags up the Waiohine, up the Waingawa, the Ruamahanga and he said, well, we're prepared to give you 2/6 a pair for their feet. Then he wrote to me and said would you be prepared to give us the stomach contents so we can analyse them and see what's there? Oh yes, I can do that. So he gave me the jars and we went up the Waiohine and I gave him the stomach contents and he was thrilled to get them ... They became quite enthusiastic about this to the extent that they gave me a permit to take my shotgun and a .303 into the forest reserve ... My mother and I used to go up the Waiohine, Waingawa and Ruamahanga and I found it a great experience, a great outing ...[25]

There was money to be had if you knew where to go. Bull recalled that his best day's bag was 62 shags in less than an hour, on a lagoon out the back of a friend's farm. 'That was a fortune,' he marvelled.

While shags were numerous and the money could be good, this was not always easy work. After one particular episode, Bull drew the line at some recoveries.

> ... in the Waiohine in October, November, if you knocked a shag down and [were] trying to recover it, the water was ice cold. I remember knocking one down — it was only 10 feet away from me and I stripped off, dived in and got it, but I had to break the ice before I could get through the water. After that, I said recovery of shags in very cold conditions is not on.[26]

Bounties were also paid by station-owners on pigs and, in some cases, deer. Rural workers often supplemented their incomes with pig-culling, and could sometimes do very well out of it with a bit of sleight of hand. Merv Addenbrooke, working as a bush contractor in the central North Island in the 1920s, was supplied with ammunition to keep the pigs down, as well as being offered sixpence a snout as a bounty:

*One place we worked [was] on the boundary of two districts, where one side paid sixpence a tail, and our side paid sixpence a snout. We knew the contractors who were a couple of miles over the boundary and arranged with them to keep both tails and snouts. We met about once a fortnight to exchange tails for snouts. We did extremely well and so did they. Nobody felt ashamed of the deception, as our bosses were rather hard men.*[27]

When acclimatisation societies needed to begin culling their deer herds, bounties were paid on those as well. In 1906 the Otago society offered 27 pence per head for stags with malformed antlers. By 1910, their herd was growing at such a rate that bounties were not effective and they moved to employing cullers. Into the 1920s other societies, realising their responsibility to control herds and responding to pressure from local farmers, gradually began paying out bounties on deer tails, and the Department of Internal Affairs also adopted this policy in the later years of that decade. Over the last three years of the 1920s the department paid out bounties on 47,000 tails, mainly to weekend shooters and high-country shepherds glad to augment their wages in this way while they worked their main jobs.[28]

In the post-World War Two period, when all browsing animals were identified as accelerating erosion (see Chapter 5) — erroneously as it turned out — a bounty was introduced on goats for government shooters. The tally in the first season, 1946–7, was so much greater than expected that the department retrospectively reduced the bounty per tail and was faced with a near mutiny among its hunting staff.[29]

Selling skins and furs offered similar work and bounties for private hunters. Rabbits formed the backbone of the fur industry in New Zealand until very recently, and although trapping or shooting them was a very small part of controlling the 'rabbit nuisance', selling pelts was an income stream for many people.

Records of the numbers of skins exported begin in the 1870s. In 1877 just short of one million skins were exported, but by 1879 this had risen to 5.4 million, the vast majority coming from packing houses in Dunedin and Bluff. It was in the early twentieth century that the 'new world' fur

Above: Specimen collectors hunted most often to supply museums and naturalists, but many bird skins were bought by garment makers. Thousands of kiwi skins were used to make muffs, cuffs and collars. Even colonial museum officials and some of New Zealand's best known naturalists could not resist having birds skins made into garments for their womenfolk.

exporters such as Canada, the United States, Australia and New Zealand really came to prominence, as Europe's dominance of the world fur industry was destroyed by World War One. During the war more than 12 million rabbit skins were exported to Canada from Australian and New Zealand packing houses, where they were sold as Canadian fur on the American and European markets. In the 1920s, New Zealand rabbit-skin exporters supplied United States fur companies, with furriers travelling to North America to set up agreements and keep up with the latest fashions. For example Dick Simpson, who established Alaska Furs in Dunedin in the early 1920s, travelled with furrier George Stewart of JK Mooney & Co to New York in order to find an agent for their furs. Simpson reported back that the prevailing fashion in New York in 1924 was the 'full swing style coat, with very full sleeves, small collars and extreme fullness at the shoulder line' and that arrangements had been made to get regular mailings from a New York fashion house of their latest patterns.[30]

Rabbits weren't the only fur export. Hare skins were supplied in smaller numbers and were usually counted under rabbit skin exports. Stewart estimated that in the 1940s New Zealand exported between 100,000 and 200,000 skins a year to the top-hat makers of London.[31]

Possum skins were not traded legally until after 1921, although before this it is thought that poached possum skins were slipped in among rabbit skins in reasonably large numbers. GM Thomson estimated that in 1912, 60,000 possum skins were taken in the Catlins district alone.[32] After 1921 the 'Opossum Regulations' required the stamping of all possum skins and in the next two decades the numbers of skins stamped increased from 25,000 in 1921 to 400,000 in 1945.[33] Stewart noted a preference for Otago and Southland possum skins for the fur trade because the colder climate meant the animals had thicker fur. North Island possum skins generally went to the mill trade, where strips of the furs were laid under fine threads to prevent them catching on the machinery during weaving.

Possum trapping for the fur trade provided and supplemented many people's incomes. When Addenbrooke was unemployed in the 1920s, he trapped possums. In the 1940s, when growing up, conservationists Ben Thorpe and John Riseborough both trapped possums in the winter. Thorpe helped his father, an Otaki market gardener, with the traps during the school holidays and Riseborough earned enough (along with blackberry-picking in the autumn) for his first two years at college in Wellington. In the 1950s, Wairarapa student Brian Woodley earned enough from trapping possums to buy his first rifle, and from the 1960s he and his wife Anne trapped possums for more than 20 years to supplement Woodley's income as a freezing works engineer. Woodley estimated that in the two decades to 1989, when the bottom fell out of the fur market, they trapped about 15,000 possums, Anne often dropping their children at school then laying her lines. (The family thinks she was the first woman in New Zealand to have her cyanide licence.) Going back the next morning to collect them, she would then have 30 dead possums cooling on the floor of the garage for Woodley to skin when he got home from work, then she would tack them out on a skin stretcher to dry. On average, they were paid $4.50–5.00 a skin, with the record exceptional price an astronomical $26.50.[34]

### Protecting possums

*Ken Francis worked in the 1920s as a government forest ranger, protecting possums from poachers:*

Our endless patrols produced very few successes and we never caught the big boys who organised the opossum poaching. They used cyanide which was banned because it killed everything that inhaled or tasted it, including several men. The powdered poison was laid out on a tiny pile of bran or flour scented with aniseed. The men died through licking cigarette papers while using the powder, and it was a very quick death.

These poachers ignored closed seasons and the necessity for skins to be Government stamped before sale (a few used counterfeit stamps). They sent their skins to England concealed in wool bales, the compressed skins covered with a thick layer of wool. These 'hot' bales bore a code sign for easy recognition in London and were exported by a well-known Dunedin firm who bribed one of our officers to keep them supplied with information regarding rangers' movements and proposed raids. Coded signals went out over the birthday greetings of the broadcasting programme, warning poachers to lie low, the announcers, of course, completely ignorant of their involvement.

On patrol we dated and indelibly initialled every skin we saw; it was like punching a time clock. When I was in London later, visiting a famous warehouse which displayed skins from all over the world, I saw a line of opossum skins bearing the initials I had pencilled on them 19,000 kilometres away in the Waiohine Valley. When I told a buyer this, he grinned broadly. I guess it did sound unbelievable.'[35]

Exporting feathers and bird skins for use in fashion was an important trade in the late nineteenth century. There was a massive American market for feathers for millinery, as feather-trimmed hats were all the rage. Albatross feet were sold for tobacco pouches, and their wing bones were in demand as pipe stems. Bird skins were used to make muffs.[36]

Kiwi skins were also highly prized for fashioning into muffs. William Docherty, one of the hunters who collected birds for Julius von Haast in the 1870s and 1880s (see Chapter 5), had a sideline in selling kiwi skins for muffs. The naturalist Thomas Potts found this alarming, but other, more prominent ornithologists of the time did not. Walter Buller and William Fox both bought kiwi skins for muffs. John Enys, a member of the Canterbury Museum committee, sent his mother 'four kiwi skins . . . for making muffs and cuffs' in 1874. James Hector, the geologist, surveyor and head of the Colonial Museum, sent five kiwi skins via Thomas Kirk, director of the Auckland Museum, to furrier Janet Yardle of Ponsonby in 1872, who sewed them into 'a tippet [a small fur cape] and muff'. Kirk's letter, which accompanied the goods back to Hector, made a tongue-in-cheek remark about making sure 'poor Kiwi' were protected 'against the vanity of titled ladies of fashion'. None of these men had any qualms about the hunting of kiwi for fashion, at least not for a few more years.[37]

Collecting bird skins could earn a man a considerable income in the late nineteenth century, but it was a difficult life, usually combined with other activities such as prospecting or road-contracting and carried out in remote parts of the country. Haast paid out a great deal of money over several decades to skin collectors, with prices based on rarity and demand on the international market to which Haast sold the skins. Docherty, based at Okarito, was paid well for providing large numbers of skins and eggs:

*9 Ka-Ka Pos £9, 2 dozen Kiwi skins £7.4.0, 1 dozen Kiwi's skeletons £3.12.0, 6 Rowi skins £6, 4 Towi's skeletons [varieties of kiwi] £4, 1 Ka-Ka Po egg 10/-, 2 Kiwis eggs £1, 2 Ka-Ka Po skeletons £1.10.0, 2 cases lined with tin (this is the money I paid 15/-) 26 Bird skins at 4/- each £7.4.0. Total £40.15.0.*[38]

Haast's receipts and letters to Leo Barnes, a bird-hunter based on the West Coast, indicated some prices and numbers received: in July 1873 Haast offered four shillings apiece for some birds and 10 shillings for a 'white crane' (kotuku); the next month, a consignment of small birds was received and 16 shillings paid out for 16 skins. A year later, in June 1874, Haast increased

Barnes's payments to £2–2 shillings per dozen bird skins 'because your skins are always done in very good order'.³⁹ WJ Wheeler, based at Jackson Bay, took over collecting for Haast when Docherty's supply petered out. Some fragments of the agreement between him and Haast indicate 'Roa [Kiwi] skins and skeletons 20s; kakapo 8s; kiwi 8s; kaka and pigeon 5s; ducks and divers 6s; all sea birds £2-10s per dozen; all small birds £2-5s per dozen'. The most Haast ever paid Wheeler in one bill was £25.⁴⁰

The trade in deer skins did not start until after the beginning of deer-destruction campaigns in 1930. The government, in an attempt to recoup some of its expenditure on wild-animal control, explored and developed a skin market to which government and private shooters alike contributed. A trial of

Above and opposite: The lifting of protection on deer in 1930 and the development of a skin market encouraged thousands of hunters into the hills. Between 1931 and 1956 the Department of Internal Affairs offered a bounty to private shooters and a bonus to government shooters for every skin brought in. While the skin bounty provided a powerful incentive to hunt deer, the effort involved in retrieving and carrying skins limited the number of deer a hunter could shoot in a day. When the Forest Service took over deer control in 1956 it dispensed with the skin bounty.

**150 Hunting**

the skin bonus among government shooters in 1931 was deemed successful, with skins being recovered from 60 per cent of deer shot and 'indications are that the prospects of establishing a definite market for deer skins are bright'. The department also sent 800 pairs of deer eye-teeth to the New Zealand High Commission in London in the hope that a European market could be found for them, and sent antlers to China.[41]

Private shooters took up the skin bounty with enthusiasm. In 1937 the department raised the bounty for skins from 1 shilling and 7 pence to 2 shillings and threepence to reflect the higher price they were receiving from skin-buyers. In response, there was an upsurge in letters to the department requesting details of skin bounties. The department sent hundreds of copies of a circular, outlining conditions of purchase and how skins should be treated, to government buildings in many towns, to survey camps and milling companies, and to almost 200 individuals all over the country who were already involved in skin hunting. In addition to this, the department's files for 1937 are full of letters asking for details about the payment, the availability of ex-army rifles and ammunition at reduced rates for skin hunters, and sometimes for other information. J Bennett wrote in July 1937:

*Dear Sir,*

*Would you send me all particulars concerning deer hunting? My mate and I are wonting [sic] to have a go at it. If you could tell me the best locality and the price of skins I would be very gratefull [sic], also about guns and ammunition.*

*Yours truly*
*J Bennett, Paparatu STN*
*Manutuke, Gisborne*[42]

Letters were written directly to Internal Affairs Minister Joseph Heenan, to 'Captain Yerex' (Frank Yerex, the director of the department's Deer Control Section) and occasionally to local acclimatisation societies, who forwarded the letters to Heenan's office. It seems the department was seen as a clearing house for enquiries about deer destruction generally, and the files reflect a high level of interest among men who often wrote on behalf of themselves and their mates. There were letters from ex-gold prospectors or those hoping to combine prospecting with skin-hunting, and some in rudimentary handwriting from rural workers who included the newspaper cutting they'd seen and asking for more information. There were letters from farm-owners requiring shooters to clear deer off their land, and letters from men seeking work as shooters on stations. Some letters asked whether there was a market for goat and pig skins, and several letters asked that the tail bonus that was available to government shooters be extended to private shooters. Canterbury skin-hunter J Kellor wrote several times to the department on this topic in 1937–8, arguing that in response to hunting pressure, deer were moving into more remote areas from which it was difficult to recover skins. If the government wanted these deer destroyed they needed to make it worth the while of men who were prepared to work in the back country.[43]

Others wrote to argue for a higher skin bonus for men who were 'serious'. W Clingin from Routeburn Station had shot for the government as a single man and then turned to skin hunting when he married. He argued for a higher skin bonus for men 'who have proved they are making an honest endeavour to get skins', suggesting that for men who shot over 100 deer a season the government could afford to pay up to 3/6 per skin and 'still be making a saving'. He had carefully calculated what it cost the government to pay a deer-culler in wages plus bonuses on 500 deer per season, then subtracted what the government gained back from the sale of the skins. The calculations took several pages and formed a very sound case.[44]

But it was not such careful and logical arguments from shooters that led to an increase in the skin bonus, but the simple facts of supply and demand. Prices for skins began to drop off in the late 1930s, causing some concern in the department. However, as with most commodities, the outbreak of war brought about an unexpected upsurge in demand. Demand for deer skins had increased to such an extent by 1941 that while the government had paid out £2162 in bonuses to private shooters, it had received from the skin traders a massive £16,000. The department raised the skin bonus in large steps from 2 shillings and 9 pence in 1941 to 5 shillings and 9 pence by December 1943.

The increased demand was mainly from the aviation industry. Various uses for skins are remembered by the hunters of this era: the use of deer hides as part of a double-layered fuel tank which reduced the risk of explosion if the tank was punctured by a bullet; upholstery; lifejackets (because deer hair is hollow, the hides float); and the use of deer leather for pilots' gloves and jackets. During the war there were appeals in the United States to hunters to donate the hides of any deer killed to the war effort for pilots' clothing.[45]

The resulting increase in the skin bonus was very attractive for hunters, but the downside for the department was that young men who could handle a rifle were by and large needed elsewhere, and the army had greatly reduced the amount of ammunition and rifles available outside the defence force. While the bonuses rose, the price of ammunition more than doubled in the same period, from 10 shillings and sixpence to 22 shillings per hundred rounds.[46]

With the end of the war, the price of skins fell and several other factors saw the trade in deer skins decline. By the 1950s deer numbers had grown to such an extent that the government abandoned all thoughts of making money from the skins and adopted the simple policy of killing as many deer as possible. Government shooting was then taken up by many hunters. The skin industry was also well and truly overtaken by the trade in game meat.

A significant change for the fur industry came with the lifting of protection on possums in 1956, which freed trappers from the restrictions of licence requirements. By 1958, however, an even larger obstacle to those earning an income through skins was created when the Forest Service began experimenting with the aerial application of 1080 poison (see Chapter 5).

Above: Deer skins became more valuable during World War Two, when they were used to manufacture double-skinned fuel tanks which reduced the likelihood of fire if the tank was punctured. Skins were also used in the manufacture of pilots' clothing and lifejackets. While skins became more valuable, the numbers of hunters shooting deer in the New Zealand bush dwindled: young, fit men who were handy with a rifle were needed elsewhere. These men are from the 75th New Zealand Bomber Squadron, pictured in England in 1942.

**154  Hunting**

## The first shooters

*Much has been written about the first generation of government shooters. Names such as Bert Barra, Teddy Davison, Bert Vercoe, Jack Mead, Archie Clarke, the Thomson brothers and Alex Munro make regular appearances in organisational histories of deer control and in published reminiscences. Many of these men had been promoted to field officer by the 1940s. They worked for, respected and were loyal to a man known as 'the Skipper', George Franklyn (Frank) Yerex. But there were many other government shooters who did their jobs without becoming legends. Many, such as Norman Hardie and Harry Scott, were just boys when they began culling, and many used shooting as part of a group of seasonal jobs on which they relied.*

Above: While Frank Yerex, the head of the Department of Internal Affairs' Deer Control Section, had relied on a supply of men who already had the requisite skills to be government shooters, World War Two, urbanisation and competition for skilled hunters from the skins industry all depleted the numbers of men who could walk into the job. In response, the Forest Service established hunter training camps. Here, HJ Ollerenshaw instructs trainee hunters at the Golden Downs camp in 1958.

**Bringing home the bacon**

# Earning a government wage

If private hunters were earning their income through piecework — being paid per pound of meat or skin — the other substantial group of people earning income through hunting were wage-earners working for the government. Government shooters received a base wage plus, up until 1957, a substantial bonus for skins (and after 1957 a smaller bonus for tails only). This bonus system was effectively a sliding pay scale, rewarding skill and effort. Skin bonuses were paid where a shooter managed to recover deer and skin them, then carry the skins to camp, where they were cleaned, dried and packed out for collection from a more accessible spot. When deer were shot in a location too remote or precarious to be skinned, their tail was sufficient evidence of their demise, for which the shooters were paid a smaller bonus. The more deer a culler could shoot and the harder he worked, the more skins or tails he retrieved and the bigger his bonus.[47]

For their six-month season in the early 1930s, deer-cullers were paid £3 10 shillings per week (equivalent to around $350 today). They could use their own rifles if they met specifications or they had to buy an ex-army .303 out of their first pay. They were allowed three rounds of ammunition, plus a bounty of one shilling and sixpence (about $5.50), per skin retrieved. This sounds a pitiful amount when one considers the labour of recovering an animal, skinning it and carrying the skin back to camp to be dried, then carrying sometimes more than 50 kg of skins out to the road end. However, seasonal tallies in the 1930s could be up to 1000 deer per season, earning the culler a healthy £75 in bonuses (around $7600).

The first Deer Control Section shooters were employed by the Department of Internal Affairs in 1930 and were deployed in southwest Otago. The Forest Service also employed shooters near Makarora, at the head of Lake Wanaka, but this duplication of effort only lasted the 1930–1 season, when the government's Economy Committee assigned all deer control to Internal Affairs. Government shooters very quickly developed a reputation for being 'hard men', which was not surprising given the conditions under which they lived and worked. Until the post-World War Two period, when huts were built in most areas for cullers, shooters lived in primitive tent camps or under tent flies, in some of the wettest areas of the country. Shooting on the tops meant there was no firewood and men could go for days without a hot meal. For example, Russell Boughton, shooting in the 1940s, was trapped in a three-day downpour in the Moeraki Valley in Westland. He filled a jam tin with water

Top: The corner office? A Forest Service hunters' tent camp in the upper Nealeburn, Fiordland. Aerially dropped along with supplies, the tent comprised canvas over a frame of poles cut from the surrounding beech forest. Corrugated iron formed the chimney for the covered fireplace. Such camps were temporary homes for hunters working in remote corners of their blocks. 'It was a good spot,' recalls Ian Buchan, 'the only downside being the black plague that inhabited the area as well and the friendly keas which used to wake us up at day break every morning trying to tear the canvas apart. We used to take turns to get up and hurl firewood at them.' Above left: More substantial accommodation was provided by the Forest Service in the form of huts such as Parariki in Haurangi Forest Park. Note the meat safe at the door. Above right: Cullers were well provisioned, as can be seen from this interior of Stonewall Tent Camp in the Haurangis.

**Bringing home the bacon**

and heated it over a candle to make a hot drink.[48]

The job also demanded enormous stamina. In 1939, Jack Mead and Bert Barra set out from Jackson Bay in Fiordland and tramped through the Cascade, Arawhata and the Pike valleys through to Big Bay, then on to Martins Bay, Lake McKerrow and finally to the Upper Hollyford Valley. Their supplies ran desperately short and they were glad to get to Davey Gunn's place on the Hollyford River, where they restocked their supplies.[49]

Even after World War Two, when physical amenities such as huts and air-dropped supplies improved shooters' conditions, the terrain in which they worked made their working lives vastly different to those of other public servants. Bert Vercoe, acting director of the Deer Control Section during World War Two, asked for a higher bonus to be paid to the men working in the Burke River region near Haast because of the difficult terrain:

> I have to advise that part of the area is the Burke River which is being shot by two men[. It] is entirely tail country and a very difficult piece of country to shoot, with the result that the two men shooting it have been having a much harder job than others on adjoining country. In addition they have to carry all their food and ammunition all the time and I would recommend that the bonus for this particular block be raised from 1/- to 1/6 per tail.[50]

In his book *The Deer Wars*, wildlife scientist Graeme Caughley relates the conditions encountered by Forest Service tahr hunters in the 1960s, much of which would have applied to many shooters working in the South Island high country. Working in Westland involved 'a lot of technical climbing and rope work. The weather was deplorable and its implications serious. Fog often dropped on shooters when they needed all the visibility they could get'. Shooters were often at risk:

> Fly-camping parties were frequently trapped for one or several days by the flooded streams of side valleys. Even a shower could cause problems by turning a shooter's otherwise safe descent route into a slippery nightmare. The nor-westers were dreaded. If one were to catch a pair of shooters up high on a face there was little chance of them getting off it alive.[51]

The lead man on a party such as this carried enormous responsibility. Each man undertook shooting work knowing there were personal risks attached, but a lead man was responsible for the safety of all of his men. Some men decided the weight of that responsibility was too great, especially in ludicrously difficult country. The lead man on the Westland party described by Caughley took the author up Splinter Creek to show him the access his hunters had to the hunting area:

> The access is up the creek which soon peters out in rock slabs. [We] were finally stopped at a rock overhang, the only way around it being across a sub-vertical slab about five metres wide and with no holds. First bounce was 150 metres below . . . Ian grinned: 'Watch.' He made a wide leap to land his left boot on a pressure hold, pivoted on it without touching the face with his hands, and hit another further across with his right boot. A little hop as he changed feet and then a very controlled push-jump to land his right boot on a ledge the width of his finger. From there he could get at a gut leading around the overhang . . . . The other shooters had used this route several times that season.

Ian, the lead man, had been feeling the strain of this trip because of its dangerous terrain. Having unnerved Caughley and impressed upon him the difficulty of the assignment, he 'became almost cheerful'.[52]

Persistent rain and mountainous terrain in the South Island, difficult bush in the North Island, loneliness, cold, flood and constantly demanding physical work meant that men who stuck at deer-culling for more than one season came quickly to be regarded as legendary. There were not many of them. Starting with three men in 1930, the Deer Control Section employed 50 hunters by 1937. In 1939, with the permanent status of Director of Deer Operations secured, Frank Yerex had a staff of 14 field officers, a clerk, storeman and nearly 100 hunters in the field. In 1942, when the war had reduced the numbers of young, fit men to shoot for the government in the hills at home (as opposed to shooting for the government in Europe), the Deer Control Section's shooters were down to 20 men.[53]

One of those few was 16-year-old Norman Hardie, who became one of New Zealand's foremost mountaineers. His brother Jack had been a government shooter in the Landsborough Valley in South Westland, where 'he was highly successful . . . and brought back great tales of the country'. Jack Hardie joined the air force when World War Two broke out and in 1941, as soon as University Entrance examinations finished, Norman Hardie took Jack's pack and rifle and reported to the Boyle base camp near Lewis Pass.

> Two short, elderly ruffians and a spaniel bitch emerged from the beech forest, looked me over, grunted and opened the door. Their mail had arrived in a bag that had

*disgorged with me from the weekly bus. There were two items in the mail. The first was a racing paper with lists of horse performances for the previous month and details of the next month's races. After they filled in the betting forms they put them in the mailbag for the driver to collect on his return journey the next day. Then they looked at the second item. It was a short note from the Internal Affairs Department advising that a new man would be arriving on the bus — no name, age nor instructions. This was me.*[54]

Jack McNair, a 60-year-old culler who had been with the department since the 1930s, was one of the men. Vic Keen, the other, took Hardie around the back of the hut and set up a target about 100m away. Having never fired a .303, the rifle kicked Hardie hard on the first two shots, but by the end of the group of five shots he had it under control. 'There was a grunt and, "You'll come right"'.

Hardie had never skinned a deer either. The method McNair taught him went straight to the heart of government shooters' concerns: on the body of a stag, McNair avoided all the muddy and smelly bits around the belly and didn't bother with half the neck nor the legs. It was a quick and dirty operation:

*It was explained to me that we were paid by the numbers of skins not by weight or quality. Why fill a pack with five big stinking coats? Do it this way and one can carry out seven skins for the same amount of work. Normally they would not bother to skin a stag unless it was near the path of an incoming field officer. The hinds and yearlings are easier to skin and lighter to carry.*[55]

Working above the bushline on loose scree soon confirmed McNair's advice about taking skins only from the smaller deer and tails from large ones. After several weeks, Hardie was transferred to shoot with Jock Findlater in the Lake Sumner block further south. The directions to this new block struck Hardie as enormously haphazard: 'Climb up that hill, veering a little left. See a small lake, called Mason. Go to where its outlet meets the South Hurunui, ford it and walk south-west two miles. The hut is hidden in the bush.'

Findlater was a Scotsman who had served in the British Indian Army. He had installed some innovations at his hut that made life much more pleasant: pulleys in the high beech canopy meant meat could be hauled in a sack into the cool air above 'blowfly level', as could a safe for the butter. As with the previous hut, there was nothing to read, something which Hardie found difficult. At least with Findlater conversation was reasonable and covered more than racing and drinking but, in common with McNair and Keen, he wasn't much interested in the war. Desperate for news of the conflict, Hardie eventually walked out to the nearest homestead to collect the mail and newspapers.

By February 1942, Hardie decided he needed to think about his future. Findlater advised him to go on to university; with 'his experience of the British Army, he considered hostilities would go on for a long time and I would eventually be involved. He advised that I leap into higher education and when my call-up came, I would be partly qualified and would get a reasonable army job . . . Besides, the politicians were promising bursaries for returned soldiers when all this ended'.[56]

Although Hardie's field officer informed him there would be no one to replace him, he decided to follow the advice of his older mate. He continued to shoot for skins as a private hunter during his university holidays.

The requirement for hunters to skin or tail the deer they shot greatly limited the number of animals they were able to shoot in a day, so the Department of Internal Affairs had to find a balance between incentive and economy. A bonus for tails was added to the schedule in 1931, along with an 'overriding bonus' to the lead man of each team of threepence per skin and half a penny per tail for all the deer shot by that group.

In 1931, when public service pay rates were cut by 10 per cent across the board in response to the worsening economic situation, Frank Yerex requested that the department reduce the shooters' base wage but not their bonuses. He wrote, 'It is difficult to convey an impression of the extremely difficult nature of this work. I know of no other work that approaches it for hardship, strenuous exertion, long hours, heavy loads, exposure, danger and lack of opportunities for change or relaxation.'[57]

Yerex's forms used when interviewing for positions as government shooters reveal the kind of man he was looking for. Questions about physical attributes and fitness were the first order of the day: age, height, weight, general state of health, past injuries, illnesses and physical weaknesses. Then came a range of questions about shooting experience and outdoor occupations: how many years' shooting experience, how frequently you shot, how long did you go out for and the localities you shot, giving 'details of actual country shot over'. Details of other outdoor activities were required 'such as mountaineering, tramping, sheep mustering, prospecting, trapping, other shooting etc'. Then tallies of deer were noted: what was the largest number of deer you had shot in a day, a week, a month and a season?[58]

Government shooters worked for the Department of Internal Affairs until 1956, when control of deer was transferred to the Forest Service. Shooters worked all over New Zealand and on various territorial islands.

## Cullers — no ordinary public servants

Conditions of Employment
  Only those who are physically fit and healthy and able to conduct operations in all weathers and classes of country will be engaged.
  Considerable experience of deer or other rifle shooting, proficiency with a rifle and a high standard of bush-craft are essential.
  The working hours . . . will normally be from some time before daybreak until some time after dark . . .
  Hunters will be required to live in tent camp (or huts when available) . . . Hunters must provide their own bedding, food and clothing . . .
  Pay will be at the rate of £3.10.0 per week, plus a bonus of 1/6 per deer skin . . . Hunters will be paid for, and required to work, six full days per week.
  The Department will supply rifles and ammunition up to 3 rounds for each skin handed in; all ammunition used in excess of this quota will be charged at 1½d per round.
  Hunters will be required to carry the skins . . . of the animals shot, as instructed, to camp or prearranged depots and all such skins etc will be the property of the Department . . .
  No alcoholic liquor will be allowed in camp . . .
  Hunters will be required to comply with the rules laid down . . .
  The Department will dispense with the services of any hunter who does not give complete satisfaction in respect of his work, observance of the rules and carrying out of the orders of the Officer-in-Charge or whose presence is inimical to the spirit of goodwill and co-operation which is essential to the success of the operations and the congeniality of camp life.
  — Department of Internal Affairs, 1930[59]

'We pay you seven-pounds-ten a week and ten bob a skin,' he said. 'Five bob if you just bring in the tails. You'll get five shillings a week dog-money if your pup turns out any good. We supply the ammunition but if you use more than three rounds for a kill then you pay for them. Anything else you want to know before I boot you out of here?'
— Barry Crump, *A Good Keen Man*, 1960

Deer cullers will shoot their own venison, pork, pigeons, and trout. Deer cullers will be supplied with salt, tealeaves and condensed milk by the Department of Internal Affairs. Any luxuries they must pay for out of their own pockets. If they work hard and don't whinge about the tucker, the field officer may issue them a small handful of rice or macaroni for Christmas dinner. Deer cullers must not expect lavish treats like this too often. The issue of Highlander Condensed Milk is one tin per man per day. Any man caught flogging his mate's condensed milk will be dog-tuckered, his name will be expunged from the Daybook, the blade of his skinning knife will be snapped, and his rifle will be dropped in the deepest part of Lake Waikaremoana.
— Jack Lasenby, *The Tears of Harry Wakatipu*, 2006

## Stuffing birds and turning barrels

Apart from meat and skins, there were other incomes that private and government shooters could get from deer hunting: Chinese herbalists bought tails, velvet antlers, pizzles and sinews. A variety of other occupations also profited from hunting: gunsmiths and gun sellers, and taxidermists represented the before and after of the hunting process.

By the 1940s, Chinese merchants were paying well for deer products, most notably velvet antlers, deer tails (the scent glands of deer are under the tail)

Above and opposite: Dispensing with the skin bonus reduced the workload for government shooters and freed them up to spend more time hunting. While shooters before 1956 had to skin their deer, carry the green skins back to camp, dry them and then carry them out to the road, in the early 1970s Forest Service hunter Ian Buchan (right) just collected tails as proof of his tally.

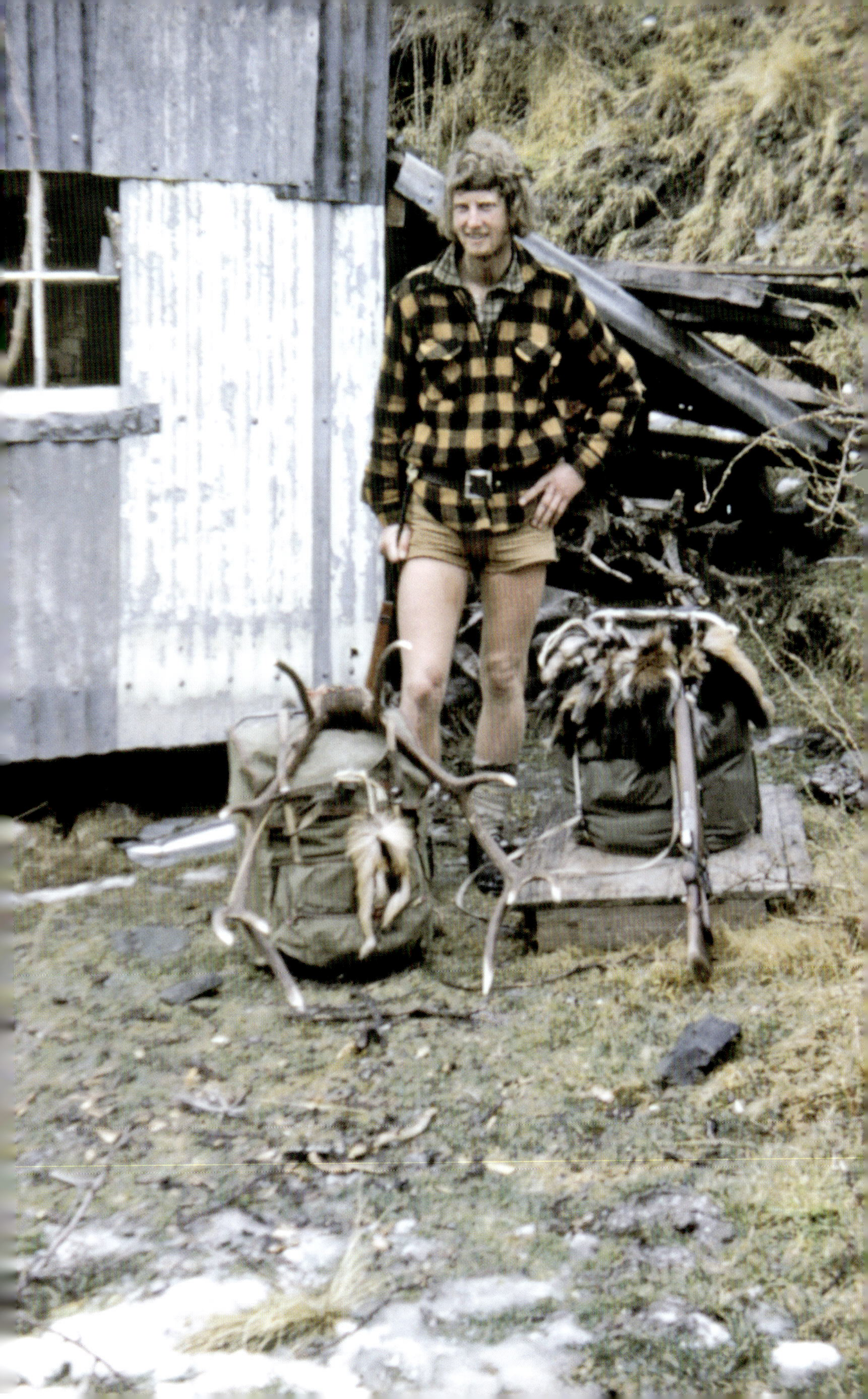

# Harry Wong

*Harry Wong came from an area in Canton known as the Four Counties. His Vivian St shop was a community centre and focal point for local Chinese from 1930 to 1970. He traded mainly in basic foods that were the mainstay of the Chinese community in Wellington — tea, soya sauce, tinned and dried foods, salted vegetables, many spices and condiments and salted fish and duck in oil. Wong's son-in-law ran the Hong Kong side of the business. Harry also exported. Wong's son, Harry junior, recalls:*

Periodically hunters came to the shop with smelly sacks containing deer tails and antlers, which my uncles Yee Kew or Wong Tien bought to export to Hong Kong and China. Our shop was well known in hunting circles and the hunters all called my uncles Harry even though that was not their names. The deer velvet and tails were used to produce medicines for manly vigour and enhance sexual prowess ... At the back of 145 Vivian Street was a drying room for the deer tails. It was a two-storey shed with 2 heaters going 24/7. As you can imagine it stunk. But for all that it was a very lucrative business fetching very high prices for those days.[60]

Above: While the government paid a skin bonus, other merchants, especially Chinese traders such as Stratford trader Dong Chong (left), purchased deer velvet, antlers and tails with the scent gland intact for export to China.

and sinews. These were used in a variety of medicines, although the sinews were also used for soup. In 1862, a member of the Acclimatisation Society in London reported eating soup made from deer sinews at one of their meals involving an enormous and exotic range of foods from around the world. 'These deer sinews from Cochin China took a monstrous deal of boiling . . . when served up they were good eating, but glue-like.'[61]

In New Zealand, many Chinese businessmen were involved in the export of deer products in the twentieth century. Harry Wong (Wong Sheung) in Wellington, George Ting in Ashburton and Hop Yick Cheong in Christchurch were all early traders in deer parts. However, in the 1960s during the venison recovery boom, game processors began to trade directly with overseas markets and Hong Kong firms made contact directly with the New Zealand Deerstalkers' Association to facilitate the private shooters' trade. These arrangements generally squeezed out the local, small-scale Chinese traders.[62]

Guiding was (and remains) another way to turn bush skills into income. Maori guides were most common in the early colonial period, although very few records remain of their names or under what terms they worked. As discussed in Chapter 1, Maori guides were integral to surveying and exploring, and their role included hunting. Robert Bain, who surveyed part of the West Coast in 1863, relied heavily on local Maori encountered along the way to guide his hunting expeditions. Anchoring in Ship Cove in Queen Charlotte Sound his party made arrangements with local Maori to go pig-hunting 'should the weather not allow of us going to sea'. Poor winds continued for some days and 'we spent the time during our detention in fishing, shooting and hunting wild pigs which abound here'.[63]

Maori guides also led and fed Ernst Dieffenbach, Lieutenant-Governor Edward Eyre, Charles Heaphy, Thomas Brunner and Leonard Harper.[64] Commercial traveller and recreational sportsman R Thomas paid a Maori guide to take him on a duck shooting trip when in Otago in 1885. His guide clearly knew the lagoon very well, guiding Thomas into a flock of 300 or so ducks, whereupon Thomas shot 50 birds in a matter of hours.[65] In Montagu Cradock's 1905 *Sport in New Zealand*, a contributor who was surveying in the Ureweras, 'a very rough, inaccessible, and little-known district covered almost entirely with dense birch forest [sic]', had several Maori guides as well as a local pakeha. 'My party included, besides myself, three Maories [sic] and one white man (at least he was fairly white, considering he had been all through the Maori war, he had lived amongst the natives ever since); but as he was an incomparable pig-hunter I could forgive him for not worrying much over his morning tub.'[66]

More pakeha began earning their income from guiding once deer-stalking became a domestic and international tourist attraction. These guides were often men who had spent a great deal of time in particular locations, knew the terrain, the conditions and the weather and, most importantly, understood when game would be found and how to find it. In his *Red Deer Stalking in New Zealand*, Thomas Donne wrote that overseas stalkers should expect to pay a guide 25 shillings per day, and expect a two- or three-week contract to cost between £20 and £30 per man.

Guides differed greatly in background and experience. Roderick McGillivray, who guided visitors on Te Awaite station in the Wairarapa in the 1890s, was described as 'an excellent stalker, having served his apprenticeship with that fine old sportsman the late Lord Tweedmouth in Guisachan, Inverness-shire'.[67] South Island guides such as Leslie Murrell and Jim Muir were more home-grown. Murrell had been brought up at Manapouri on the edge of Fiordland, and grew up knowing the country intimately. In 1914 he enlisted with the Otago Mounted Rifles, serving in France during World War One. Murrell guided many wapiti hunters into Fiordland in the 1930s, including well-known Wairarapa hunters Ken and Alec Sutherland, Herbert Hart and Vivian Donald (see Chapter 4). Muir, similarly, grew up at Hawea Flat and was so accomplished in the mountains that in 1913, at the age of only 18, he guided accomplished hunter and author Major Robert Wilson. Muir also enlisted in World War One and served in Egypt and France, where he was an ambulance driver and so reliable that his colonel would not let him transfer although he had been accepted for training by the British air force. When Muir came home he managed one of Wilson's North Island farms for a few years before patching together a full-time living from rabbiting, deer culling and guiding. He was only in his mid-fifties when he died from cancer in 1949.[68]

EJC (Ernest) Wiffin was a guide who had celebrity clients, most famously the novelist Zane Grey, whom Wiffin took game fishing in the Bay of Islands. He was a guide for members of the British aristocracy in the early 1930s, organising specialist stalking guides, equipment, porters and camp cooks. Wiffin was engaged by the travel agents Thomas Cook & Son to guide Lord and Lady Latymer into South Westland in 1930. Latymer had sent a long list of instructions for the trip, the most important among them that he wanted to 'get among the heaviest heads in the Dominion', which meant Wiffin had to do some quick negotiation to secure exclusive access to a block in South Westland only a month before the season opened. However, this block proved 'most unsuitable for a lady, and was so bad in fact, that [guide George Humphreys] positively refused to take a woman onto it'. Good luck and sharp ears while at the pub meant that Wiffin was able to exchange the block for another — he overheard some stalkers saying they were not going to take up their block and would forfeit their fees.[69]

Wiffin's role was to ensure the safety and comfort of his guests. His son was engaged as camp cook and he was very satisfied with Humphreys as chief guide. Wiffin's connection with Grey also brought a bonus to this trip:

> I had brought with me a tent which was given to me by Zane Grey. It differs from tents which are popular with New Zealanders, being complete with poles and all

Above: The Murrell brothers (pictured here), along with Jim Muir, Ernie Wiffin and Con Hodgkinson, worked as guides for wapiti and red deer stalkers in Fiordland and South Westland. Guiding was a specialised occupation and paid relatively well for short periods. This photo from Herbert Hart's album records a trip with Viv Donald to Fiordland in 1925.

**Bringing home the bacon** 169

*necessary equipment. The tent is made by Abercrombie & Fitch of New York. It is shaped after a pattern of an Arab's tent, and may be erected in ten minutes. It weighs about 25 lbs and it defies the heaviest of weather. Having this tent with us, we were enabled to provide passable quarters for Lord & Lady Latymer.*

The men's concerns about Lady Latymer's ability to manage a month in the Landsborough Valley were put to rest on the second day of their trip when the river had to be forded many times.

*Lady Latymer and I were to be the next to cross. We watched the progress of the first two, and saw them reach the other side before we made the attempt. We saw that the water was well up towards the saddle flaps, and I could see that Her Ladyship was not relishing the task, and I rather think it was her first experience of the kind. If it was, she showed remarkable courage and presence of mind. I know many younger women who would not have ventured that crossing. This episode removed any doubts that we may have had, as to the ability of Her Ladyship to do the strenuous work required of a deerstalking trip.*

Several men were earning money from the trip: Wiffin and Humphreys were joined by stalking guide Con Hodgkinson for a week; Wiffin's son Jack and Jack Denniston were the porters, carrying bundles of gear weighing 25–35 kg each over very difficult terrain between camps; and Wiffin junior was also camp cook. Closer to civilisation there were two more porters who came up to help for a few days.

It was rough country in which to be a porter. Wiffin described one day as being so hard that it took six hours to travel eight miles. The porters had to bring everything up to the 'flying camp' from base camp because the bush and terrain made the use of horses impossible. 'This is a sooo dreary job, one day up from the base camp with supplies, returning the following day with any heads that have been taken. Everything has to be done by manpower from Harper's Bluff'.[70]

Opposite: Lady Hester Frances Latymer quashed her guides' fears that she was not robust enough for a month's stalking in South Westland with a heroic river crossing on the second day of their 1930 trip. This was their base camp, designed to be home for over a month. The large tent flies are suspended over a frame of poles from the surrounding bush. The high-slung canvas keeps the camp dry while leaving room to stand up as well as to light a fire.

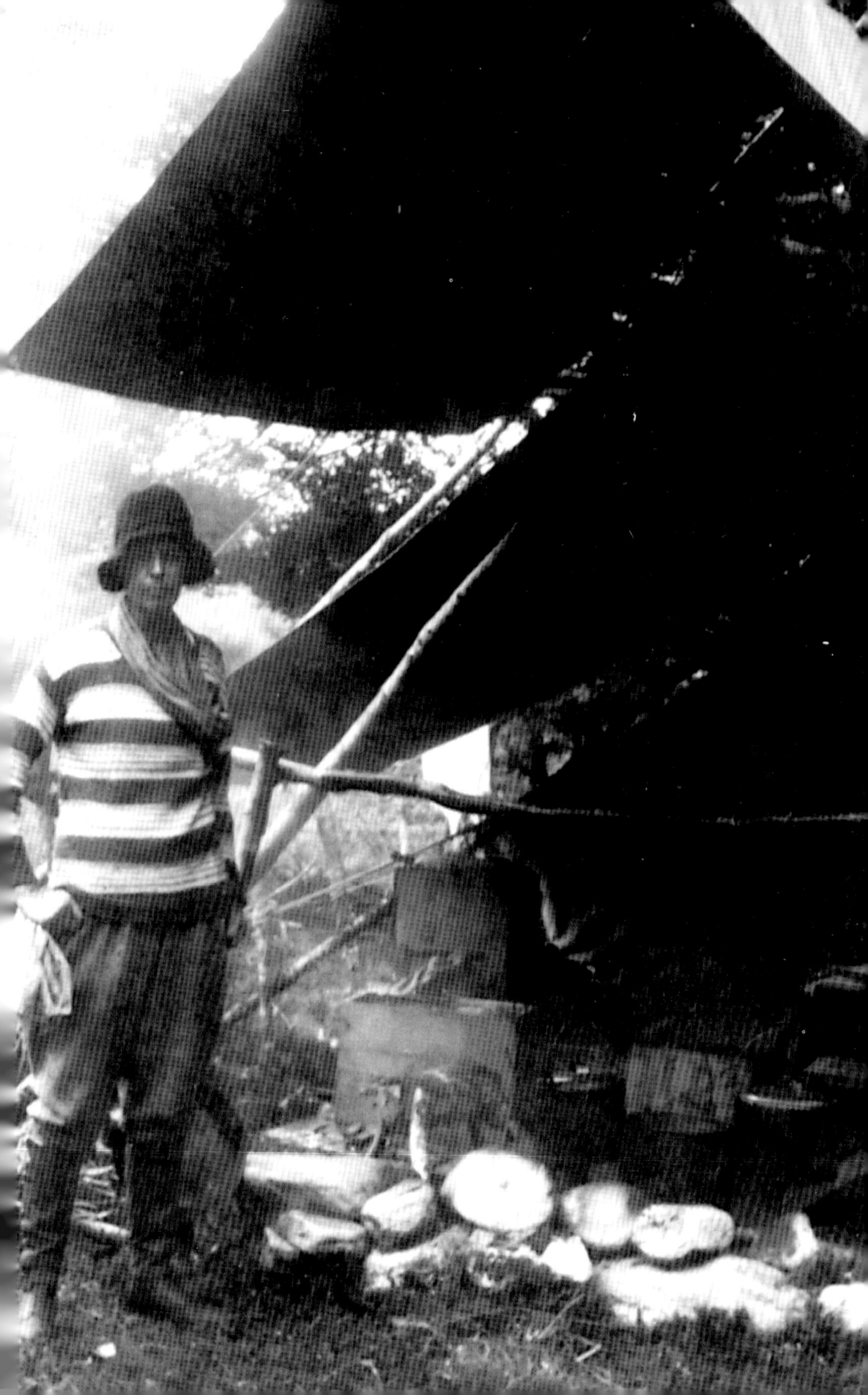

### John McLeod Ross

The taxidermist and deer-stalker of Martinborough, is known all over the British Empire as one of the most expert taxidermists and skilful stalkers in the Australasian Colonies. For many years he has made a close study of the nature and habits of the deer, and is regarded as a reliable authority on matters pertaining thereto. Mr Ross was born in Caithness, Scotland, in April 1857, and during his early years saw much of deer and the manner of their capture in the Highlands of Scotland. After leaving school he went out as a shepherd, and at the age of sixteen came out to New Zealand. His first employment was rough pioneering work in connection with the clearing and fencing of the back-block stations. During this time he did a large amount of deer stalking and deer head and skin curing, and becoming skilful in the work, he determined later to devote his entire attention to it. During recent years many tourists have visited Martinborough, and Mr Ross has invariably been employed as their guide in the deer stalking expeditions. At his home in the town Mr Ross has facilities for carrying on his work as a taxidermist, and always has a large number of fine heads in various stages of curing.

— The Cyclopedia of New Zealand, *1905*[71]

How early taxidermists learned their trade is not an easy question to answer, except to say that it was a matter of practice. Ross Galbreath in his biography of naturalist Walter Buller suggests that some books outlining different methods of preservation and insect-proofing were widely read in the colonies. Charles Waterton in his *Wanderings in South America* recommended corrosive sublimate or mercuric chloride for preservation, and William Swainson's *Taxidermy, Bibliography and Biography* recommended 'arsenical soap'.[72] Arsenic was commonly used in the process right up into the 1960s. (Because of this, more than one taxidermist met an early death from slowly being poisoned by his trade; on a more macabre note, a few also used arsenic as their method of taking their own lives. In 1882 Invercargill taxidermist James Morton swallowed arsenic, and Frederick Fuller similarly committed suicide in 1876 after a battle with the Canterbury Museum to be reinstated in his job.[73])

Taxidermy was a fairly widespread trade, ranging from high-end furriers to amateurs and enthusiasts. At the top end were taxidermists such as brothers St Clair and Hector Liardet in Wellington (who won prizes for 'fur and feathers' at the Philadelphia Exhibition in 1876), Alexander Yuill in Christchurch, William Smyth in Dunedin, E Spencer and Sigvard Dannefaerd in Auckland, and MJ Jones of New Plymouth, who had worked at museums in Brisbane and Sydney. AS Jacobs in New Plymouth advertised that birds, fish and animals would be 'mounted in the highest style of the art'. John King worked in Wanaka, and John Jacobs worked in Masterton until being declared bankrupt in July 1895.[74] (Was he the 'AJ Jacobs, taxidermist' who was fined £5 six months later in the Masterton court for killing seven huia and a kereru?[75]) Further down the scale were those Galbreath described as small-town 'bird stuffers'.[76] AW Avery in Marton was one; in West Taieri, a Mr Waterfall was reported to be 'adept at stuffing birds, mounting insects, a taxidermist of no mean ability, but he only did this work in his spare hours'.[77]

The files of the Wildlife Service also reveal many taxidermists operating around the country in the twentieth century, because for a short period taxidermists were required to be licensed through the service. After 1955 this requirement was dropped but laws remained around the mounting of protected species and game birds. In the 1950s the Wildlife Service wrote to all its conservators and to acclimatisation societies for information on taxidermists in their areas and opinions on how much illegal activity was being carried out. The replies reveal that in the mid-twentieth century, taxidermy was still of wide amateur interest, with several conservancies replying that the local taxidermist only worked 'as a hobby' (as in the case of Peter Crawford, a 15-year-old Rotorua schoolboy). In addition, the replies revealed long-standing career taxidermists such as I Talbot in Ohai, Southland, who had first registered as a taxidermist in 1932 and was still working as one in 1959.[78]

**Saving his dinner**

In the little town of Arundel there is a taxidermist who is gifted with wonderful presence of mind. Here is an instance:

Some time ago a gentleman called at his shop with a cock pheasant, which he desired to have skinned, stating at the same time that he did not require the body. This quite suited the taxidermist who thought the pheasant would do for his dinner on the morrow.

However, later in the day the gentleman called again, and said that he would take the body away. The taxidermist replied that it was unusual for customers to take the bodies away, but that he had no objection, and he fetched the bird, which his wife had put on a plate and covered with flour.

'Ah!' exclaimed the gentleman. 'It looks very nice, but what is this white powder with which is it covered?'

'Oh! That,' replied the taxidermist, quietly, 'is arsenic. I always cover the bodies with that until I can dispose of them.'

'Ar-arsenic,' stammered the gentleman. 'Why I thought that the bird would be good to eat. Thankyou, I won't trouble to take it away with me. Good day!'

The taxidermist saved his dinner.

— *Otago Witness*, 1905 [79]

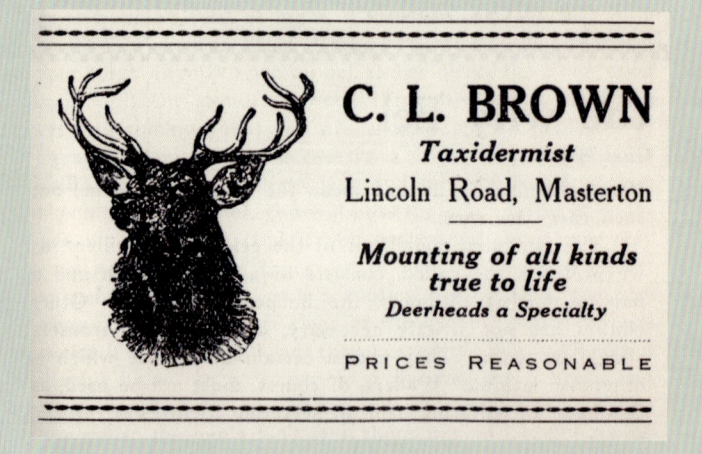

**C. L. BROWN**
*Taxidermist*
Lincoln Road, Masterton

*Mounting of all kinds true to life*
Deerheads a Specialty

PRICES REASONABLE

Many gunsmiths in early New Zealand were military armourers. As with taxidermists, there were also a variety of whitesmiths (those who worked in tin and finished metal goods) and talented amateurs who did gun repairs, although they were not always considered worthy of the term 'gunsmith'.

In *The Fishing & Shooting Gazette* in 1931, 'Tangaroa' complained that gun-making was rapidly becoming only 'a mere assembling of machine-made components'. He wanted to pay tribute to those English gunsmiths who 'were to gun-making what Gainsborough and Turner were to painting or Shakespeare to literature'.[80] In reminding readers of the art of gun-making, he cited the example of a man who was skilled at woodwork who bought a small wood-cutter in order to 'checker' his son's rifle (cross-hatch the stock to improve the grip). 'He started alright and the checkering was well enough done, but he did not know how to stop. When he had done the grip as far as he

Above: Taxidermy is a craft learned on the job. A surprisingly large number of amateur taxidermists worked in New Zealand as well as those who pursued it as a profession. Museums usually employed in-house taxidermists and many others worked in provincial towns all over the country.

**Bringing home the bacon** 175

wanted, not knowing how to finish, he kept going until he had checkered the whole stock from one end to the other and all round; it was a funny looking job and I think his son had to grow a beard to save his cheek from being sawn off.'[81]

Most sporting goods companies were offering gun repairs by the 1910s. WH Tisdall, A & W McCarthy's and Hammond & Turner all sold British- and American-made rifles and shotguns and offered repairs. Specialist gunsmiths were also operating by the post-World War Two period.

Collings & Brady in Wellington began almost by accident in the 1960s. In 1961 Din Collings, an engineer and tool-maker, became seriously ill with pneumonia compounded by a burst lung ulcer. When he was finally released from hospital, his doctor recommended six months off work to recover and that Collings should not return to factory work. To pass the time and to earn a little money, Collings, a father to six small children, began doing machining jobs for friends, mainly repairing and maintaining firearms. Din's wife Viv Collings recalled, 'That's how the business started. He was always doing odd

Above: Skins and antlers were both money-earners. The government paid a skin bonus and antlers were sold either to Chinese merchants for the traditional medicine trade or for use in other industries such as cutlery manufacture. Gunsmiths also earned their income from hunting. In this photo the rifles are both ex-military .303s but one has been cut down by a gunsmith to a sport model while the other remains a fully wooded military model. Converting rifles to 'sporters' was a large part of gunsmiths' business after both wars.

This page: Collings & Brady gunsmiths is a Wellington institution. Established over 40 years ago, the family business continues apace in the original workshop beneath the Collings's house.

**Bringing home the bacon**

jobs for people but the doctors suggested he get outside for a while, for a couple of years. So he did outside work for a couple of years and then he said he would catch up on all these jobs, and he's still catching up!'[82] Collings dug out a workshop underneath the family home, where the business is still located today. Viv learned how to cut down ex-service .303 rifles to 'sport' models so she could help with the business. Two of Din and Viv's four sons have become gunsmiths.[83]

Pilots were another group making a living on the fringes of the hunting enterprise. Pilots first began to work for the government's Deer Control

Above: The rise in the number of experienced pilots in New Zealand after World War Two and the increasing number of aircraft meant that flying into the hills to hunt became viable for those who could afford it. Even before the explosion of the venison industry, some pilots were making part of their living ferrying hunters in and out of remote areas. Here, a wapiti-stalking party is being dropped into George Sound in a Grumman Widgeon.

Section immediately after World War Two. In 1946 materials for a high-altitude hut were air-dropped into Mount Crawford in the Tararuas; the first deaths of pilots engaged in this work occurred in Fiordland exactly one year later.[84]

'Popeye' Lucas was one of the first pilots to fly for the section after World War Two. He had flown for the RAF during the war, having been rejected by the New Zealand air force in 1935. Back home, in the late 1940s Lucas tried to get the Department of Internal Affairs interested in using planes to support deer-cullers and experimented with parachutes for supply drops. Lucas began working for the Forest Service in the early 1950s, flying hut materials into remote areas and dropping supplies. 'Supply-dropping was to become one of our most important jobs, providing a good, steady income and helping us to fully utilise our aircraft.'[85] Lucas's Auster aircraft could carry just over 200 kg 'plus a thrower-out' (very often 'Fearless' Ron Fraser of the Deer Control Section) but the De Havilland Dominies could carry three times that load.

This was not always a good thing for the men on the ground. In 1966 Jim Kane was meat-shooting out of the Clark Hut in Grebe Valley, Fiordland. He was packing out carcasses on horseback when pilot Bill Black in a Dominie roared overhead and 'Forest Service supplies began to rain down unexpectedly'. Government shooter Lindsay Dickson complained once that his supplies had been dropped too far away. 'The next time pilot Bill Hewitt dropped the supplies in by plane the bag of flour dented the roof, and the chimney was destroyed by a box of ammunition.'[86]

## Making ends meet

For many hunters, piecing together an income over the years involved all sorts of hunting: government shooting, private skin- or meat-hunting, pest control, trapping and guiding. Harry Scott was born in 1918. When Scott was 15 he went to the local cullers' camp, where Yerex and Bert Vercoe were in charge, lied about his age and asked for a job.

> *Captain [Yerex] asked 'how many deer have you shot?' I said 300 and I said I can show you the receipts for the skins I've got from Dunedin. OK, away you go, so I started off. I think I was the youngest culler, because in those days the cullers were mainly musterers and high country men . . .*[87]

Harry Scott began culling with Donald Bell and George Fitzpatrick in the Albert Burn area near Wanaka. Fitzpatrick had been a culler on Molesworth Station in the 1920s, one of the high country musterers that Yerex was fond of employing. He had been paid half a crown (two and a half shillings) per tail on the station and could make £1 per day on bounties alone. He had also sold skins and slinks (the delicately spotted skins of unborn fawns) to the Forest Service at Hanmer.

After two months working with Fitzpatrick, Scott was sent to the Matiri area, in what is now in the south of the Kahurangi National Park:

> There weren't many deer there; we spent three months in there, I got about 300 deer ... Well I complained there was no deer, so Bill Chisolm — he was our field officer — he moved me onto the Victoria River, from the Buller ... right through to the Rahu. Well it was virgin country, never been shot. I took 860 tails off there in 4 months, and skins, a few skins I'd carry down ... I had two other chaps with me but I was the leading hand.[88]

Scott missed out on skin bonuses because the country was too remote to make carrying skins out practical, but Deer Control Section wage books show he made more in tail bonuses and his 'overriding bonuses' for being the lead man than in wages that season.

Scott spent the off-season shooting rabbits and deer on his family's farm near Wanaka. The family also made money by selling shooting rights to stalkers during the 1930s. 'We had lords and dukes and generals and colonels and majors from India and everywhere. Yes, I remember Lord Latymer, he was a nice chap, he'd just talk to you naturally, and his wife too. She used to go way up into the Blue [River] and everywhere.' He also shot skins privately during the winters.[89]

In 1940 the skin bonus went up to half a crown per pound from 1 shilling per pound because of the extra demand from the aviation industry. Scott's calculations were that skins weighed about 3–3½ pounds so he was getting '7/6 or 8 bob a skin. Well, if you knocked out 20 deer for the day ... you'd knock out £20 some days — that was *fabulous* money in those days'. The money Scott made from deer shooting went into farming. He wanted to buy his own farm and he had a widowed sister with children who needed support. 'I wasn't a drinker and not much of a smoker,' he commented. Other cullers spent their money on various pursuits. Scott shot one season in the Poulter River valley with Ted Davidson, a much older culler — one of the original generation. Scott described Davidson as 'a broken-down gentleman from

North Canterbury. He'd lost his property in the Great Depression, like a lot more. He was a great polo player. That's where his money went'.[90]

Grant Fitz-William has made an income from hunting since 1965, when he was 15. He and his mates would drive south from Auckland to shoot deer and sell the meat.

> *In those days you could nail a few deer and sell 'em off. And that was the days when you had to give a name for your tax so Rob Muldoon came up fairly often and Bill Rowling came up fairly often and was put down on your tax forms. I think they shot more deer in New Zealand than anyone else if it went to the tax man.*[91]

Fitz-William signed on to the Forest Service when he was 18 years old, shooting mainly goats and pigs in the Kaimai Ranges.

> *I got interviewed in Auckland by a guy called Keith, who was the head ranger there then and he asked a few questions and said, okay, you've got the job. So I went straight into the bush for a month. We were living in a tent camp, so you had to cart everything in and build your tent camp and you stayed there for the month and for that you got paid something like about $200 and you had to buy your own food out of that. You used to get three rounds of ammo a tail.*

After two seasons with the Forest Service, like many government shooters, Fitz-William went meat-hunting:

> *It was a good idea to go meat-hunting, but we never made any money out of it, because we used to go and shoot a few deer and then go and spend the next few days in the pub playing pool and when the money ran out, we'd go and shoot a few more. So I really wasn't in it to make the money, I was in it for the lifestyle. I just loved being out in the hills . . . although for meat-hunting, it was fairly handy sort of stuff. You didn't want to have to carry them too far, so you always struck the easier bits you know around the back of Mangakino there with the logging and things like that. The deer would always come out the logging side. Of course it was poaching then, but you'd sneak in there, nail one or two, and rush out. But we were always pretty cheeky, figured it was New Zealand and we were New Zealanders and it was bush and it should be ours.*

Over the next 30 years, Fitz-William hunted privately as well as professionally for the Department of Conservation and was area supervisor for the Mid-Wakitipu Pest Board. 'All that land you can see from Queenstown — Mount

Nicholas Station, Walter Peak, Cecil Peak and Halfway Bay, back to the Lakes plus the Greenstone — it was all my area. I got *paid* to go and wander around it.' By the time he moved to Golden Bay to carry out possum monitoring and some shooting he was getting 'a bit bush sick. You need a break out of it, especially when you're not getting out on the tops'.

Possum monitoring is hard physical labour. The gear is heavy and bulky to carry and trap lines must be laid regardless of the terrain.

> *I was going up the hill one day thinking, 40 traps in your pack, hammer and nails, and lunch if you can fit it in. It's a couple of kilometres over the tops to the ridge where you're heading to do your four lines. It takes a full day, perhaps, to get way back out there and I was thinking, 'this is a young man's game'.*

Fitz-William retired from DoC and began a small possum-skin tannery. 'I wanted to stay in touch with that side of my life, getting rid of possums and pests which I've done most of my life.'[92]

> **I switched to a 222 when I went into the Forest Service, because that was a calibre they used, and I bought a cheap junky Sportco 222. I think it cost me a hundred or something like that, because I wanted a gun that I could knock around. When you're rushing through the bush after dogs and you're going through supplejack and stuff, I used to throw the gun first and walk after it, you know, crawl and scramble the way through, pick your gun up. The worst part was when you threw your gun like that and you came and found it barrel first in the mud. So it was off down to the creek, wash it out. Also when you got to a waterfall you could throw your rifle over into the shallows and clamber down or jump off into the middle of the pool and swim to the other side and grab your rifle and carry on, you know. So you wanted something that you could knock around and you didn't want a scope on it.**
> **— Grant Fitz-William**[93]

Jocelyn Rae has lived and worked on the edge of hunting enterprises for much of her life. She grew up in the 1950s in a hunting family near Waikanae, north of Wellington. Her love of horses led her to her first job in Queenstown as a horse-trek guide. In the winter she led packhorses for private meat-hunters on Waterloo Station, packing in supplies to camps and packing out deer carcasses, and in later years in the Takatimus.

*We'd go and live in a little hut way out the back, it was a two-day horse ride to get in there, and then the hunters would go off hunting up into the hills and once I had a load of deer I had two packhorses to bring those out. That was the whole carcass then, and that was being sold to Germany. That was before the helicopter hunters or deer-farming and that was pretty amazing.*[94]

It was the mid-1960s and there were plenty of deer about:

*I'd take six deer to a horse, normally, depending on the size of the deer. One time we'd been way up the valley and the guys had come across a big herd and let fire and got a heap of deer and we loaded up both horses to the hilt. I was feeling sorry for them, it was such a heavy load. I was walking along leading them down the valley and we came around the corner and there was another big herd of deer so the boys let rip again. The horses got such a fright that they bolted and the deer all sort of fell off as they went. They went all the way back to the hut, with me traipsing along behind, I didn't feel sorry for them after that.*

Attempts to make life at the hut more comfortable were difficult with horses involved.

*I'd loaded up the packhorses at the homestead with the goods, flour, and all our food to last another few weeks. I'd decided it was time I took a bathtub out for myself. I was sick of the cold creek, and we had one of those big old tin tubs. I had it nicely tied on the top, with all the gear and we took off. Something clanged against it, and the old draughthorse didn't like the sound too much and he bolted then and bucked all the way across the paddock, and I remember flour and all sorts going for miles.*

Being in the bush could be magical, though.

*I remember going out hunting with the guys and running out of light and camping, making a bed out of tea tree I guess on a ridge in the dark and waking up in the morning being above the clouds. The clouds were filling the valley and then as the clouds cleared I was sitting up on this ridge and looking down, and I could see the deer coming out in the clearings. The boys had taken off early to hunt and from the ridge I watched them shooting the deer, which nowadays I couldn't do, but back then that was pretty exciting. That was what you were supposed to do with deer. But then I realised that this ridge we were sleeping on was a razorback ridge — it was pretty horrifying but fantastic.*

Rae moved back to Queenstown and flatted with two hunters and a helicopter pilot. It was a wild life in some ways. Some days 'they came back with bullet holes in the helicopters' after being shot at by runholders. Perhaps not without cause; venison was extremely valuable and rumour had it that helicopter hunters were never out of beef.

*These guys would come home and they were making huge money from all their deer hunting and Dave always had wads of $100 notes in his back pocket. He'd pin them on the wall and say, here Jollie, this is for the shopping. I'd never seen a $100 note before that and it was just mind-boggling.*

There was, however, a less glamorous part of being a young woman in a meat-hunters' flat. 'I was supposed to be cook and bottle washer at home and their clothes would be *so* covered in blood . . . because they'd jump out of the choppers and gut them on the hill. You could literally stand the trousers up . . . they were that thick and dried, caked with blood.'[95]

Many other high country and farming jobs eventually led Rae to Golden Bay where she met Grant Fitz-William. In 2004 they opened their possum-skin tannery, The Naked Possum, in Bainham in Golden Bay. Using natural tanning methods they make possum leather, adding value to the possum-trapping industry and continuing to earn their living through hunting as well as doing their bit for conservation.

# Earning an income

The sheer diversity of ways an income could be made from hunting meant that it infiltrated New Zealand life in all sorts of areas. Because of the seasonal nature of the work and because it was hard physical labour, few people made a long-term career of hunting. Rather, it was one of a range of rural jobs that went towards making a working life. While the helicopter era was one of high adventure, it is the government cullers who entered the popular imagination. Surely no other branch of the public service contributed as they did to the national legend.

One of the reasons they did so was because hunting was and is an adventure. As a Department of Conservation hunter commented to me, 'If I wasn't being paid for it, I'd still be out hunting.' While many people were motivated to hunt in order to provision their families, communities and camps and hunted to earn a shilling, a third motivation was that hunting was recreation. It could be work, but it could also be play.

ID: 4

# Sportsman's paradise

Filling the pot or earning an income were not the only reasons people hunted: it was adventure, it was challenge and it was fun. Along with camping, tramping and fishing, hunting has long been a recreational pursuit for New Zealanders and tourists from overseas — indeed, the Department of Tourist and Health Resorts spent a great deal of the first half of the twentieth century promoting New Zealand as 'the sportsman's paradise'. Some wealthy New Zealanders travelled overseas to hunt, joining a long tradition of 'sportsmen' throughout the British Empire. Hunting was also the impetus for a great number of other recreational activities: reading, writing and even shopping.

Hunting was seldom a discrete recreational category, with many hunters enjoying a range of related activities including photography, tramping and mountaineering. Also blurring the distinction were the various government departments concerned with animal control pouring millions of dollars into creating tracks and huts, a hunting infrastructure that has benefited government shooters, private hunters, trampers and mountaineers alike.

> **A lot of my time in the bush wasn't for meat-hunting, it was just to be out there and go and have a look. You might trip over that stag that's got the huge head or something like that, that you'd never know about. But I just enjoyed being there, you know, whether I saw anything or not, just to be out there and watch. — Grant Fitz-William**[1]

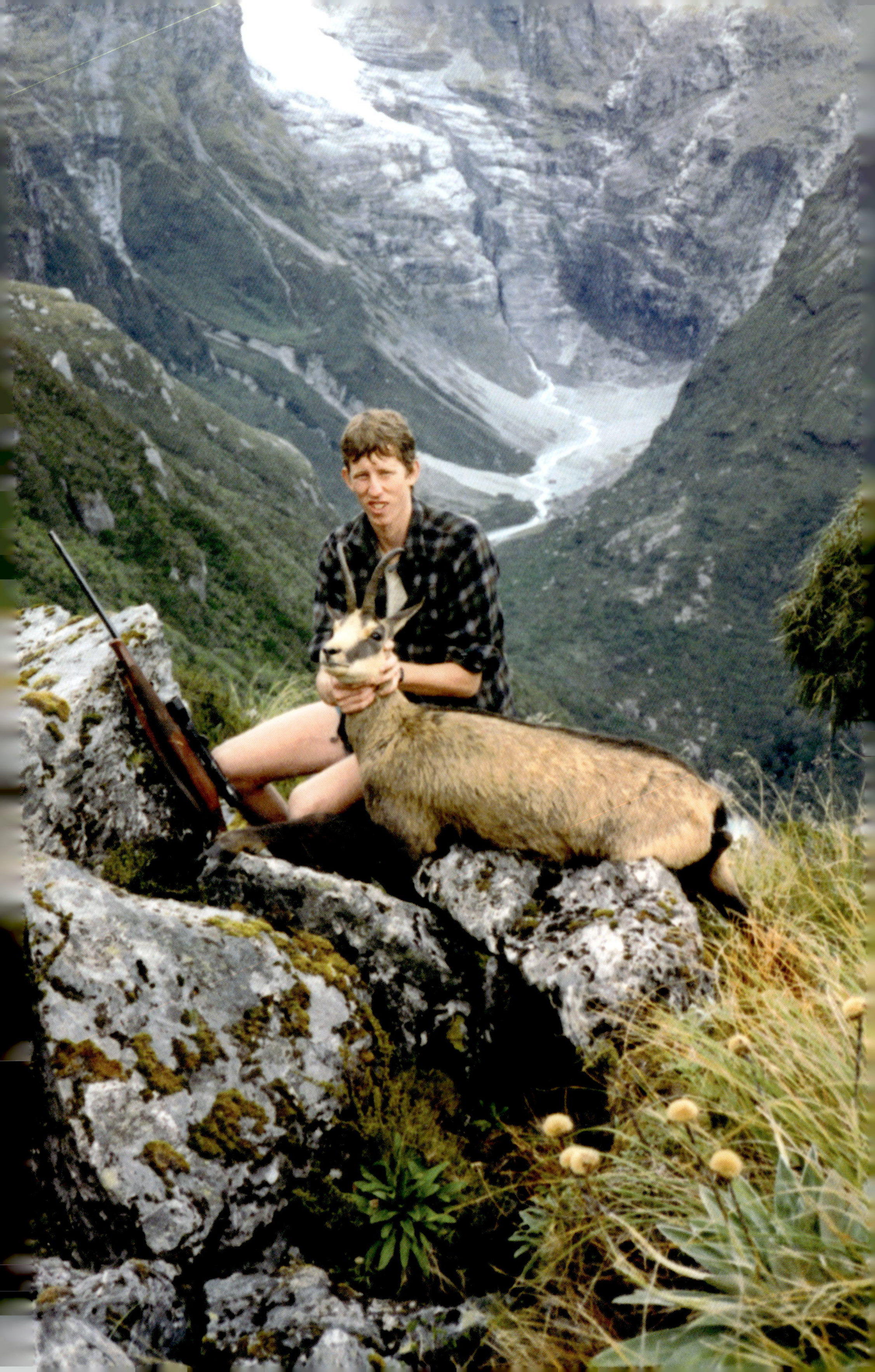

**Shooters came [to the Blue Mountains] from all over New Zealand, camping out for a week or ten days. It was a splendid holiday and great sport. The average shooter, even one you had never met before, became a friend for life after the first camp. The same chaps came back year after year . . . — Robert Shearing[2]**

**In the '50s hunters and trampers in the club shared the transport, but once they got to a place they'd do their own things. When we did the trip down the Wangapeka, half of them were hunters and half would have been trampers . . . You'd have a base camp and you'd do trips from there. But everybody sort of cooperated and worked in together and it was great. — Viv Collings[3]**

## Out for a shot at home

When asked why they hunt, New Zealand hunters often give long, rambling answers that reveal complex motivations. They enjoy the physical exercise, the socialising and the honing and maintenance of bush skills, as well as the satisfaction of bringing home meat and, in many cases, of carrying on a family tradition. Most recreational hunters will tell you that the most important part of hunting for them is being in the bush. In recounting hunting trips or major expeditions, descriptions of the bush, the terrain and the views are integral. Most hunters interviewed had favourite places to hunt. Many also spoke about the thrill of encountering an animal.

> It's a reason to get out in the bush or the tops, which I would want to do even if I didn't hunt. Then there's a sense of adventure and exploration. When you get off the track you're never quite sure where your hunt will lead or what you might find. But most of all it's the challenge of pitting your knowledge and experience against a wild animal's highly tuned senses. The process of hunting is about predicting where and when the animal will be and what it will be doing, then taking account of the weather, wind and lie of the land, working your way into a position where you encounter that animal on

Opposite: Adventure and challenge are two reasons people hunt. Alpine terrain can be difficult to hunt over, but the rewards can be immense. Bruce Wenden on Blue Lookout with Lambert Glacier in the background, 1989.

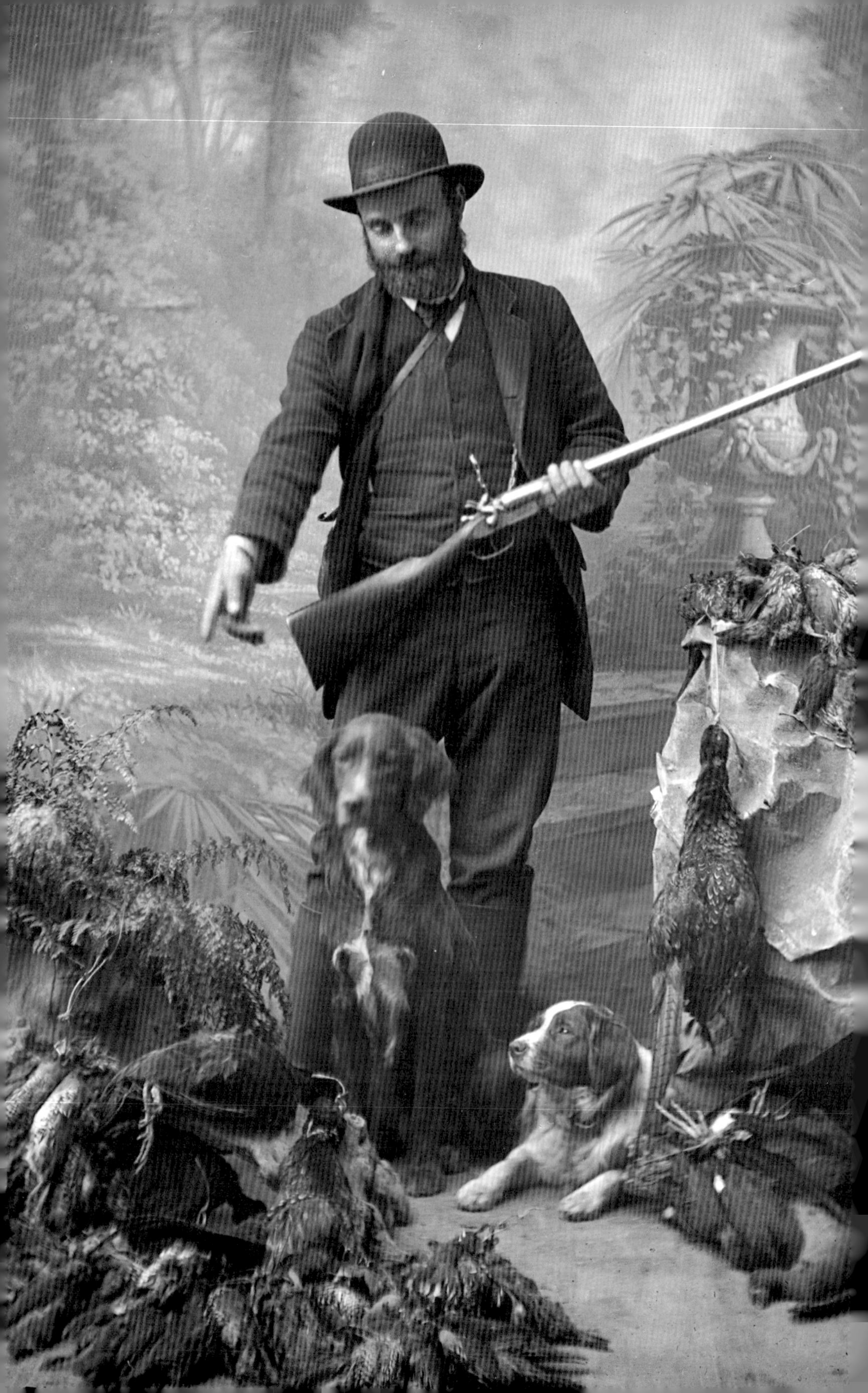

*your terms, if only for an instant. When you start out, killing is really important because that is how you measure your skill as a hunter. Nowadays I'm satisfied to just get close to them. Sometimes I just sit and watch because deep down I find them fascinating. I shoot only what I can carry, and it's often with regret that I pull the trigger.*[4]

Research conducted from the 1980s onwards has consistently demonstrated that trophy heads are less important to most recreational hunters than a good day (or weekend) in the bush and a bit of venison to take home. Given the decline of plentiful, high-quality trophies among New Zealand's deer populations, the primary reason that hunters continue to shoot during the roar (the rutting season) seems to be social. It's an opportunity for hunting mates to go into the hills together. Similarly, even in times of falling bags, duck hunters continue to make an event out of opening day.[5] These surveys have also revealed that hunters in New Zealand are overwhelmingly male and that the age range is very broad, although most were between 20 and 40 years old. Married men outnumbered single men in these surveys, perhaps confirming

Opposite: The distinction between those who hunted for recreation and those who hunted to provision their households is often a false one. Adventure and enjoyment can be had while stocking the larder. When Mr Birch succeeded in getting his dog to sit in the right spot, this photo would send a strong message about the bounty of the colony, the opportunities to richly provision the household and the sport that could be had in New Zealand.

Above: This cigarette card described pig-hunting as sport but upper-class British visitors to New Zealand disparaged it. There was a strong class element to the 'sportsman's ethic' and some hunting fell outside it. Pig-hunting was pursued and described in enthusiastic terms by many other settlers, however.

**Sportsman's paradise** 193

the anecdotal link between hunting and provisioning. Other striking conclusions of these surveys were that 'more hunters continue their sport into married life than appears to be the case for trampers', and that hunters 'differ most markedly from other forms of back-country use in that they are more representative of general New Zealand occupational and educational levels'.[6]

It is clear from the letters from immigrants quoted in Chapter 1 that it is almost impossible to separate out purely recreational hunters from pot-hunters even in the late nineteenth century, when hunting for survival was less of a priority. Alexander Bathgate, in his comments on 1870s Otago, observed:

> The sportsman may get a very good day's duck-shooting in different parts of the country. The grey duck and teal being plentiful in places, while the noble paradise ducks are very abundant among the stubble in some parts of the interior. In the swamps there is also the pukaki [pukeko], or swamp-turkey, a bird which rises well and affords good sport.[7]

Mr R Thomas, a commercial traveller, wrote of an Otago duck-hunting expedition in 1885. He clearly regarded this as recreation, being paddled in a kaiwaka by his Maori guide, silently gliding through the reeds, hearing 'the cries of duck and whistling of Teal and Widgeon at no great distance ahead of us . . . Peeping through my screen I saw a sight that made my heart rejoice. Fully 300 Grey Ducks, quite a number of Teal and ten or a dozen Black Swan were within gunshot.'[8] Thomas was well versed in an imperial sporting ethos:

> Before opening fire, I lay for a few moments watching the family party. It was almost a shame to disturb them, but this view did not influence me for long, as anyone fond of sport with the gun can well imagine. Sentiment in this sport is all very well for the ultra-humanitarian, but does not, for any appreciable length of time, influence the British gunnery on the warpath at the opening of the game season; whatever men of other nationalities may think on the subject. It was not my intention to shoot for the pot, or in other words, take sitting shots — I would give these birds a sporting chance on the wing.[9]

Within a few hours, Thomas had shot 50 birds.

Canterbury runholder Lady Mary-Anne Barker wrote extensively of recreational hunting, although she found that while she enjoyed the chase enormously she could not bring herself to shoot wild cattle. 'My hunting instincts only lead me to the point of *reaching* the game; when it comes to that, I always try to save its life, and if this can't be done, I retire to a distance and stop my ears; indeed, if very much over-excited, I can't help crying.'[10]

She held fewer qualms, it seemed, when it came to birds. She lamented that when shooting whio, or blue mountain ducks, on the Waimakariri River, '50 per cent of the birds were lost for want of a retriever bold enough to face that formidable river'.[11]

The term 'sportsman' was attached to a particular ethic or code of practice. Nelson hunter Newton McConochie well remembered his father's definition of a sportsman, defined by his Scots heritage:

> A sportsman is one who takes his full measure of game with the least possible suffering to his quarry. Also it is his duty to remember that if it had not been for the foresight of those of earlier days, it would not be your privilege to enjoy the bountiful hunting in which you can now indulge. Therefore it is your duty to conserve your game so that a similar privilege may be enjoyed by those that follow on.[12]

Until recent decades the term also carried class connotations. Charles Hursthouse made this very clear in his books about colonial life, written in the 1850s, in which he disparaged pig-hunting as a low-class activity, only fit for 'pork butchers' and something in which a 'sportsman' would not be interested.

Above: A day off in a working men's camp was time for a haircut and a shave, catching up with the papers, a bit of larking about and some hunting. After working hard all week, provisioning trips after pigs or wild cattle provided many men with a day's recreation. The image shows workers from Prouse & Saunders' flaxmill, Paturau, ca. 1906.

**Sportsman's paradise**

Note his sarcastic italics: 'The *sportsmen* get together two or three mongrel curs, take hatchet and musket, and proceed to beat the woods in some remote locality: the pig started, the curs worry him for half a mile through the thicket til they bring him to bay, when the ragged Nimrods labour up, cut the poor brute's throat and bag him for the pot'.[13] His pronouncement that there was 'nothing to shoot' in New Zealand (see Chapter 1) was as much about who was doing the shooting as it was about the game available.

Hubert Ostler, who went on to become a Supreme Court judge and a pillar of the acclimatisation society, was a very keen pig-hunter in his youth when he was a bush contractor in the Otaki district in the 1880s.[14] Hursthouse would have been horrified by the stories Ostler later recounted about setting off after a pig armed with nothing but his woodsman's axe, but Hursthouse's view was not universal. Other nineteenth-century writers referred to pig-hunting as a 'rough-and-tumble bit of excitement' and 'one of the most exhilarating and intensely exciting species of sport that any lover of the true charm of dangerous adventure can wish for'.[15] Lady Barker also wrote of Canterbury working men spending their spare time going after wild cattle, partly to provide variation in a monotonous diet, but also because cattle hunts could be fast and sometimes dangerous.

Hursthouse might have been also perplexed by Lady Barker's entire chapter about 'pig-stalking' in her *Station Amusements*, first published in 1871. She made it clear that this was not pot-hunting; it was part of the duties of a responsible pastoralist. 'It was much too hot in summer to go after wild pigs. That was our winter's amusement, and very good sport it afforded us, besides the pleasure of knowing that we were really doing good service to the pastoral interest, by ridding the hills around us of almost the only enemies which the sheep have.' Many more stalkers and sportsmen would have taken offence at her description of pig-hunting, however, and her comparison with what were considered much nobler pursuits:

*The sport is conducted exactly like deer stalking, only it is much harder work, and a huge boar is not so picturesque an object as a stag of many tines, when you do catch sight of him. There is just the same accurate knowledge needed of the animal's habits and customs, and the same untiring patience. It is quite as necessary to be a good shot, for a grey pig standing under the lee of a boulder of exactly his own colour is a much more difficult object to hit from the opposite side of a ravine than a stag; and a wild boar is every whit as keen of scent and sharp of eye and ear as any antlered 'Monarch of the Glen'.*[16]

As discussed in previous chapters, there was a great deal of free food to be hunted in New Zealand and large numbers of labouring and working-class people availed themselves of those opportunities denied them in England. Recreational hunting was no different, although working-class hunters were much more likely to combine pot-hunting with their recreation. While the hunting undertaken by Francis McDiarmid and the bush workers in his West Taieri community in the 1850s and 60s was obviously for the larder, plenty of wild pork allowed for the occasional trophy hunt, in this case of an animal that would not have made good eating. Francis's daughter Elizabeth wrote of two young men who hunted for a large, elusive boar.

*They named him the 'General'. His lair was somewhere up in the gorge, above Mr A Mann's house, but this big boar was shot at last ... by Mr Alex Adam (son of Mr James Adam of Tokomairiro) and Mr George Duncan (founder of the NZ and Australian Cable System). I do not know which of their shots [killed the boar] — perhaps both were successful in this. Those two young men while spending a holiday with my parents ... went for a day's pig hunting, and after having an exciting time, shot the 'General' and brought home his head in triumph.*[17]

That hunting for leisure was enormously important for rural workers is revealed in the many contemporary accounts. Bush workers, despite toiling in difficult conditions during the week, still hunted on their days off. Settler Philip Kenway wrote of timber workers in the Wairarapa in the late nineteenth century, they would 'work mightily all the week, and instead of resting the seventh day, they would be off cattle hunting miles away among the precipitous ranges, and after a whole day's rough and most arduous bush clambering, would come gaily up the long track to camp, "humping" on their backs the most surprising loads of good beef.'[18]

Hunting was also the chosen recreation of many city workers. City-dwellers had ready access to butchered meat, so had less need of hunting for food. But they were also living and working in environments which, for the nineteenth century and some of the twentieth, were regarded as unhealthy. Getting out into the bush for a hunt was considered a healthy recreation for city people, as were other popular outdoor activities of the time: picnics, sea bathing and, by the 1930s, tramping.

These activities all cost money and time, though. Apart from work outings, getting out amidst nature required the organisation of transport and accommodation of some sort. Huts in the bush, often referred to as whares, were one way of solving the accommodation problem, and areas such as the Orongorongo Valley (between South Wairarapa and Wellington) and the Wainuiomata Valley became dotted with private whares in the 1930s.

One city-dweller with a whare in the Wainuiomata bush was Fred Whitley, whose 'shooting diary' records more than 40 years of weekend shooting around Wainuiomata, beginning in the late 1880s. Whitley and his friend Thomas would catch the train from Wellington to the Hutt Valley, then walk 22.5 km to the farm of Dave Dicks, where they would shoot birds and pigs. In the 1890s the men ventured into the Orongorongos in pursuit of goats, but pigeons and kaka were always among the weekend's bag. In the 1890s, Whitley and his friends leased land from farmers and built whares so they would have more comfortable accommodation.[19]

Above: The building of a 'whare' or private hut gave hunters a more permanent and comfortable place to stay in the bush. It also reinforced ties with a particular place and many hunters and their families and friends used their whares for decades and sometimes several generations.

## Fred Whitley's whare

*While rural people had hunting opportunities on their doorstep, city-dwellers had to have the means and time to travel to hunting spots. That they did this in large numbers indicates how important hunting was as a recreational pursuit.*

Fred Whitley's diary illustrates how important recreational hunting was to him. He lived and worked in Wellington but for nearly 40 years, from the late 1880s to the 1920s, his diary recorded only his weekend hunting in the Wainuiomata area, and his annual week's holiday at Hinakura in the South Wairarapa; he never went further afield. His diary never mentions his occupation nor his family, except briefly when he mentions sharing venison with some recently arrived cousins.

Beginning with visits to the bush at the back of Dave Dick's farm at Wainuiomata in the 1880s, Whitley and the friends he made over the years built two whares in the Wainuiomata hills, the first of which was destroyed in a flood. The land for the second whare was secured on a 20-year lease. The men paid shares on the lease and the building, and on supplies; Whitley recorded in his 1900 diary the purchase of 16 pounds (7.3 kg) of bacon 'for the whare. All shares paid'.

In 1915, he went shares in a motorbike with his friend Ernest Wiffin so they could make the journey to Wainuiomata more easily. (Up until then they had taken the train to the Hutt Valley and walked or hitchhiked.) The friends spent weekends hunting, track-clearing, maintaining the whare and enjoying meals together. Venison was shared out, often with friends in town, and there were a great many meals eaten together back in town. Skins were tanned, used as rugs and made into bags by a saddler on Lambton Quay. Guns were swapped and sold. Dogs were bought at sales, sold, swapped, lost, mourned and occasionally, if they were no good, destroyed. Transport evolved from train travel and walking in the early years, to horses, motorbikes and then the occasional car journey in the early 1920s.

Many friendships were made through hunting and snippets about them in the diary give us a wider picture of men's networks at this time: Sid Tisdall, a local businessman who had a whare in the Akatarawas, Jack Clarke (wounded at Gallipoli in 1915), Jack McCormick (killed at Gallipoli), Colonel Esson (veteran of the South African War), Ernest Wiffin (a member of the local acclimatisation society and, in the 1930s, a hunting and fishing guide to aristocrats and movie stars — see Chapter 3), and Alec and Ken Sutherland (sons of Wairarapa farmers who went on to become well-known and highly successful wapiti hunters).

After a lifetime of hunting, Whitley's diary peters out in 1925 and he died, probably from a heart attack, in 1928.

Above and opposite: Neville 'Stag' Spooner and his brother Tory spent as much time in the bush as they could. Part of a large Wairarapa family, the boys left school as soon as they were old enough. Hunting and fishing were a large part of their lives and so were drawing and painting. They produced sketchbooks of major weekend trips and painted a panoramic view of the Tararuas as a frieze around their bedroom. When war broke out in 1939, both brothers enlisted, and sent home many, many letters, especially to their mother and their hunting mate Horace Anderson. The envelopes the brothers sent home were always highly decorated and they had several designs commercially printed in Cairo which they presumably sold to other soldiers. Hunting was a constant theme in Stag's art. When he returned from the war he joined the Deer Control Section, dying in the bush while at work at the age of 28. Tory also died young, aged 32, also in the bush and from the same heart condition that afflicted all of the Spooner brothers.

**200 Hunting**

## Taking the Yanks out

Wairarapa hunter Walter Day and his friends had an enterprising way of keeping up with pig-hunting during World War Two when petrol-rationing threatened to curtail their sport. Local farmers were crying out for men to come and dispatch the ever-increasing numbers of pigs on their land, and Day ran the Shell fuel depot in Masterton. For some years, a little petrol could always be found to go and do the job.

When the American troops arrived and the fuel depot came under strict military supervision, Day and his friend Norm Bull simply started to take the 'Yanks' out shooting.

'Oh, we took out a Major and a Captain from the medical unit at Paekakariki. They supplied the fuel. If we took the Yanks out we'd go round Palliser Light House — an ordinary car couldn't get there, but those four-by-fours, I'd never seen anything like them, they'd go across sand. We had the dogs and the know-how. We had quite a lot of hunting and got to know a lot of fellows . . . Over the years of the war we got over 1000 pigs . . . and about 250 deer — Norm's still got the records.'[20]

A childhood in the bush often involved hunting of some sort. Hunting was, and remains, an adventure for many children. Many people I spoke to while researching this book spoke of going into the bush with their fathers and older relatives, learning to shoot by starting with rabbits and graduating to goats, then deer; of being in the thick of it and of simply tagging along. Several hunters connected time spent in the bush as a child with their skills as an adult. On growing up in Te Horo, north of Wellington, Dave Marino commented that by the time he saw his first deer he knew how to stalk, because as a child in the bush 'you're always sneaking up on something'. Central North Island hunter Fred Richards described running down goats on foot with his mates when they were children and Sonny Te Ahuru and his friends hunted wild cattle on horseback in the Tongariro forest.[21]

Hunting was an important ingredient in the general excitement among the Cameron boys that preceded the visits of their Uncle Will to their Wairarapa farm in the late nineteenth century: 'He was fond of pig hunting

Above: Anticipation of the opening of the game-bird season could infect a household. For many New Zealanders, duck season represents an important social and family time.

and pigeon shooting and occasionally would take a few days off from farming to spend with us at his favourite sports. The whole family looked forward joyfully to his visits.'[22] The boys were allowed to accompany their uncle on hunting trips. 'Johnnie and I carried the bag of shot pigeons. Usually about 20 pigeons were shot for the use of the household. However the day before he left about 40 pigeons would be shot to give him a fair number to take away with him'.[23]

Even in the increasingly urbanised twentieth century, hunting continued to be part of children's adventures. Chris Laidlaw wrote that there was really only one thing he and his father did together, 'when I was 10 or 11 years old: rabbit shooting'. These expeditions were very popular, writes Laidlaw, 'particularly if you could sell the meat a local butcher'.

*Dad was enormously enthusiastic about this. He had hunted rabbits ever since he was a boy and had become something of a crack shot with the old family .22. He would clean the rifle for days beforehand and count out the ammunition that he kept in a special drawer in his bedroom. He taught me how to shoot and where to position yourself to get the best shot. I loved every minute of it. It is difficult to remember how many times we went roaming into the hills of the peninsula, perhaps a dozen or so. My first kill came after countless misses and I remember insisting we take the rabbit home and cook it . . . On those expeditions, the gulf between me and my father was eliminated for a few exhilarating hours.*[24]

Sometimes it was the sense of adventure or excitement rather than actually participating that impressed children. They were often on the periphery of hunting activities, especially if they were a little young to be tagging along. Growing up in a hunting family, Jocelyn Rae enthusiastically described family camping trips in the summers of the 1950s and 1960s, during which her father and uncles would leave camp before dawn to go into the bush. 'The fathers would all go off hunting and the kids would all play and the mums would all do the cooking as was done in those days. The men would bring back the meat.' She recalls the excitement for the children of her father's weekend hunting trips:

*During those early days, my memories of Dad are our uncles coming to stay in the weekends, and the men going off hunting. They had an old Volkswagen truck, with a cover over the deck, and the excitement of when our dads came home, rushing out, rushing into the back of the truck to see what they had, and then the mounds of meat and skins. Back then they used to hang the skins to dry, so around the back of our garage at home, there was all these racks with deer skins drying. They must have got a lot of deer in those days. The smell of venison and skins drying is still very, very vivid in my mind.*[25]

## Muriel Henderson

*Muriel Henderson has been a keen duck-hunter all her life. Raised in Southland in the 1940s in a bird-hunting family and with three brothers, it is no surprise that she has continued to hunt all her life. The opening day of the duck season has been a family occasion for as long as she can remember, but it has not been without its costs.*

I don't know how I managed when I think back because I went duck-shooting even though I was raising five children, and I used to have a big family breakfast before we left at five o'clock in the morning. Everyone would come to my house for a cooked breakfast — it had to be a really good breakfast. Then we'd go out shooting and we'd get home just at dark, tired and hungry, wet clothes and whatnot, [and] hang the ducks up. But then I'd have to pluck them and cook them too later. And I had to make the lunches! I think I must have been fairly strong.[26]

## A different kind of shooting

From the 1920s, cameras became a more common part of hunting equipment. Photographic records in archives and libraries all over New Zealand are full of hunting photographs. Wellington hunter Fred Whitley got his first camera in 1919. The photo albums of trampers and hunters Gavin Wallace, Ben Iorns and Fred Furkert all concentrate on the 1930s and early 1940s, with extensive records of trips in the Orongorongo Valley, the Tararua Ranges and South Westland. As the technology allowed, 'home movies' were also made of hunting trips. Earnest Adams filmed hunting activities as early as 1928; Frank Tate recorded his hunting trip to New Zealand on 16mm film in 1936. There was an explosion in amateur filming of hunting in the 1950s and '60s, as well as the productions of the Government Publicity Studio and the National Film Unit.[27]

Jocelyn Rae's father owned an 8mm movie camera, and a great family ritual associated with hunting was watching films of hunting trips, particularly his annual South Island trips. 'That was always pretty exciting, watching his adventures on film. We'd pull out the screen, and all the family and the cousins, we'd all get together and sit there watching these, these great expeditions they did to the South Island high country.'[28]

A great number of hunters are photographers and some have given up the rifle altogether in favour of the lens.

# Men of means

Trophy-hunting stands out as a clearly defined form of recreational hunting. Apart from shooting smaller beasts for food along the way, trophy-hunting is all about the 'head' — the antlers or horns — or, in more exotic circumstances, the skin or tusks. Specimen- or trophy-hunters tend to be very selective, observing and passing over inferior animals, disturbing them as little as possible and only shooting once they have located a specimen of acceptable quality.

Before the lifting of protection on deer, tahr and chamois in New Zealand in 1930, the only legal form of hunting of these animals was licensed stalking.

Stalking licences cost between £1 and £5 depending on the district and the pedigree of the herd. The numbers of licences issued each year and the bag sizes (how many animals or birds that could be shot by each licence holder) were restricted. A stalking licence usually allowed the taking of between two and four bucks or stags.

Accounts of trophy-hunting were published in great numbers from the advent of licensed hunting in the 1870s: newspapers and illustrated weeklies reported regularly on the seasons and results. From the 1960s onwards many books have been devoted to 'the halcyon days' of New Zealand stalking between the 1890s and 1930. These accounts depict a group of relatively wealthy people, able to travel to distant parts of the country for weeks at a time and to pay for travel, supplies, guides and eventually taxidermists. There is an emphasis in these stalking reminiscences on the central and southern parts of the South Island, which tended to produce the finest antlers.

Deer-stalking in the South Island has had two distinct features: it has

Above: For many, hunting has been recreation pursued to the point of obsession. Viv Donald drew an enormous amount of satisfaction from his trophy-hunting and, for obvious reasons, the Donalds' dining room was legendary among Masterton children growing up in the 1950s and '60s.

**206  Hunting**

involved more women than most other kinds of hunting, and it was the kind of hunting that the New Zealand tourist department promoted with great fervour. Women were a prominent part of some stalking parties into difficult South Island terrain. These women came from families wealthy enough to afford them leisure, and they were very often horsewomen, and therefore able to participate more easily than women of other classes.

Margaret Donald, the 14-year-old daughter of veteran stalker Vivian Donald, shot with guide Leslie Murrell in South Westland in 1922. Novelist Ngaio Marsh joined a stalking party in 1923 and wrote about it for the Christchurch *Sun*. Mercy Money-Coutts, who later became a noted archaeologist in Crete, accompanied her father, Lord Latymer, into South Westland in 1933, three years after her mother had completed a similar trip.

Above: Thomas Donne, director of the Department of Tourist and Health Resorts, made it his mission to promote New Zealand as 'the sportsman's paradise'. Thousands of pounds were spent on brochures, posters and exhibiting deer heads at international expositions. Overseas stalkers were regular visitors to New Zealand and they contributed significantly to the tourist economy. From 1930, however, protection on deer was removed and so began a decade of wrangling between those who saw deer as an economic asset and those who wanted them destroyed to protect the environment.

In the 1920s, Hawke's Bay runholder Mrs Ethne R Herrick was judged by the legendary guide Jim Muir 'to be the best shot, man or woman, he had ever hunted with'.[29]

Stalking and trophy-hunting in New Zealand were major tourist attractions. When Thomas Donne was put in charge of the new Department of Tourist and Health Resorts in 1901, he was of the opinion that 'we have some of the grandest scenery in the world, but we have practically not yet begun to advertise it'. His contemporary the Reverend WC Oliver agreed, adding that 'there are in this colony three things that should bring to our shores, in growing numbers every year, men of means and leisure, *viz.*, magnificent scenery, over one thousand rivers and streams well stocked with trout, . . .

Above: Moose were liberated in Dusky Sound, Fiordland in 1910. They were purchased from the Canadian government by the Department of Tourist and Health Resorts. Moose never thrived, however: the diet and climate did not suit them and they had to compete with the more adaptable red deer. (It has also been suggested that the moose's large and sensitive nose was especially susceptible to sandfly bites). In 1924 the first licence to shoot moose was issued, but it was 1929 before the first one was legally shot. Between 1929 and 1952 only three bull moose and two cows were shot; two of the bulls were shot by EJ Herrick, seen here carrying his first trophy across the Seaforth River, guided by Jim Muir. The third and last bull moose shot in New Zealand was by long-time government shooter Percy Lyes.

and herds of deer'.[30] Thousands of pounds were poured into both stocking New Zealand with appropriate animals and publicising the opportunities this gave to overseas sportsmen and women (see Chapter 1). The *New Zealand Illustrated Tourist Guide* published in 1925 contained dozens of references to 'deer, pigs, ducks, swan, hares, pheasant, quail and curlew in abundance for the gun'. It was illustrated with mounted heads of pigs and goats as well as deer and photographs of hunters with piles of antlers, and included advertisements for sporting goods and ammunition. Sections included 'Salmon Rivers and Deer Country', 'Sport in Otago' and 'Sportsman's Paradise'. Advice to tourists warned that 'it is to be remembered that in New Zealand stalking is real hunting, not a dress parade of gillies [Scottish highland guides], ponies and suitably-garbed parties engaged in fashionable exercise'. Indeed, the booklet went on, a stalker should hire a guide and 'preferably he will have a companion, for two means more than company in difficult country. He will wear the roughest and toughest clothes he may possess, and should be prepared to spend nights in bivouacs beneath the stars'. These privations would, however, be fully enjoyed by a true sportsman and 'when he has bagged his really exceptional head [he] will value the prize all the more for the strenuous hours, the rugged, primitive life he has lived in securing it'.[31]

Overseas hunters and stalkers came to New Zealand in large numbers before the beginning of the deer destruction campaigns of the 1930s. Donne quoted many overseas sportsmen who had visited New Zealand in his *Red Deer Stalking in New Zealand*. As well as recording many New Zealand hunters, deer-stalking authority D Bruce Banwell writes of hunters coming to Fiordland from Britain and India.[32] British magazines contained many articles on stalking in New Zealand by recently returned sportsmen; AE Leatham wrote in *Blackwood's Magazine*, 'I doubt whether anything in the way of sport can surpass red deer stalking in the highlands of Otago. Gorgeous scenery! A climate so bracing that a man can walk from sunrise to sunset without feeling unduly tired! Glorious trophies in the form of stags' horns, far surpassing anything to be found in our own country! What more can the heart of a hunter desire?'[33]

That Donne was convinced of the value of overseas hunter-tourists to the New Zealand economy can be seen in his books promoting the sport. In his 1924 book *Game Animals of New Zealand*, he constantly promoted the number of deer to be found in the bush. Even a paragraph on illegal shooting is turned to promotional advantage:

*One resident of Nelson shot such a large number of stags in the earlier days of their acclimatisation that their antlers were displayed throughout his home from the front door to the backyard fence, and even adorned his fowl-house. It is asserted that some of the residents shot stags of any age or size and that hinds did not always escape the bullet ... The shooting had one good effect, as it caused some of the deer to seek less noisy and disturbed quarters further afield, so that little colonies were formed which extended from time to time until the Nelson and Marlborough provinces were fairly well stocked by natural expansion.*[34]

Even in the early 1920s, Donne was anticipating the battle he would face with the anti-deer movement, presenting a justification for the presence of deer that would echo through the decades. He asserted in *Game Animals* (published two years after Allan Perham's report on the damage done to forests by deer — see Chapter 1) that

*to endeavour to exterminate the deer, as is suggested, would be a calamity of more than local importance. It is, of course, known that deer browse on shrubs and plants but their destructiveness to forests is infinitesimal in comparison with that caused by fire ... It might be pointedly asked, how many travellers visit New Zealand to view shrubs and plants as against those who are attracted there by sport? In any case there are more trees, shrubs and plants than a man could look at in a hundred years.*[35]

When the Deer Control Section was established in 1930 and the destruction of deer became government policy, there was almost a decade of wrangling between the Department of Tourist and Health Resorts and the new section. In the early 1930s, the tourist department continued as long as it could to include stalking in its publicity: it continued to print leaflets in the 'sportsman's paradise' vein and to exhibit animal heads at expositions and exhibitions. The High Commissioner to London's publicity department continued to set up stalls displaying mounted New Zealand deer heads; *The Dominion* carried a picture in September 1935 of such a display at the Aldershot Command and District Horse Show under the caption 'Advertising New Zealand'. This particular picture had been clipped by the Under-Secretary's office and sent to the Minister of Internal Affairs with a note: 'Your attention is drawn to the above display in which deer heads figure prominently . . . You have already taken this matter up with the Departments of Industry and Commerce, Tourist and Publicity on several occasions with, it would appear, no definite results either in New Zealand or abroad. The above photo is evidence of what is still going on in England'.[36]

The Department of Tourist and Health Resorts had argued that it could continue advertising stalking and attracting visitors on this basis as long as it apprised potential tourists of Deer Control's operations. A 12-month trial of the coexistence of hunting-tourism and government deer-shooting operations was not a success. Internal Affairs continued to receive complaints from sportsmen. 'In connection with this overseas publicity I may mention that a friend of Captain Percy, ADC, some six months back spent £600 in coming to New Zealand for deer-stalking on the strength of posters advertising deer-shooting attractions, only to find when he came here that his presence in deer country covered by our operations was naturally not welcomed.'[37] Eventually a memo was drafted for the Prime Minister's office to send to the High Commissioner to London clearly making the point that 'the presence of individual sportsmen in areas (naturally those with the greatest deer populations) worked by the Departmental parties seriously interferes with the work of those parties'. Commercial skin-hunters, it was also pointed out, were also less than enthusiastic about overseas sportsmen in the bush. As a consequence, overseas stalkers would be discouraged. 'They readily acknowledge when faced with the facts the necessity for the Government's campaign but are very bitter in their complaints about the continued featuring of deer stalking in government publicity'. The Minister of Internal Affairs decreed that 'experience of the [past] 12 months has very definitely shown that the interests of sportsmen conflict with the settled Government policy with respect to deer'.[38]

The High Commissioner's office was requested to stop advertising deer-stalking, but the Tourist and Health Resorts publicity department continued producing materials promoting New Zealand as a stalking destination for several more years. In a 1935 brochure 'New Zealand: Scenic Playground of the Pacific', the 'many varieties of deer' that flourish in New Zealand were noted, deer-stalking was advertised as one of the sports 'obtainable under ideal conditions', and most blatantly,

> *A Wonderland for Sportsmen* — *in deer stalking the Dominion offers a greater variety than possibly any other country in the world. Ranging from giant moose and wapiti, the species available include also red and fallow deer, sambur [sic], chamois, Himalayan thar, and Virginian [white-tailed] and Japanese [sika] deer. Owing to the rapid increases of deer herds in New Zealand of late years, stalking may be had without payment of licence fees, it only being necessary to arrange for permission to shoot over the properties it is desired to visit.*[39]

Despite frequent memos on this issue from Internal Affairs to Tourist and Health Resorts, and from the Prime Minister to the High Commissioner, an advertisement in *United Empire* in March 1938 advertised activities that could be had on one's next 'carefree three or four month holiday trip to New Zealand' as 'incomparable trout and salmon fishing, deep-sea angling for sword-fish and deerstalking'.[40]

The onset of World War Two put an end to all thoughts of carefree trips to New Zealand, and stalking tourism did not recover. The decimation of deer numbers by the commercial venison industry in the 1960s also put paid to any thoughts of reviving this kind of tourism. More recently, however, private safari parks and guiding companies offering deer-, tahr- and chamois-stalking are rebuilding New Zealand's international reputation as a destination for elite stalking holidays.

### The wapiti block

*The 'wapiti block' is in Fiordland National Park and constitutes approximately 172,000 of the park's 1.2 million hectares. Apart from a brief period when protection was completely lifted, access to hunting wapiti has been allocated in blocks to which stalkers gain access through the purchase of a licence. (Currently these blocks are assigned through a ballot system for the roar, as is the case with other popular hunting areas such as parts of South Westland.) The achievements of hunters and their guides in hunting in this environment sets it apart from stalking in other parts of the country. It is the most mountainous and least explored region of New Zealand, with the added factor of it being the wettest part of the country, receiving up to 6m of rainfall per year.*

Above: Herbert Hart and Les Murrell battle the terrain in the wapiti block, 1925.

# No licence required

While the lifting of protection on deer all but destroyed the international component of hunting-tourism, it opened up deer-stalking, and the hunting of tahr and chamois, to a wide range of New Zealanders.

A great number of reminiscences of rural life from the 1930s onwards include descriptions of hunting as part of leisure-time activities. Low wage-earners — mill hands, farm workers, bush contractors and city factory workers and tradesmen — were freed from the restrictions of licence requirements and positively encouraged to shoot deer by the government and farmers. They took to deer-stalking with enthusiasm.

Bill Monk, born in 1919 into a large and extended farming family in the Reikorangi Basin north of Wellington, talked about his youth as including country dances, swimming, badminton and tennis as well as days when 'the men would take the boys out' eeling, fishing and hunting: 'we spent much of our time hunting'.[41] As with many families, hunting was a part of every family holiday for Viv and Din Collings and their children. Viv and Din met in the early 1950s when Viv joined the hunting section of the Wellington Tramping & Mountaineering Club as a young woman just out of school. Din was a toolmaker and engineer and made Viv her own .303 when they got married. He also made scaled-down rifles for his children as they grew up. Rifles were a constant companion on their trips into the bush over decades.

Above: In the 1930s, '40s and '50s, the distinction between hunting and tramping was far less marked than it is today. Tramping parties often carried rifles and venison stew was a common trampers' dinner. This party is enjoying bracing conditions in the Tararua Ranges.

Sportsman's paradise

While many individuals and families enjoyed the freedom brought by unrestricted hunting, those stalkers concerned with the quality of trophy heads were not so enthusiastic about indiscriminate shooting, nor the language of 'eradication' that was used by some groups. In 1938 a group of trophy-hunters formed the New Zealand Deerstalkers' Association, although with the interruption of World War Two, the association did not gather momentum until the late 1940s. While the association's formal membership never came close to reflecting the numbers of recreational hunters in the community, the support it could muster around particular issues carried substantial weight. For example, in 1960 it managed to get 80,000 signatures on a petition calling for the banning of 1080 poison (then being trialled by the Forest Service), offering instead the services of 4000 recreational hunters free of charge.[42] The group also had informal agreements with the Forest Service giving recreational hunters the run of blocks not seen as critical to government control operations. One example in the 1960s was the Mohaka River block in the Kaweka Ranges in Hawke's Bay: it was a wilderness area with poor access and no huts, and it was set aside for a time for recreational hunting alone.[43] An extension of these arrangements was the establishment of 10 formal Recreational Hunting Areas (RHAs) in the early 1980s under the Wild Animal Control Act (1977), in which no government control or commercial harvesting would take place. This was, in part, a response to the rapid reduction of recreational deer-hunting

Above: Summer holiday activities included hunting for many. Hunting provided food for the family while away from home, and with a bit of luck there was meat to take home at the end of the holiday.

opportunities by the commercial venison industry, as well as an official recognition of the importance of recreational hunting to the community.

### The beginning of a lifetime's hunting

*I left school at fifteen and started work the next day at the local sawmill. The wages were £25 a fortnight, a fortune! Enough to buy a .303, a skinning knife and 50 rounds of ammo. At the end of the first week I borrowed 10 shillings from Mum and, armed with a letter from Dad giving his permission for me to buy a .303 rifle, I went to the Greymouth Police Station and obtained the necessary permit. God, the next week went so bloody slow, it seemed like a month . . . Friday, knock off time, collect pay, on the bike, home, bath, catch the bus to town and around to Pegely's Sports Shop to begin the gun selection process. There are so many to choose from. I finally settle for a cut down sporting model [ex-army .303] for £18. I also purchase a knife, sheath and steel, £2, and fifty rounds of ammo £4. Back around to the police station to register the rifle. I didn't go to the movies and caught the early bus home. I walked in the door proudly brandishing my fine new rifle. 'Haven't you forgotten something?' Mum asked. I replied, 'No, I've got my knife and my ammo.' 'What about your board?' was her reply. Oops, £7 a week plus the 10 shillings I borrowed. 'I'll pay it with next fortnight's board.' . . . I went to bed that evening with my rifle on the floor close by, and slept little. Leapt out of bed at 4am to find Mum making breakfast — bacon, eggs and toast — plus a few sandwiches to take with me. Goodbye came with all the advice: 'Be careful, make sure you carry the rifle on half cock, make sure you know what you are shooting at, look out for the shafts that the miners dug looking for gold.'*

*I was off. Pack on back, rifle slung over the shoulder and knife on the belt. I rode my bike to the mill and then set out on foot . . . I arrived early at the lookout. It was still quite dark. Sitting down . . . I waited. The dawn came slowly. The birds started their morning song as shafts of light began to filter through the trees. Time ticked on, and at about 7.30 I decided to walk down the track and look under the willows that grew along the river's edge. As I stood, something caught my eye on the fringe of First Island. A patch of brown. As I watched, it moved and disappeared. My heart went up a gear . . . As I waited and watched, a hind emerged from the gorse. The deer waited briefly and set off across the river bed towards the willows, closely followed by a second one . . . I went down on my hands and knees and crawled up a slight rise. There, not more than 50 yards away were two deer browsing on young willow shoots. I developed a bad*

> *case of 'buck fever'. My hands were shaking, my mouth was dry and my eyes watered. Sliding the rifle forward and pulling the butt back against my shoulder, I took aim. Christ, I could hardly see. I wiped my eyes and tried again. This time I could see the foresight, place it in the v of the rear sight and then carefully train them on the deer. Now sqeeeeeze the trigger. Nothing happened. The bloody rifle was on half cock! Pull the hammer 'click'. The closest hind's head jerked up and it looked straight at me. I pulled the trigger. BANG! A cloud of smoke obscured my vision. I jumped to my feet. There in front of me lay my first deer struggling hopelessly . . . I ran to where the wounded animal lay struggling. Its large brown eyes looked at me and I have to admit I felt a wave of pity for the gallant beast. I dispatched it quickly with a shot between the eyes.*
>
> *Pity gone, elation took over. I danced around my kill. If anyone had been watching they would have thought I had gone mad. I arrived home late morning with a pack full of venison and a large deer skin. I was king.*
> — Edgar J Russ[44]

Lifting the protection from deer provided legislative encouragement to hunt, but more practical encouragement came in the form of government-built huts and tracks that opened up the bush to a wide range of trampers and hunters. Early clubs, such as the Tararua Tramping Club, had often followed deer trails through the bush, but these informal routes remained rough and inaccessible to many because they were unmarked and certainly not mapped.

In the late 1930s, the Physical Welfare and Recreation branch of the Department of Internal Affairs was established, promoted by the then minister, Bill Parry, who was himself a keen hunter. One of Parry's ideas was the construction of a network of tracks that would enable New Zealanders to access the bush without needing to belong to a club. New Zealanders were assured that tracks would be made accessible and 'huts would be an "easy day's march apart", making the trips and the scenery available to the inexperienced tramper, "who while wanting no luxuries likes a bit of comfort"'.[45]

The selection of areas where track construction would begin was dictated by deer-control operations; Parry's idea was that cullers would work over the winter (their down time) in their blocks constructing tracks. The first two areas chosen were the Tararuas and the Southern Alps, and large numbers of tracks, particularly those in more remote areas, were constructed by government shooters. Departmental politics made the whole operation

Rabbit Shooting - Wairarapa
August '58

Top: Until very recently, hunting, holidays and tramping were very often combined. At left is the Collings familiy and friends; at right, Viv Collings and three of her boys are pictured on top of Mt Hector, Tararua Ranges.
Above: The construction of huts in the back country was done in part to encourage more recreational hunters into the bush. The network of huts and tracks created in particular by the Forest Service was a great boon to other groups wanting to use the outdoors. This is Styx River base camp near Hokitika, 1959.

**Sportsman's paradise**

fraught, however. Battles of will between Forest Service supervisors, Internal Affairs shooters and contractors meant that by the time the first tramp over the Harper Pass was planned at Easter 1940, the track was complete but only one of the five huts was finished. This did not dampen the spirits of the 40 cheerful trampers who christened the track.[46]

Apart from these few areas, the construction of huts by government agencies was not carried out with recreational trampers or hunters in mind until the 1960s. Some early bush huts had been constructed by tramping clubs, but most were constructed by hunters employed by Internal Affairs and then the Forest Service, for their own use. Huts remained basic, even primitive. Early huts were constructed from materials hewn from the bush or carried in on the backs of men or horses. With the advent of aerial drops in the late 1940s, hut materials could be flown into more remote areas, and as early as 1947 there were trials of dropping prefabricated huts for hunters to assemble:

> The structure was broken down into sections with a maximum length of 3 feet, the inch-thick wooden walls being clad with RNZAF-surplus Dural sheets, which also formed the roof and the chimney. The interior was fitted out with bunks, a table, chairs, a vermin-proof cupboard and a plastic window, and the whole structure was held in place against the inevitable gales on the open tops, by heavy-duty tie-downs.[47]

In 1954, the establishment of a national park in the Tararua Ranges was opposed by tramping groups not wanting to see the area developed and wilderness values lost. Instead the Forest Service suggested a trial of a 'multiple-use' or 'forest park' area where recreational hunters and trampers could have access but Forest Service hunters would control animal populations. The trial was enormously successful (although many of tramping club members still resented the loss of what they saw as wilderness).

> In 1958 there were 26 club huts throughout the range but only three government huts for wild animal control; during 1960–62, the Forest Service built 10 new huts and by the end of the 1960s the figure stood at 14 new huts and 10 two-person bivouacs. In addition, scores of new tracks were cut, most giving access to the tops via subsidiary spurs and ridges.[48]

From the mid-1960s another 17 forest parks were opened to recreational users and from the 1960s huts throughout the country were built with multiple purposes in mind.

# The long shot

For all the importance of New Zealand's domestic hunting traditions, it is important not to neglect the practice of travelling overseas to hunt. Over the years New Zealanders have hunted in Australia, Africa, North America and, most ironically, given the introduction to New Zealand of so many game birds and animals from Britain, Scotland. While the government's tourism agencies promoted New Zealand as offering all that the English game parks, Scottish highlands and North American forests had in the way of game, and the big game-hunting experience of India and Africa *without* the dangerous animals, the lure of those places persisted for many who could afford such holidays. The 1930s represented a break in this kind of overseas hunting. The New Zealand stalking 'industry' so rigorously promoted by the government declined significantly and momentum was gained in wildlife conservation in the traditional destinations of sport hunters such as Africa.

After a successful shooting holiday in Scotland in 1923, Daniel Riddiford, heir to a Wairarapa sheep-farming fortune, engaged his friend Michael Lindsay to rent on his behalf accommodation for the 1927 grouse-shooting season. With a budget of £2000, Lindsay secured both the country house on Strathmore estate and Thurso Castle for several months.

The Riddifords enjoyed a great amount of bird-shooting and socialising over their months in Scotland. Their shooting diary recorded that between early August and mid-September 1927 the Riddiford party shot 2105 grouse, 234 snipe, 15 partridge, 199 hares, 52 rabbits and four stags, and caught 16 salmon.[49]

> **The castle is situated on the Bay of Thurso, within a mile of the Town and Railway Station of Thurso, commanding extensive views of the Coast scenery and the Orkneys. It is handsomely furnished and contains — Entrance Hall, 5 public rooms, Billiard Room, Secretary's Room, 25 principal bedrooms, 10 dressing rooms (4 of which have plunge baths), 13 servants' bedrooms, 3 bathrooms, 10 WCs, Servants' Hall, Housekeeper's Room, Kitchen, Pantries, Larders &c., as well as stabling, a large Garage and Kennels. The Castle and Offices are lighted with Gas except for the Public Rooms. Good Drainage.**
> — E Paton & Son Shooting & Estate Agency advertisement, London, 1925[50]

> ## Why go abroad for Big Game?
>
> Arnhem Land, North Australia —"One of the world's wild spots"—is a sportsman's paradise.
>
> Buffaloes, Crocodiles, Kangaroos, Wallabies and myriads of small game abound. Excellent sea and river fishing.
>
> *Buffalo Hunting in Arnhem Land*
>
> During the months of June, July and August
> An opportunity will be offered for
>
> ## Big Game Hunting in Australia
>
> Personally conducted Hunting Parties to Arnhem Land, North Australia
> Under the direction of an expert Buffalo Shooter
>
> A five weeks' trip, Sydney to Sydney, by rail and motor, embracing 5000 miles of travel.
> **Inclusive Price £143**
>
> Full particulars from
> THE SECRETARY,
> Commonwealth Railways,
> 623 Collins Street,
> MELBOURNE, C.I. (Australia),
> or
> **RAILWAY DEPARTMENT**
> WELLINGTON, N.Z.
>
> *This 20 ft. Man-eating Crocodile's troubles are ended. The huge reptiles are numerous on the banks of the rivers in Arnhem Land*

In 1926, Herbert Hart, a Brigadier General during World War One and a respected Carterton solicitor, went on a three-month safari to North Rhodesia (now Zambia), with friend and fellow hunter Vivian Donald. Both were extremely keen recreational hunters, and for Hart the trip to Africa was something of a return journey. Lying about his age, he had enlisted for the South African War and arrived in Durban just as hostilities ceased in 1902. His diary from the 1926 safari is full of comparisons between his trip in 1902 and what he was seeing nearly 25 years later.

Above: The hunting tradition in New Zealand has included the pursuit of hunting opportunities overseas, usually in other parts of the British Empire. Some sailed to Britain for bird-shooting, others travelled to Australia's Northern Territory.

Hart and Donald travelled by steamer from Wellington to Sydney, where they 'saw the Zoo & Museum, studying the identification & anatomy of African animals, particularly where to shoot them'.[51] From Australia they sailed to Durban, travelling north by train on the Rhodesian Express, then by barge up the Luapula River. The journey from New Zealand to the Luangwa Valley (now a wildlife sanctuary) took over six weeks, and once in the valley they marched between 20 and 35 miles (32–56km) per day between hunting areas. Their group comprised more than 30 porters (the equipment and supplies having been divided into loads of around 23kg) as well as guides who tracked animals for the two shooters and the all-important cook.

This was a trophy hunt and after the second day's shooting Hart and Donald agreed to shoot only trophy specimens. Consequently, periods of three or four days would pass without them shooting anything. Even so, during the three-month trip they shot an extraordinary array of animals: waterbuck, reedbuck, warthog, puku and sitatunga (both antelopes), buffalo, impala, duiker, hartebeest, a large antelope that Hart called a tessebe, eland, elephant, rhino, lion, zebra and hippo. Horns, tusks and hides were dispatched back to the nearest town to be salted.

There were moments of high adventure. Twice Hart wrote in his diary of near escapes from charging wounded buffalo and stampeding herds. He was charged by a wounded bull elephant that 'came straight at us through the thicket as if it were paper . . . the niggers all thought I was a goner. After about 10 mins they all turned up, jumped for joy and shook hands'.

The stalking of elephants through 3m high elephant grass also provided a fair bit of tension. It was not elephants they found in this grass but a group of hippos. They shot four in one afternoon, which brought two problems: the need to dispense an enormous amount of meat before it spoiled, and a race against the lions to recover the meat and the tusks. The entire camp moved down to the edge of the elephant grass and a messenger was dispatched to the nearest village. The next morning 200 villagers arrived to take away the meat, but by then a large pride of lions had also arrived. When the camp's guides went down to the swamp to remove the hippos' tusks, 'there was a terrific roar and some lions dashed away through the trees'. The solution to this problem came from another part of the empire; Hart wrote in his letter-book that they had decided on a platform lookout in a tree, a technique 'often adopted in India for tiger shooting'. Nonetheless, the camp was very vigilant for several days and nights while the hippo meat was dispatched.[52]

## Salisbury Hut

Salisbury Hut was built in the 1920s on the tablelands between Mount Arthur and the Cobb Valley in the Nelson region. Typical of huts of its day, it was visited constantly by trampers, hunters and musterers. The hut book records groups of trampers, often including more than one recreational hunter, parties of women trampers, government shooters and private skin-hunters. Generally these groups coexisted happily. Venison stew was often on the menu for hut visitors and notes in the hut book provided newly arrived hunters with information about the movements of the local deer. Both red and fallow deer were common in the area.

**5.1.38** Ruth Beatson, Denis Brereton, JG Brereton, Patricia Brereton, Hector B Coleman

Arrived here tonight from Flora where we stayed last night, spending a more or less (mostly less) comfortable night. Jack spotted a deer just at the edge of the bush before we came to this hut, and Hector, our hunter, shot it.

**Thurs 6th** Raining until about 10.30am when it cleared and we set out to explore the Pot Holes, Sphinx Gully and Cave and Richards Cave — all very interesting. Saw 3 deer quite near the hut — Jack shot one . . .

**Fri 7th** . . . saw 4 deer altogether . . . had to hurry down as some suspicious looking clouds appeared in the west and before we reached Balloon rain had set in. We had a quick cup of tea and left for Salisbury reaching here a bit wet but quite happy and after a spot of rum and a super venison stew we were feeling 100 per cent.[53]

In April 1938, M Chapman, V Chapman, J Chapman and A Ray, all of Motueka, and J Halford and Yvonne Jones from Auckland arrived at the hut. 'The deer stalkers went out yesterday, saw 10 deer but returned empty handed as well as wet and hungry, must all be dud shots in this party.' Five days later, still with little luck, one of them commented, 'A stalker's life is not a happy one!', confirmed in April 1940 by a stalker who must have been flicking back through previous entries: 'You said it brother 26.4.40.'

Other hunters had more luck.

**4th June [19]38** King's birthday weekend, W McClaren, J Frank and A Simister [?] from Nelson City. It's a hell 'er way up here but it's worth it. Sunday went off well with an all day shoot. Got up early and went through Pot Holes. Shot two deer and arrived back at 11.30 O'clock. Had dinner and went over table land through Cundires out to Balloon. Saw one deer... Monday morning white frost. Cook breakfast and are leaving for home "sweat" home.

Just returned from Balloon and surroundings after a week hunting noise in the gullies. Shot 12 deer, one good head. No deer on tops, all in the lower areas. Weather perfect. No joke carrying water from lower creek in billies. V Wylie, J Parkes, J Chapman.

Venison stew was on the menu for most parties who visited Salisbury, even if they were non-hunting trampers. If there was a hunter at the hut, then stew was on the menu for all. Joan Collier, Maisie Arthur and Isabel and Jack Sixtus arrived to venison stew in April 1939. A few days later, WK Barker and EBO Shone saw six deer, shot two and 'arrived hut wet and hungry; 4pm waiting for stew to cook, 5pm still drizzling, meat still stewing, stomach still fasting'. The rain and the wait for the stew went on for some hours, all recorded by the hungry hunter. Audrey Kirk and Brenda Bishop of Auckland were treated to stew when they reached the hut in February 1940. 'Heard a gun shot as we came insight of the hut and thought, "well I would rather die quickly than a slow process of pack carrying". That shot proved to be a true one for Mr Hole fed us our first taste of venison.'[54]

Above: Salisbury Hut with Gordon Pyramid behind.

There were rare points of conflict between users of Salisbury recorded in the hut book. In late December 1939, a group of New Year's trampers arrived to find 'Woodshed occupied by 8 particularly virile and pungent deer skins and most of this from the Cobb to Mt Arthur. What a hell of a stink! Is this a reserve hut or a skin and hides depot?' The reply was posted immediately below in government-issue blue pencil: 'With apologies, MM Chisolm, Govt Shooting Party, Wellington, GG Hole, Govt Shooting Party, Wellington, J Hughes, Govt Shooting Party, Murchison, JA Mead, Govt Shooting Party Wellington'.[55]

There was also sometimes conflict between hunters, especially when the market for skins was paying well as it did during World War Two. The area around Salisbury was hunted quite frequently during this period, mostly by high-country shepherds and musterers who passed through the area. The Lewis brothers shot 16 deer between 29 December 1940 and New Year's Day 1941, but the Win brothers were musterers who hunted the area intensively.

> So we are back again from up the mountain
> Salisbury where we went
> We got our skins and hides and tails, although the barrel's bent
> We are heading for the bottom, where there's a bath and shave
> And the company of our people whose companionship we crave.
> The weather has been marvellous, we have seen no rain
> And as soon as we get over it we'll be coming back again.
> 32 skins RL Win, MJ Thorn, WN Franklyn, Trevor G Win [56]

And they were back again. The Wins overlapped with a tramping and hunting party in February 1944, recording their daily deer tally in the hut book alongside entries by the tramping party.

**3 Feb** Arrived from Flora about fiveish wet as, well wet anyway. Shot doe where we came out of bush. Had a cuppa and toured around potholes. Raining harder outside and even more inside. Both chimneys down. Had a royal feed. Deer's fry, onions, spuds, johnnie cakes and rice. 8.30pm The breakwater has busted 2 in[ches of] water inside hut and slowly rising. 8.45 still gaining. 9.15 the tide is now receding.

**4 Feb** Still raining. Shot 1 stag fallow, in nearest pothole. Started on chimney in men's end of hut. 1pm raining harder . . .

**5 Feb** Finished on chimney. Left for Gordon's knob. Arrived back and found Art Win, Fred Win and Vic Win in possession of hut [Win's writing] 3 red + one fallow

**6 Feb** Raining again. Drovers left for home. Both fireplaces in working order. Most leaks stopped in roof, walls nailed up, ditch dug. [Win's writing] 2 red 3 fallow[57]

Another five red deer and one fallow were recorded by the Wins against other people's entries before February 9, possibly filled in on a return trip. It was probably the Wins' working of the area that led to this entry in the hut book in March 1943:

**27.3.43** Arrived at Salisbury hut 4pm shot fallow stag in pot holes No Deer Roaring

**28.3.43** Went to Balloon. Shot two red stags. The place is not worth shooting any more, all deer gone over seas.

**29.3.43** Had another look to see if any have been invalided home. Have stalked over here for the last 25 years and don't think they will see me in the next 25 years. Disgusted. Going home. GE Heath, P Fenemor, K Mytton, L Chathman, R Heath[58]

One of the delightful aspects of the Salisbury hut book is the amount of verse written by trampers and hunters. One example appeared early in the book.

**17th April [1938]** A Inder, B Knowles, FK Knowles Dunedin
When we awoke in the morning
The sun was shining bright
And low [sic] and behold a deer
Came stalking into sight

So out of bed and grab the gun
That deer just looked and looked
What did he care for paultry [sic] man
But he ran like butchers hooks

One good deed that dear deer did
As he gazed across the mire,
He terminated an argument
As to who would light the fire.[59]

> Our cook, who incidentally is also our interpreter, is a perfect gem. For breakfast he gives us fried steak, liver, kidney or rissoles either with or without eggs, for lunch we have a haversack ration of sandwiches, but for dinner at 7pm he exceeds all expectations. Soups, roast or stewed meat with onions and sweet potatoes (poultry twice a week), and a never-ending variety of sweets, I don't know how he does it. He has one specially attractive sweet, he calls a custard, but it looks like and tastes like a blancmange and is a rare treat after a 20 mile walk with the heat running up to that of a hot January day at home.
> — Herbert Hart, North Rhodesia, 1926[60]

In 1930, trophy-hunters J Holmes, Alic McKinnon and Harold Thomas travelled to North Rhodesia to the Bangweolo Swamp area of the Chambeshi River system.[61] A series of articles about their trip was published in the *New Zealand Fishing & Shooting Gazette*. Lions were encountered very early in the trip, although Holmes noted that the numbers of game in general had dropped significantly from his previous trip in 1925. Buffalo, eland, sitatunga, reedbuck, elephants, zebra and kudu all made an appearance on the trophy list of this party.

In a reminder of the dangers of these kinds of trips, Holmes visited the grave of his companion on the 1925 trip, William Twigg, who had died 'after encountering a lion'.[62] Twigg's grave was 'well looked after, as also were the other three graves. All of these graves are of hunters who have met their death in the Mpika district. We also inspected a small hospital, built and kept up by Mrs Twigg, in which everything is ready for taking in a patient at a moment's notice. I found the same Native Red Cross man in charge of it, who had helped me nurse Mr Twigg. He seems to take a pride in keeping it in first-class order'.[63]

Overseas hunting declined dramatically in the 1930s and '40s due to the strictures of the economic depression and the outbreak of war. For

Opposite: Herbert Hart and Vivian Donald went to the Luangwa Valley in Zambia (now a wildlife reserve) for a three-month safari in 1926. Hart and Donald's Rhodesian safari was a trophy-hunting trip but a by-product of it for local people was a very good supply of meat. It was and remains usual African safari practice for local villagers to take the meat from animals shot, in this case elephants.

Sportsman's paradise 227

many of these hunters, domestic stalking of wapiti, the only species of deer that remained protected, in Fiordland became much more popular. The establishment of private game parks overseas in the 1960s opened up possibilities of safari hunting again, albeit on a much more limited scale.

## Armchair hunting

Hunting has always been the stuff of stories. Published hunting tales appeared in a wide variety of media, from foreign newspapers to children's books that were presented as Sunday School prizes in small-town New Zealand. British publications such as *The Field*, *Gun & Game* and *Country Life* carried hunting stories from around the empire, including New Zealand, in their travel sections from the 1870s. Local daily newspapers too reported regularly on acclimatisation society meetings and on the openings of deer and wapiti seasons. The opening of duck season was, and remains, an event worthy of notice for New Zealand's media.

Early twentieth-century illustrated weeklies, too, carried stories about hunting. The *Weekly News*, *The Free Lance*, *New Zealand Graphic* and *New Zealand Illustrated Magazine* all carried stories and photographs of hunters and hunting. The *New Zealand Listener*'s regular columnist 'Sundowner' wrote many articles about hunting and fishing from the 1930s to the 1950s, and in the late 1940s a series of articles and letters in the *Listener* were sparked by the visit of Harvard Museum scientist H Wendell Endicott and his assertions that deer were assets to the New Zealand economy. In an article in 1947, Endicott warned against making the same mistakes in game management that the United States had made and appealed against the New Zealand government's policy of deer destruction. In reply, letters from readers demonstrated a considerable strength of feeling about deer destruction, sporting interests and conservation of the bush.

More specialised newspapers and magazines also developed around tourism from the 1920s, featuring 'sportsman's paradise' stories alongside those about the scenic delights of various parts of New Zealand. *New Zealand Railways Magazine,* published by the New Zealand Government Railways Department from 1926 to 1940, often contained stories about hunting which, interestingly, tended to focus on pig-hunting rather than deer-stalking. This may have been because the readership of the magazine was considered to constitute people of modest means, or because the department had taken seriously the call to cease advertising stalking as a pastime once the deer destruction campaigns began.

The other kind of specialised magazines that developed in the first half of the twentieth century were hunting magazines: the *New Zealand Fishing & Shooting Gazette* began in 1927, published by New Zealand's acclimatisation societies, and ran until 1956 (the current incarnation of the magazine is *Fish & Game,* published by Fish & Game New Zealand). Local content was the mainstay of the *Gazette*, but it did feature stories of big-game hunting overseas, and carried advertisements for safaris in Australia's Northern Territory. Another publication, *New Zealand Rod & Gun*, had a brief appearance in the 1930s. From the 1980s more magazines appeared and now there is a raft of specialised hunting magazines, published variously by enthusiasts and lobby groups, all underpinned by advertising from firearms, specialist equipment and outdoor clothing manufacturers.

Hunting books were a staple of imperial fiction and especially imperial children's adventure books. The figure of the 'great white hunter' was central to the books of Sir Henry Rider Haggard, Rudyard Kipling and American authors such as James Fenimore Cooper. While adults enjoyed travelling the empire through these novels, these kinds of books were also considered morally improving for children, and many New Zealand children received adventure hunting stories as school and Sunday School prizes. For example, Whenua Kura School presented Edward S Ellis's *On the Trail of the Moose* to Daniel Oldham for passing Standard Two in 1897; RM Ballantyne's *The Gorilla Hunters* was presented by Balclutha Primary School in 1901; Fred Furkert was awarded *Adventures in Many Lands* for attendance at Kilbirnie Presbyterian Sunday School in 1916; GM Fenn's *Nat the Naturalist* was Allan Scott's reward for regular attendance at Lincoln Presbyterian Sunday School in 1912; and New Zealand's own adventure story, *The Bush Boys of New Zealand* by the Reverend James Millar Thomson was presented to Barbara McDonald for her regular attendance and good conduct at Wanganui's St Paul's Presbyterian Sunday School in 1910.[64]

By the 1930s a swag of non-fiction hunting books were available to New Zealand readers also. 'Tangataroa', in a 1931 column in the *New Zealand Fishing & Shooting Gazette*, commented that 'the world has produced some hundreds of hunting tales during the last 25 years', going on to list authors such as big-game hunter FC Selous, hunters-turned-conservationists Paul Kruger and Harry Johnson, Theodore Roosevelt who 'made up for a lot of misdemeanours' by writing *African Game Trails*, and Frenchman Edouard Foa, 'who took such dreadful chances, such as shooting the lions in the open by torchlight, that his adventures are irresistibly funny'.[65] Tangataroa recommended a large group of books about hunting in Asia, from *Himalayan Game Hunting* to *Sportsman's Book for India*, and a few books on North America, but he concentrated on the literature about Africa. He also referred to books about ballistics and firearms, ending his round-up of the explosion in hunting publications by commenting, 'Again, let me say, "It is not all of shooting to Shoot"'.[66]

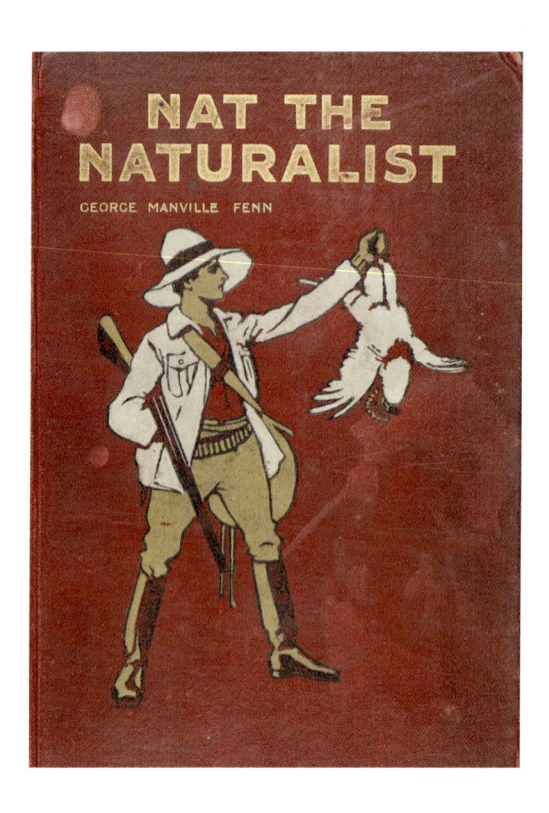

Hunting books were not written solely by English authors, or just in the imperial adventure mould. One of the remarkable products of New Zealand's deer-destruction campaigns and the shooters it employed is the number of books that were written by this group of men about their experiences. Graeme Caughley estimates that of the generation of government shooters who shot

Above: Hunters have also been readers and writers. In the late nineteenth century the popularity of juvenile fiction exploded and hunting was the focus of many stories. Magazines focusing on outdoor pursuits, particularly fishing and shooting, proliferated in the early twentieth century and continue to be very strong today. In New Zealand a particular literary tradition exists in the many books written by ex-government shooters, of which *A Good Keen Man* by Barry Crump is the best known.

for the Forest Service, 25 per cent of them have had works published and, on average, they have each written two books. The most famous, perhaps, was Barry Crump's semi-autobiographical and humorous *A Good Keen Man*, first published in 1960 and reprinted six times. More recently, for younger readers, Jack Lasenby's Harry Wakitipu – the laziest, condensed-milk-swilling packhorse ever to set foot in the vast untrodden Ureweras — continues the tongue-in-cheek look back at the deer-destruction days. But the overwhelming number of books written by ex-government shooters were non-fiction reminiscences. Surely no other government department could boast such a literary record.

Private meat-hunters and trophy-hunters have also written many books including, recently, cookbooks. There are 189 separate subject headings on the National Library catalogue for 'hunting, New Zealand', representing more than 400 books in the collection, in addition to many more magazines, newsletters, children's books and audiovisual materials. Reading about hunting remains an absorbing pastime.

## Retail therapy?

From the earliest hunting publications, advice was dispensed about 'the right' or 'essential' equipment. Colonists' guides, early sporting adventure stories and advertisements in magazines all showed that there was shopping to be done.

In the mid-nineteenth century most colonists brought their firearms with them from Britain; if you needed a new one after arrival there were few avenues other than buying second-hand privately or from the government armourer. By the late 1890s, however, along with the rise of general department stores, several sporting goods outlets had established themselves around the country, selling firearms and ammunition as well as an array of newfangled items such as 'rucksacks' and sleeping bags (which would today be considered the most basic of necessities). The strength of the mail-order business saw extensive catalogues produced by such stores. Until the 1940s most stores had a separate catalogue for shotguns and rifles, sometimes combined with a few pages on other winter sports such as golf.

A & W McCarthy's was established in 1862 and in its 1902 mail-order catalogue advertised 26 shotguns, including muzzle-loaders, and 34 different models of rifle. From 1914, catalogues included advertisements for deer rifles.

**127A.—GRASS SUITS.**

FRONT.   KNEELING.   BACK.      FRONT.   STANDING.   BACK.

These Suits save the trouble of digging a whare when duck shooting; the shooter can also change his position, if he is not in the flight of the ducks. A duck will not detect a shooter in this suit. Price, **10/-** each.

( 75 )

**SPECIAL STYLE SIDE EJECTOR BICYCLE RIFLE.**

Cartridges cannot go by post; we can forward by rail or Express Company.

We are prepared to furnish this rifle with 16-inch barrel and full magazine. (We also have these rifles with 20in. barrel, which makes a really nice little Repeating Rifle for a lady. The barrel is, however, too long to go in bicycle.) It is of convenient length to strap within a diamond frame. The magazine will be 16in. in length. Weight of rifle, with 16in. barrel, 5lbs.

521—Price, with round barrel, **£4 5s**; with octagon barrel, **£4 10s**. CAPACITY—16 short, 12 long, 10 long rifle cartridges.

We can furnish canvas case, as shown, leather bound, complete with straps, of proper form to fit securely within a diamond frame. Price, **7s. 6d**.

**To Clean.**—The action must be taken apart—which heretofore has not been easy in the case of repeating rifles. The thumb-screw on the right-hand side of the action can be unscrewed, and the entire side of the receiver removed. The carrier and breech bolt can be taken out; from the breech bolt may be taken the firing pin and extractor. The finger lever can be slipped off its pin, and the ejector removed from its slot. The whole action is then entirely apart. Not a tool is used in doing this. To take rifle apart and put it together again requires but a fraction of a minute.

This feature is a valuable one, as the action can be thoroughly cleaned in two or three minutes, and when it can be done so easily, the action is cleaned more frequently, and the result is a better working gun and more lasting satisfaction.

It will be observed that as the breech bolt can be removed, this allows the shooter to clean the barrel **by inserting the wiping rod at one end and drawing it clear through the barrel.** It is a very valuable feature in a small bore rifle, to be able to clean the gun from the breech.

Rifle Apart to Clean.

Another valuable feature is, that owing to the removable side plate, if the action becomes clogged because of dirt, defective ammunition, a bullet slipping out of the cartridge, &c., the side plate can be unscrewed, and the trouble remedied in less than a minute.

Top: A & W McCarthy's of Dunedin and Invercargill, 'importers of sportsmen's sundries', advertised this grass suit in its 1902 winter catalogue, along with 26 models of shotguns, 34 models of rifles, 15 models of pistols, decoys, gun-sights, field glasses and watches which kept 'fair time' and stood 'rough work'.

Above: The Marlin 'Bicycle Rifle' was one of the more specialised examples among the many models of firearms for sale in the early twentieth century.

WH Tisdall's 1914 winter catalogue included 22 shotguns and 21 rifles, seven of them advertised for deer-stalking. New Zealand hunting conditions became the focus of advertising from this period, and while the firearms themselves continued to come from British and American factories, companies began to stress their care in choosing which models would be available for sale in New Zealand. Kelly Ltd's catalogue in the early 1920s stated in the 'sporting rifle' section:

> For this list we have selected what we believe to be the most practical arms for the game and conditions to be found in NZ. The largest game animals are the moose, the smallest, if you want them, are mice. Firearms suitable for these extremes and all in between are listed in this catalogue. Most New Zealanders know what they want, but where you think we can help in the selection it is our job to do so and of course, a pleasure, too.[67]

Large numbers of new firearms remained available through catalogues throughout the 1920s. In the 1929 Hammond & Turner catalogue, 32 models of shotgun and 35 models of rifle were available. No other company of this period offered such a large array. In 1931 they offered a special 'New Zealand model' made by American firm Iver Johnson.

The economic depression of the 1930s had an inevitable effect on the sale of guns, with catalogues stating in their preambles, 'In view of the prevailing economic conditions, the question of whether we should or should not publish our annual catalogue of Shooting and Winter Sports equipment has received the very earnest consideration of our directors . . .' Hammond & Turner were forced to stop offering free postage on mail-order items, citing the increasing costs of tariffs and customs duties:

> Today English Sporting Goods are costing on average 15% more than before, while the increase in respect of foreign goods averages 25% . . . Let us all remember — Prosperity Always Returns. There is no need to be pessimistic. Statistics show that the average wealth per head of New Zealand's population is greater today then ever before. Therefore, let us cooperate by carrying on as usual.

Tisdall's 1937 catalogue pointed to a different problem, stating 'Rifle prices are subject to alteration at any moment owing to the increasing cost of metals. Rearmament has completely upset the metals markets in Great Britain, the United States and on the continent.'

In the wake of World War Two, the firearms market was flooded with ex-army .303 rifles which were cut down by local gunsmiths and sold relatively cheaply. Viv Collings of Wellington learned basic gunsmithing during this period. 'There were so many .303s around from after the war. That was one of our jobs — we had all these fully-wooded military weapons, and we'd cut them down into sporters. We did about 30 a week for Whitcomb and Caldwell [sports shops]. It just was never-ending'.[68]

Firearms weren't the only things for sale in these mail-order catalogues. After all, a well-made British or American rifle could be expected to last for 20 years of regular hunting, and there could hardly be much of a profit in that. The catalogues are both fascinating and amusing in the range of accessories and outdoor equipment offered. In catalogues up to the 1920s, knives, gun cases, ferret muzzles and collars, decoys and shooting clothing all made appearances. Shooting coats were advertised in nearly all catalogues of this period. Camp chairs and stools made an appearance in the 1916 Colonial Ammunition Company catalogue, and by the 1920s rucksacks and sleeping bags were common.[69]

Most catalogues offered gun parts, sights and ammunition. This was especially so in the case of the Colonial Ammunition Company who proclaimed in their 1916 catalogue:

> The CAC Ltd alone control the complete operation of shotgun shell manufacture within the Dominion, and the pronounced excellence of CAC cartridges, over locally loaded imported factory-made shells, is obvious. Similarly, imported loaded cartridges suffer severely by comparison with the CAC product owing to the extremes of climatic influence to which they are subjected ... the excessive heat of the tropics having a pronounced deteriorating effect on cartridges loaded in the Northern hemisphere.

The ammunition section of their catalogue filled four pages.

# Hunting as recreation

Recreational hunting was the fulfilment of the aims of acclimatisation societies and commentators such as Charles Hursthouse. It was hunting for the sport of it. Trophy-hunters were usually well off, could afford the time and expense of long trips both within New Zealand and overseas, and had the wherewithal to have their trophies tanned or mounted and displayed. Up until the 1930s, the government invested significant resources into promoting New Zealand as a 'sportsman's paradise', and hunting was important for the tourist economy. It also bound New Zealand into the web of empire in very real ways.

Alongside the wealthier locals and tourists, however, were thousands who headed off hunting to break the monotony of their working lives, to enjoy the adventure of it, and to be in the bush. Rural and bush labourers as well as those working in the city were drawn to the outdoors for their leisure. With the popularisation of tramping, hunters shared huts, tracks and trips with increasing numbers of people. Again, the government had a hand in promoting the outdoors as healthy leisure for the masses. Resources were put into hut-building and off-season government shooters cut tracks to make the wilderness that bit more accessible.

Wider social developments were reflected in other ways. The growth of consumer culture and the rise of specialist outdoor equipment meant that hunters began to peruse catalogues and shop by mail order. Changing technology around photography was reflected in the increasing number of photographs taken on hunting trips. The explosion in popular literature at the end of the nineteenth century saw hunters and hunting as regular topics of children's and adults' reading alike.

Love of the bush and the popularisation of being in the wilderness as a form of recreation were tied up with changing ideas about nature in New Zealand. The development of national parks, along with increasing calls from botanists and bird-lovers for the protection of what little wilderness was left in New Zealand, represented a developing conservationist ethic that would dominate twentieth-century attitudes to nature. In New Zealand — uniquely — this ethic demanded the massive reduction of introduced mammals: deer, tahr, chamois, feral goats and pigs and, from the 1950s, possums. Both recreational and professional hunters came to be at the centre of the conservation effort.

# 5

# Collecting and conserving

**H**unters have long been integral to conservation in New Zealand, whether that meant specimen-collecting as it did in the nineteenth century, or killing predators and bush-browsers as it has in the twentieth. Nineteenth-century collecting was part of the broader science of classifying, identifying and displaying the natural world by flattening, pinning or stuffing it and putting it in a glass case. Consequently, most noted New Zealand naturalists and ornithologists were collectors, usually supplied with bird skins and eggs by hunters.

Walter Buller's *A History of the Birds of New Zealand* was illustrated almost exclusively with drawings and paintings of specimens that had been shot, skinned and mounted. James Hector, Thomas Potts and Julius von Haast were all involved in the extensive bird-skin trade which underpinned the development of New Zealand's museums. They were not at all unusual in this, and were part of an international trade and intellectual climate that supported these activities. Possibly the most famous example of this was Theodore Roosevelt's 1909 safari to East Africa, during which he shot over 500 animals, including six white rhino, on behalf of the Smithsonian Institute.

Potts was one of the naturalists who bridged the gap between nineteenth-century specimen hunters and twentieth-century ecologists and their diverging views on how best to preserve species. During his career he moved from ideas of preserving birds with arsenical soap to preserving them in the wild through legal protection from pot-hunters, collectors and introduced predators. In this he was joined by botanists, most notably Leonard Cockayne, and the Royal Forest and Bird Protection Society, which increased in strength throughout the

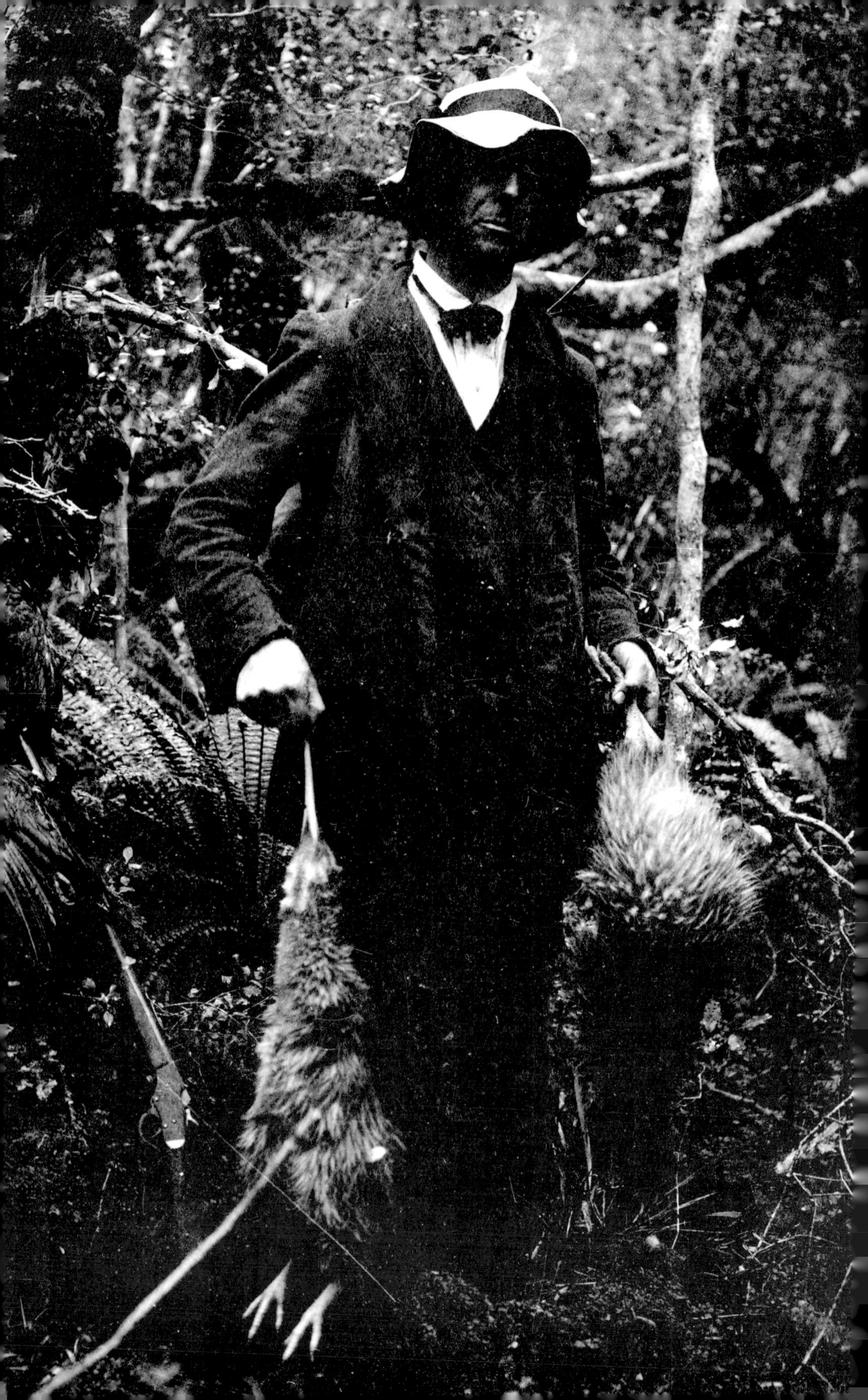

early decades of the twentieth century.

The big flip in attitudes towards introduced species that occurred in the early 1900s was not spurred only by this conservation movement but by a misplaced fear of accelerated erosion caused by browsing mammals, especially by deer. Combined with farmers' frustration at the impact of increasing deer, tahr and chamois numbers on their productivity, these were powerful motives for the government to change its mind about 'sport' animals, especially deer. Seen less as an asset to the economy through tourism nor to the character of the colony through manly recreation, deer were recast as a direct threat to the geological — and therefore economic and social — stability of the country. At its most dramatic, it was argued, the continued degradation of native vegetation by deer would produce massive flooding, threatening major towns and cities. In these early decades it was preservation of the bush as a protective layer that was uppermost in the minds of politicians. The regeneration of

Opposite: In the nineteenth century, there was a widespread belief that introduced European species were superior to, and would inevitably displace, indigenous species. Specimen collecting for museums was seen as hunting for preservation; museums were creating a record of the species that would soon disappear.
Above: Sir James Hector, director of the Colonial Museum, had a collar and cuff set made from kiwi skins for his mother, pictured here with him.

native forests and conservation of the widest range of native species possible became the focus of the government's strategy only later in the twentieth century; it was not until the 1980s and the formation of the Department of Conservation that protecting biodiversity, rather than simply maintaining forest cover regardless of species, became the primary objective of government policy in this area.

In the first instance, however, protection was lifted from deer, tahr and chamois in 1930 (and wapiti in 1934), creating a true hunting democracy for the first time. The government also established the Deer Control Section of the Department of Internal Affairs in 1930. In 1956, with the passage of the Noxious Animals Act, all deer, tahr, chamois, wild goats, pigs and, most belatedly, possums were declared noxious pests, and the government encouraged their destruction in the largest numbers possible. Hunting, then, both by government employees and private shooters, became the foundation of efforts to conserve New Zealand's bush and alpine environments.

## The naturalist-collectors

Conservation historian David Young argues that 'the practice of natural science — the taking and collecting, describing and naming of flora and fauna — was as close as nineteenth-century pakeha got to conservation science'.[1] Indeed, many naturalists, such as Ernst Dieffenbach and Lutheran missionary Johann Wohlers, were among the first to protest against the rapacious whaling industry even while they pursued the shooting and collecting of native birds as scientific specimens.

The collecting of specimens from new lands in the southern hemisphere had been vital to European taxonomy since the vast collections of Joseph Banks in the eighteenth century. Throughout the eighteenth and nineteenth centuries extensive efforts were made to establish comprehensive catalogues of plants and animals, to provide scientists with information on world ecologies. Explorers were sent out to fill the gaps in these catalogues and amateurs were encouraged to send their specimens to more learned men at museums and universities.

Museums in the colonies also adopted these practices, using locally collected specimens to not only fill their own collections but to swap and trade for less-available items.[2] Regionally specific species, such as kiwi and tuatara, became a 'kind of "currency" used to acquire other specimens from more distant places, as the extensive exchange and accession books of

Above: Julius von Haast (left) and the Canterbury Museum taxidermist Frederick Fuller, 1866. Thousands of native bird skins, fossils and moa bones (pictured here) were traded with other collectors around the world in order to build up the collections in New Zealand's museums.

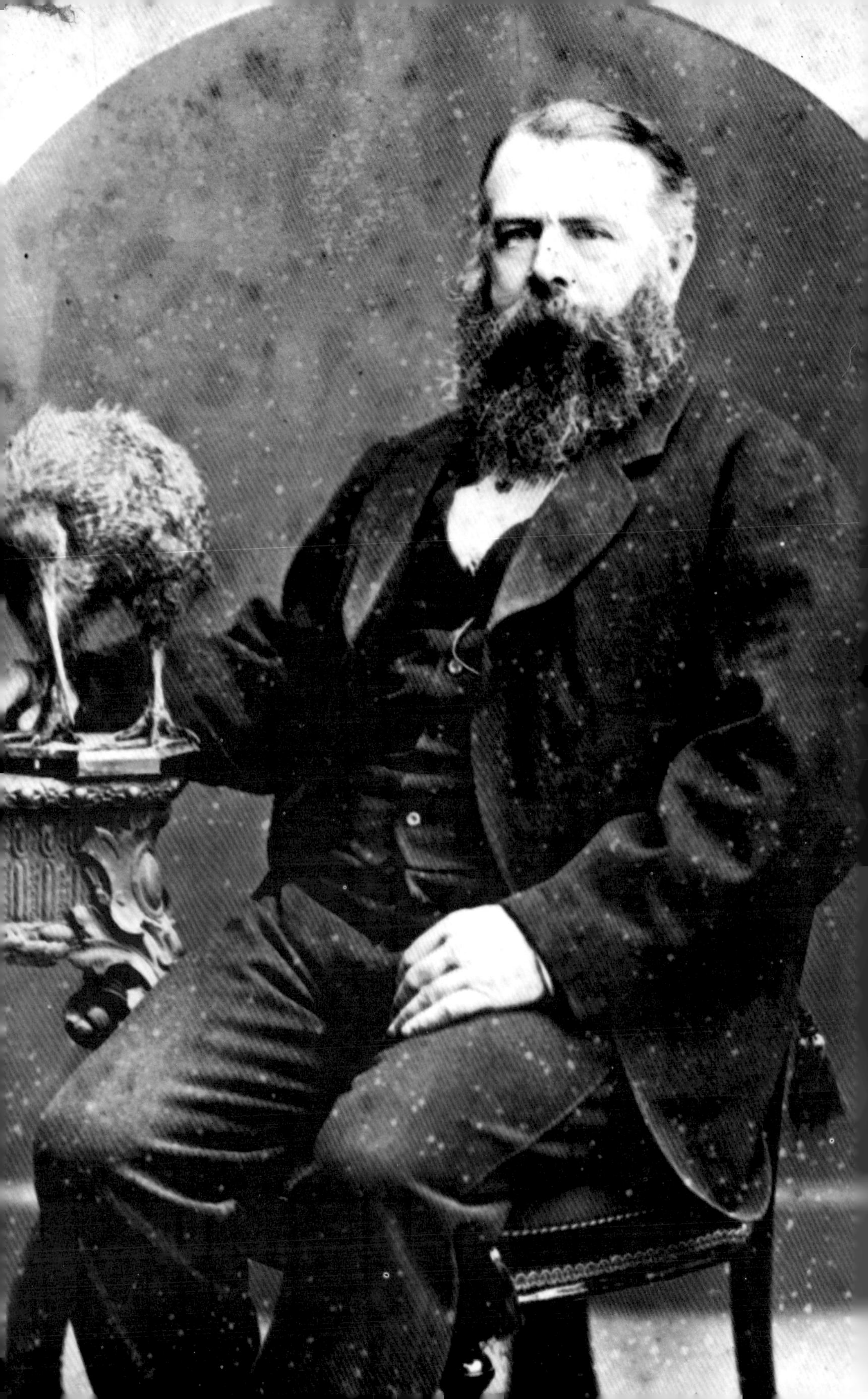

learned societies make clear'.[3] During Canterbury Museum's first 50 years, thousands of native bird skins were recorded in its exchange books. While bird skins were not the only items exchanged, Julius von Haast's trade in this commodity was the foundation of the Canterbury Museum as 'the crowning glory of Christchurch . . . of which the town and colony may well feel proud, for there is not its equal out of Europe and there are very few even in Europe superior to it'. The journalist who wrote these words attributed the success of the museum to 'the ceaseless energy and untiring perseverance of Professor von Haast who has ransacked the world for objects of interest'.[4] During his tenure, Haast traded more than 3000 native New Zealand bird skins with European and Australian museums in exchange for a remarkable range of specimens including a leopard and a lion, the bones of an extinct giant Irish elk or *Megaloceros*, a human skeleton, skeletons of a platypus, an echidna and a dugong, bronze ornaments from a prehistoric cemetery in Salzburg, the skin of a giraffe and two skulls of mummies from Thebes.[5]

All of New Zealand's noted nineteenth-century ornithologists were specimen hunters and all had items sent to them by amateur and professional collectors. Walter Buller, born in 1838, was raised at Tangiteroria, inland from Dargaville on the Wairoa River. When Buller was 13, his father allowed him to use his shotgun and he spent some of his school holidays shooting birds. It was an exciting day, the 'bright, dewy morning . . . when I shot my first Koheperoa [long-tailed cuckoo] in the old Mission garden at Tangiteroria, and found my beautiful prize lying on the sward with its banded wings and tail stretched out to their full extent'.[6] The young Buller learned taxidermy and preserved and mounted many of his own specimens. By 1870 he had a sufficient collection of native bird skins and mounts to take leave from his position as a local magistrate and write his first edition of A *History of the Birds of New Zealand*. By the time of the second edition in 1882, Buller's collection was comprehensive. As Buller's biographer Ross Galbreath notes, it would not have been difficult to have amassed such a collection by the late 1870s, as 'there were by this time many taxidermists and dealers catering for the demand for bird skins, both for ornamental cases of mounted birds to decorate fashionable drawing rooms, and for feather fashions: feather boas, muffs, collars and hats'.[7]

Opposite: Thomas Potts was uneasy about the naturalists' practice of killing what they collected. He explored and hunted with James Hector and other prominent naturalists of his time, but found the killing of birds and their chicks discomforting. His scruples made him the butt of jokes within the scientific community.

Taxidermist AW Avery in Marton sold Buller a very rare specimen of *Anthochaera carunculata*, the red wattlebird, a wayward and windblown Australian native. Avery told Buller he had shot the bird while on military service at Parihaka.[8] Buller's other collectors included Charles Robson, a lighthouse keeper who sent specimens of seabirds from Cape Campbell, and Robson's son, who sent specimens from the subantarctic Auckland Islands after visiting them on a government steamer. Nelson surveyor Jonathon Brough supplied kiwi and bush wrens, gardener William Smith 'specialised in supplying the rare Laughing Owl, which was still to be found on the Albury estate near Timaru where he worked'.[9]

Occasionally Buller shot his own specimens. In November 1882, while on Land Court business, he camped for a week at Pirongia in the Waikato with artist Gottfried Lindauer and 'three Maori Kiwi-hunters with dogs'. In that week they collected 40 kiwi and nine eggs. In 1883, Buller and his brother-in-law Gilbert Mair spent three days with a Maori huia-hunter in bush country in the Wairarapa. They shot 16 huia and caught one pair alive.[10]

The specimen trade was so expansive that in 1880 there was a glut of New Zealand birds on the market. One London dealer told Buller he would not take any more New Zealand birds because he still had 385 kakapo and 90 little spotted kiwi in stock at the time.[11]

Julius von Haast's collectors were a hard-working and lonely lot. William Docherty, who lived at Okarito, 'used to solace his loneliness by playing the concertina, and asked Haast to send him one valued at about £2 10s, in return for which he would send all the kiwi eggs he could get and the skins of two white cranes [kotuku]'.[12] WJ Wheeler from Jackson Bay provided Haast with 'skins and skeletons from the smallest upwards and eggs of kakapos, kiwis, the roa or giant kiwi, the grey kiwi and nestlings in spirits of wine'. Leo Barnes was another West Coast collector who worked solidly for Haast, negotiating local politics as he worked. Haast urged him to keep collecting, despite troubles he was having with local farmers. 'Of course do not shoot ducks etc because that would be wrong, but I do not see what difference it can make about the smaller birds. You are on the spot and are able to judge if you could have any rows which of course I wish to avoid.'[13]

Haast could not avoid rows in his own organisation, however, when a member of the museum committee raised an objection to the bird-skin trade, suggesting that it was having a detrimental effect on native bird populations. In 1878 Haast requested authority to spend £50 on bird skins, but the committee declared itself 'very much averse to the destruction of the New

**CONSERVATION WEEK '76**

Take the land
and how can the trees grow
without the trees
where will the birds go

Zealand fauna for the purpose of exchanges with other museums and would call his attention to the fact that there are other objects such as fossils which might be available for the purpose of exchange'. Haast was furious and wrote a reply that was deemed offensive, the director responding that Haast had 'manifestly misconceived the intention of the Board' and there the matter ended.[14]

Conserving species alive and in their own habitats would take decades to be accepted as the best practice. Haast's collectors continued with their work.

Collectors sometimes took live specimens, occasionally on commission. In 1877 Wheeler wrote to Haast declaring that 'I have twelve young kakapos

Above: By the 1970s 'conservation' had become integrally linked with ecology, the idea of nature as an interconnected system. Ironically this poster asked the same question Maori MPs had raised in Parliament a century earlier, when they argued that it was not hunting that was decimating native birds, but the clearance of bush habitat for agriculture.

**Collecting and conserving   247**

# NEW ZEALAND RAILWAYS

## TOURIST TICKETS

**TOURIST TICKETS**
on the
**NEW ZEALAND GOVERNMENT RAILWAYS**
(3037 MILES)
On Sale at the Principal Stations.

Over All Lines (Available for Seven Weeks) — £16 5s.
Over North Island Lines (Available for Four Weeks) £10 0s.
Over South Island Lines (Available for Four Weeks) £10 0s.
Also available on Lake Wakatipu Steamers.

These Tickets may be extended for a period up to Four Weeks at a charge of £2 10s. per week or portion of a week.

**HOLIDAY EXCURSION TICKETS**
AT REDUCED FARES
ISSUED AT CHRISTMAS, NEW YEAR, EASTER, AND OTHER HOLIDAY PERIODS AS ADVERTISED

about 5 months old and they are living in a pen together quite agreeable, and live without their native food. I think that you might venture to send them to any port in Europe without risk. They are eating at present flour, sugar, bread and potatoes'.[15] The trade in live birds, however, was severely restricted by the distances both from the bush to ports, and then from New Zealand to the rest of the specimen-mad world. It was also restricted by the unusual diets and lack of knowledge about the habits of native New Zealand birds.

In 1907, when chamois were first brought to New Zealand, five tuatara and a range of native birds including half a dozen kiwi were dispatched to Vienna in exchange. By 1909, reports from the Mount Cook guides and other observers of the chamois were all positive, in stark contrast to reports from the Austro-Hungarian Consulate that all the kiwi had died, along with four of the five tuatara. This precipitated attempts to replace the kiwi, tuatara being too rare to do the same.

South Island hunters informed the Department of Tourist and Health Resorts that kiwi were very difficult to catch and keep alive and so the price would be substantial. One South Island bird collector, Arthur Hickford, with encouragement from Thomas Donne, caught three live kiwi and asked £5 per head for them. The department was outraged and not only refused to pay but threatened him with legal action for having trapped kiwis without a permit.

Maori bird hunters at Taupo were more amenable to the prices offered by department and several letters from Reweti, a kiwi hunter, were written to 'Engineer' Birks, in charge of the government thermal park at Rotorua, organising the deal. Reweti's kiwi hunters caught eight kiwi at £1 each, four of which were kept for the nocturnal house at Rotorua. Pages of advice on kiwi housing and diet were then obtained from a ranger at Kapiti Island in an attempt to ensure these birds had longer lives than previous captive kiwi.[16]

The collectors who supplied birds to this market of museums, natural-history enthusiasts and the fashion-conscious could be seen from a variety of perspectives. On one hand, as discussed in Chapter 3, these were men making a living in difficult and remote conditions. They were also, as Thomas Potts argued in the 1880s, a kind of predator. Their impact on bird numbers, while their harvests look horrifying to us, was probably not great. Most ecologists agree that the loss of habitat and predation by cats and dogs had a much greater impact on native bird numbers than hunting during this period. But were these men also shooting for science?

Opposite: The notion of New Zealand as the sportsman's paradise was evident in this 1925 tourism poster for New Zealand Railways.

Buller's work was underpinned by displacement theory which held that old-world species were inherently superior to, and would replace, the less advanced species of the new world. He believed, therefore, that indigenous New Zealand birds would inevitably die out. While modern understandings of ecology have refined our perspectives on the interplay between native and exotic flora and fauna, Buller's work was nevertheless extremely important in the early appreciation of New Zealand's natural environment. He argued early in his career against the introduction of ferrets to New Zealand to control the rabbit menace, saying that they would devastate bird populations. In 1876 he published a letter received from a Cambridge University colleague that urged New Zealand to resist the introduction of ferrets, or 'it will then be good-bye at once and for ever to all your brevipennate [short-winged and therefore non-flying] birds, as well as to many other of your native species, which of course have no instincts whereby they may escape from such bloodthirsty enemies'.[17]

Ornithologists of Buller's generation had a raft of explanations for why native bird populations were declining but hunting was not one of them. Indeed, it was insightful of Buller to argue against the introduction of predators. Explanations that were popular in the late nineteenth century included climatic change owing to deforestation, native species' inability to adapt to environmental change or introduced diseases, and the popular idea of indigenous species being displaced by 'superior' introduced species.[18]

Besides Buller, other ornithologists and naturalists combined hunting with a proto-conservationist ethic. Runholder, naturalist and keen shooter John Enys wrote in a scientific paper in 1874 that more than 600 huia skins had been procured from Maori in the northern Wairarapa the year before, but also that 'part of the ranges had been made *tapu* by the natives for the last seven years, so as to protect the huia from being killed off'.[19] Environmental historian Paul Star argues that men such as Enys and Thomas Potts, who came from the 'landholding tradition', understood and had a great sympathy for the practice of tapu inasmuch as it resembled a closed season. 'TH Potts, who shot native game in New Zealand throughout his life, implied some understanding of this when he wrote in 1872 of the need to place flightless birds on Resolution Island "under tapu from molestation by dog and gun".'[20]

Potts represents in many ways a bridge between naturalists such as Buller, Haast and James Hector, who were convinced of the regrettable but inevitable

Opposite: After the lifting of protection on deer in 1930, a shift occurred in the perception of New Zealand as a tourist destination. The 'sportsman's paradise' promotions were replaced by publicity that emphasised scenery, tramping and skiing, as in this poster.

Famous
LAKES, MOUNTAINS, FIORDS,
Otago & Southland
South Island
NEW ZEALAND
Issued by the Publicity Branch, N.Z. Railways.

extinction of New Zealand's native species (and the importance of collecting as many as possible before they disappeared), and the botanist-conservationists who saw the New Zealand bush — and its birds — as an ecology that could hold its own against invading exotic species if it received some protection from disturbance by humans, predators and grazing animals. Potts was a bird shooter, both for science and for recreation. Indeed, he was the son of a gun-maker and his fortune was made when his father's company, Brander & Potts, was bought by the larger Birmingham Small Arms Company (BSA). Potts, his wife and the first three of their children emigrated to New Zealand in 1854, where he took up land in the upper Rangitata River in south Canterbury, eventually building up his stations until he owned more than 32,000 hectares. He was also a vice president of the Canterbury Acclimatisation Society, an original trustee of the Canterbury Museum and a Member of Parliament from 1866–70.

Potts was an enthusiastic naturalist with an interest in ferns and birds, who travelled on expeditions with James Hector and George Grey. He was a contemporary and colleague of the more famous naturalists — Haast, Thomas Kirk and Buller — but not, it would seem, friends with them. His views differed markedly from theirs and he was an object of fun within those powerful circles.

When Potts met Haast's collector William Docherty, who told him that he had already killed 2000 kiwi, Potts's response was to issue a call for the protection of kiwi. He appealed to British naturalists, however, not to New Zealand ones; in a letter to *Nature* in 1872 he asked the British public to 'help us save our birds . . . [from] the collector, the provider of rarities for museums'. Potts saw the kiwi as 'a useful check on insect life' exactly at the time acclimatisation societies were clamouring for the introduction of insectivorous birds to assist farmers. He knew, however, that 'in this colony a strong protest against such barbarity cannot be expected . . . a few lovers of nature might raise their voices against it, but their voices would fall unheeded unless backed by general opinion from without our little sphere'.[21]

Potts had fewer qualms about other birds. On an expedition to Fiordland and the West Coast with Hector and Enys in 1873, many birds were 'collected': petrels, falcons, oystercatchers and penguins. In Milford Sound the nests of several rare birds were discovered including those of the South Island kokako, presenting Potts the conservationist-naturalist with what Star describes as 'both ecstasy and agony. He could see the destructiveness of the act, yet he could not unbind himself from the ornithological practices of his day'.[22] On the one hand Potts was thrilled beyond words at finding the nests:

> ... few persons can perhaps realise the feeling of intense pleasure and satisfaction which the writer experienced when he caught sight of the nest with the parent bird comfortably seated therein; for years the search after the nest of the kokako had been carried on as opportunity offered: hundreds of miles had been traversed in this quest, among rough wood-dotted gullies and terraces of river-beds on the east and west coasts. After taking notes of the structure and its surroundings, one was obliged to disturb matters so far as to learn whether the nest contained eggs or young; as the parent bird slowly quitted her charge, two downy mites were disclosed that afforded matter for careful observation.[23]

The 'downy mites' were, of course, 'carried away from their snug quarters and offered as victims on the altar of science. At the institution thus referred to [the Colonial Museum], probably to this day, they may be observed by the curious, dangling in a jar of spirit'.[24]

Given Potts' intensely emotional responses to the discoveries of birds, it is hardly surprising that his views continued to diverge with those of the local scientific community and he became a more vocal supporter of island sanctuaries. He strongly advocated for Richard Henry's proposed bird sanctuary on Resolution Island.

Potts saw no conflict between hunting and an appreciation of the environment. His book *Out in the Open*, published in 1882, contains a chapter describing at length — partly tongue-in-cheek — the opening day of the bird-hunting season. It is part jibe at certain kinds of sportsmen, part observation on how rare several species of duck were becoming. But it is also a celebration of the kind of encounter with nature that could be had while hunting. It is 'nature writing' in the tradition of the American writers Henry Thoreau and George Perkins Marsh. Marsh's book, *Man and Nature*, published in 1864, was an argument for the retention of tree cover and reforestation to maintain and rehabilitate the soil. Potts quoted Marsh in his parliamentary speeches arguing for 'better conservation' of New Zealand's forests.

Potts, along with a handful of others —Dieffenbach and Heaphy among them — expressed in their writings an early version of an ethic of conserving systems or ecologies. Their arguments were utilitarian — Potts advocated conservation of native forests to sustain their 'wise use', not to preserve them as wilderness or for their own sake. These men, wealthy and leisured enough to pursue naturalist hobbies, were not the only ones to appreciate the connections between the loss of bush and the loss of birds, but it would take the rise of a new generation of botanists and bird enthusiasts to bring the majority of Parliament around to agreeing that native birds and forests deserved protection.

## Losing the bush, losing the birds

In order to understand the about-face on deer that occurred by 1930, it is necessary to examine the changing forces for conservation (as we now know it) that gathered momentum from the 1890s. Historians Paul Star and Lynne Lochhead have noted that it was precisely during the decades of the greatest destruction of native bush that movements began to protect it.

In 1886, the forested area of New Zealand was 8.9 million hectares but had been reduced to 6.9 million hectares by 1909.[25] Some historians such as David Young have argued that the 'settlers' lack of identification with the flora and fauna is almost certainly a reason why they were so blasé about destroying so much of New Zealand's forest and its creatures.'[26] On the other hand, Star and others have argued that the relationship between pakeha and the bush was more complex, and that while the early settlers felt awed and inspired by the

Above: Hunting and the introduction of both predators and bush-browsers were only a small part of the reason native birds declined. Overwhelmingly, the greatest damage came from the burning of New Zealand's diverse and productive lowland forests to create agricultural land.

bush they also felt morally and religiously bound to *use* the land. Added to this was the widely held scientific belief that indigenous species were primitive and therefore inevitably prone to displacement by superior exotic species. Settlers might regret the destruction of the bush but science and religion convinced them that they were only accelerating natural processes.

When arguments were made about conservation, as in Potts's speeches and writings, equally utilitarian motives were in evidence. The fear of erosion and flooding — one that was to crucially shape arguments in the 1920s about browsing mammals — was evident in the Forests Act 1874, which recognised that loss of forests contributed to 'droughts and increased downstream flooding, both of which imposed economic costs on settlement'.[27]

There were also those who argued that New Zealand's bush could be a tourist attraction. The impetus towards the establishment of national parks was given a healthy shove by the establishment of America's Yellowstone National Park in 1872 and Canada's Banff National Park in 1885. Private tourist ventures had begun in Fiordland in 1877, and the Hermitage at Mount Cook opened in 1885, the same year the nearby Hooker Valley was designated a recreation reserve. The first national park, Tongariro, was formalised in 1894, and the government made the expansive commitment of the creation of a Department of Tourist and Health Resorts in 1901. Scenery now had a government ally.

However, the new department had an agenda that soon clashed with those of conservation groups. On the one hand the department was determined to preserve areas of scenic bush, especially along major tourist routes such as the main trunk line. Thomas Donne argued that bush, 'preserved in its primeval beauty contiguous to the railway will afford great attraction to travellers . . . agreeably adorn the routes of travel [and] also serve as a last home for the rarer New Zealand birds'.[28] On the other hand, the department's primary motive was to attract tourists. While attractive scenery on view through train windows was important, so was the 'improvement' of other areas where visitors might be induced to part with their tourist dollars. So it was that even as the scenic preservation movement began, national parks were being argued for and established and conservationists were making the case for the protection of forest remnants, the Department of Tourist and Health Resorts was negotiating the release of tahr and chamois into the Mount Cook region and wapiti into Fiordland. Ideas of acclimatisation and 'improvement' had not yet been superseded by botanical conservation and early environmentalism.

## Out in the open

*Thomas Potts has been described as 'head and shoulders above the pakeha conservationists of his time'.[29] He was a keen recreational hunter, reluctant specimen collector and nature writer. In his 1882 book* Out in the Open, *Potts wrote about the close observation of nature that occurred while out hunting.*

Suppose we have a day with the shooting party, and be allowed to notice other objects of interest beside the game.

If a rail-splitter when down for his rations, took his pipe from his mouth sufficiently long to report he had seen pigeons about, the start was usually made through a corner of the wood, as there was more chance of making sure of something; pigeons, although often met with in beech forest, were not by any means numerous, as in pine woods, where totara and black pine afforded them in the season such an abundance of fattening food, attracting great flocks. These birds usually kept well up the slopes of the hill, not far from the stream for the sake of the konini berries, often they were high enough up to frequent those parts of the wood where there yet remained something of the last fall of weather, where the deep hued foliage showed still darker shades of green against a partial coating of glistening snow that seemed to have stilly crept along the topside of the branches, to reach and weigh down with its sparkling gems the outer twigs and leaves, til the rude wind with sudden twist and shake swept off the jewelled ornature. As we trudge through masses of bold stiff fronds of the common hard fern (*L. discolor*), and trample under-foot the long silky leaves of bedding astelias, we hear the bell-birds chime among the crowded orange-red drupes of karamu; the tiny wren prying for insects in creviced bark flitters from tree to tree, often hidden by luxuriant growth of lichens, their broad-lobed fronds deep golden, emerald green, or bronzed with duller brown and orange, expanding the moist air, decorating stems and branches with their rich livery, most lavishly . . . . As we push aside the damp undergrowth, we notice the green parroquets [parakeets] pressing the long tail feathers against the stem, in furcate fashion, as they ascend aloft. We hear the rush of the mountain torrent; soon through the tangled brush-wood, are seen below peeps of the silvery stream marking its hurried dash against the curbing rocks with flecks and bubbles of radiant foam. Above the murmur comes up a faint long whistle, in the turbulent pools that seethe and eddy round them, floats a small party of blue mountain ducks; these curious waterfowl turn round and round in the swirling water, carrying high sterns, like the poops of ancient galleons; for a brief space we watch the helpless creatures, then away, they are not under tapu; there might be no inclination to slaughter for mere slaughter's sake, rather a humiliating confession for an Englishman. Flap, flap, now tells the whereabouts of the wood pigeons, and we see from afar their white breasts and lustrous necklets of green and gold; soon three or four of these simple victims are potted in rather an unsportsmanlike style. The report of the guns scares a select company of screaming kakas; as they cross the leafy canopy above one gets a glancing gleam of the deep red which tricks out their russet plumage; some of these sagacious birds are killed, mostly dying hard, as if they clutched at life to the very last. A bunch or two of the game are tied up with strips of ribbon-wood bark, and hung up to some convenient bough, whence they may be fetched away when the shooters are homeward bound ... As we jog onward it does not escape notice that, on nearing the more level ground, our dog resumes his vivacity; with nose carried low he hurriedly traverses the flat; with a dull whirr, quail spring up, flying straight and rather low, at intervals with a marked pause between, a bevy is aroused. Of these a brace have been got by the dog ... These little delicacies are carefully strung on a shoulder-belt made of a strip of flax leaf. Our way now lies across a flat intersected with small creeks, where one may see large bull-heads (galaxia) lying on the stones in the shallows, till a sudden movement alarms them, and they dart away into the obscurity of the overhanging bank. Every step we take causes commotion; with a clicking sound grasshoppers innumerable make off in successive bounds; lizards scuttle away in all directions, they hasten for the shelter of grey prostrate leaves that form the decaying outwork of flax-bushes; they crawl beneath, or climb on the sides of stones, to which they cling in a wonderful manner: in the panic some tails drop off, changing the lithe and sinuous figures of the late wearers to a grotesque and abrupt ending, the organs so abandoned writhing as in gentle protest against such unseemly haste.[30]

The wider international context makes sense of this seeming contradiction. In the United States, Canada and to some extent New Zealand, sport hunting and 'sportsmen' drove early wildlife-conservation movements. The imperative of sporting hunting codes, and of the various societies that managed access to animals, was maintaining consistent populations to ensure the steady availability of game. This was, and still is in the case of bird hunting, the rationale behind the designation of seasons, the imposition of bag limits, the selling of licences and the preservation of habitat. Mass slaughter, or the killing of animals during their breeding season, was anathema to 'sportsmen' and their societies, in large part because it reduced the available game. As pioneering American biologist Aldo Leopold put it in the 1930s, the aim of managing wildlife was to produce 'wildlife crops' for 'recreational use'.[31]

In New Zealand this ethic was manifested in laws protecting some native birds and declaring closed seasons on others. Each year acclimatisation societies around the country discussed bird populations (introduced and native) and made decisions on seasons and bag limits. Along the same lines, the equivalent groups in Canada were charged with the management of game, spending a great deal of effort to control hunters who used game as a source of food, not as sport. The arguments in New Zealand, Canada and the United States were that pot-hunters were a distinct threat to the viability of game numbers because they shot all year round and, in the case of bird-hunters, trapped birds during the moult when they could not fly easily, and harvested eggs as a source of food. It was no accident then that the sportsmen's lobby was integral in the establishment of game reserves and national parks in North America. By protecting wildlife from year-round hunters in national parks, hunting could be managed and regulated, allowing some sportsmen licences to stalk game but strictly controlling the numbers of animals hunters could bag.

That the development of national parks in the United States influenced the growing conservation movement in New Zealand is clear. The American Audubon Society, founded in opposition to 'the fashion of wearing feathers and skins of birds' in the late 1880s, was cited as an example of a bird-protection society by the Governor-General Lord Onslow in 1892 in his attempts to persuade New Zealand's Parliament to protect the huia.[32] (As it was, the bird-protection lobby succeeded more quickly in New Zealand than in America, with Resolution and Little Barrier Islands being established as bird sanctuaries in the early 1890s, while Pelican Island in Florida was not established until 1903.) The Boone and Crockett Club, of which Theodore Roosevelt was a founder, was a strong supporter of the establishment of Yellowstone National Park, and was the partner of the New Zealand Department of Tourist and Health Resorts in the introduction of wapiti into Fiordland in 1905.

Donne's position, then, was not inconsistent with the wider national parks movement nor with his role of attracting international tourists in a global market. Improvements in transport had made travel to New Zealand easier and Donne's department actively promoted New Zealand at expositions and exhibitions in the United States, South Africa and, most often, Britain. Mounted deer heads and pamphlets declaring New Zealand the 'sportsman's paradise' were prominent at these exhibitions. New Zealand had it all: alps, lochs, lakes, trout rivers and deer-stalking. The natural environment was important as the stage but deer and wapiti, tahr and chamois added action for everyone, particularly wealthy tourists willing to pay for guides, licences and stalking blocks (see Chapter 4).

In the early 1900s, in North America and British colonies such as Australia, South Africa and India, a range of agencies began to take an interest in the scientific management of wildlife. There was a move away from an emphasis on laws and statutes about who could shoot what and when, to

Above: As early as the 1880s, naturalists such as Charlie Douglas were lamenting the introduction of cats and dogs to New Zealand. The bush workers in this 1904 photograph had clearly been eating venison and wild pork and most likely native birds. Typically, they also brought dogs and cats to the bush — and, probably unwittingly, rats.

more scientific arguments about ecology, and a subsequent increase in state intervention to boost wildlife numbers or preserve habitats.[33] Botanist Leonard Cockayne managed to discredit the 'displacement theory' of native species being naturally inferior fairly soundly through careful research and arguments that most of the damage to New Zealand's indigenous forests had been caused by human intervention, not just the presence of exotic species. His initial studies on the Chatham Islands were rewarded by government funding for further research into the environments that had already been designated as salvageable — Tongariro, Kapiti Island, Waipoua Forest and Stewart Island.

It was not only scientists who could see the effects of settlement on native forests. Some settlers were aware of the pressure on bird populations from bush-burning and clearing and from hunting. W Roberts kept extensive notes during 1856–7, when he travelled from Nelson to Bluff. In the preface to his reminiscences he noted that he was making 'an effort to record some items that otherwise would have been lost in the history of the colony' and provides an extensive description of the flora and fauna he encountered. As with so many early accounts of birdlife in New Zealand, his descriptions are both visual and 'gastronomic'.[34] 'There are a good many pigeons,' wrote Roberts. 'It is a pretty copper-purple bird, head, neck, and breast coppery-green, abdomen white with little pink feet. It is excellent eating, but they are seldom seen now.' He demonstrated not only the range of wildfowl settlers were hunting, but the impact that this was having on native bird populations:

> Outside the bush, there were a number of native quail. It was a small bird, reddish-brown, spotted with white on breast and abdomen. They were most delicious eating. Their eggs were nearly as large as a pigeon's egg, buff thickly spotted with brown. As they could not fly far they are now nearly extinct, for they could not escape from the bush fires or were easily shot, or caught by dogs, cats and rats . . .[35]

In the 1890s, growing up on a Wairarapa farm, Robert Cameron noted the long walks entailed by a shooting expedition with his uncle, 'often to very distant patches of bush left on the older parts of the station' because the bush had been knocked back well away from the house and the grazing land. The Cameron family's doctor suggested that the length of the walk was exhausting Cameron and his brothers and making them vulnerable to illness.[36]

May Brown, who lived about 24km from Dargaville, housekeeping for her brother and father, wrote that by the 1900s, as the bush was cleared, native pigeons became scarcer and she was glad of the newly opened butcher's shop.[37]

Explorer Charlie Douglas, even as he was 'laying in' supplies of birds for food during his expeditions in Westland in the 1880s, was lamenting their declining numbers and fearing the worst for them. 'Before we left the Copland,' he wrote, 'we saw the Tracks of a Cat. Such is the result of the advent of the white man a few more months and pussy will extend operations and the small birds will vanish forever and worse and worse the ferret is on its way up from south.'[38]

The decimation of native birds by mustelids (stoats, weasels and ferrets), introduced in the 1880s to control rabbits, brought a shift in attitudes towards native birds even by acclimatisation societies. Talk of protection and closed seasons on native birds went on alongside the naturalists' talk of collecting specimens before it was 'too late'. The notion of the loss of birds being linked to loss of habitat had not yet taken hold in scientific circles, however.

A pioneer in this field was the Reverend Philip Walsh, who gave a paper to the New Zealand Institute in 1892 putting forward the idea that forests were

Above: The supposed acceleration of erosion by animals was the principal reason for lifting protection on deer, tahr and chamois in 1930. It was not until the 1980s that the great shingle slides of the Southern Alps were understood to reflect not erosion, but uplift and deposition from the collision of two colossal tectonic plates. The minuscule effects of grazing animals played no part in this. Here, Forest Service hunter Doug Smith is packing skins down the Hopkins Valley in 1941.

systems and the destruction of one part of that system — his focus was on the undergrowth browsed by deer — led to serious consequences for the whole. He also pointed out the link between the introduction of small bird pests and rabbits, the enormous strain they had placed on farmers, the introduction of mustelids to control these pests and the consequent destruction of native birds by these predators.

But it was almost another 20 years before the government was persuaded to protect native birds, with exceptions such as the hawk and the kea, from hunters and professional bird collectors. In this period three island sanctuaries were established and the Tongariro National Park and Fiordland and Egmont reserves were created (they were later gazetted as national parks). David Young describes the late 1890s and early 1900s as 'the most active in New Zealand's conservation history' until the late 1960s.[39] It remained, too, a period of continued and active acclimatisation, with the introduction of three more browsing game animals — wapiti, tahr and chamois — and the continued introduction of possums to new areas.

## Dirt: the fear of erosion

It was not only bird-lovers, tourism directors and botanists who were pressuring the government to protect New Zealand vegetation. Farmers and foresters formed the other arm of this increasingly powerful lobby.

To European eyes, New Zealand looked highly vulnerable to erosion. Everywhere Europeans explored and travelled in the high country they found slips, scree slopes and rockfalls, especially after heavy rains. The nature of the wide, braided, gravel-filled rivers made them seem flood-prone.

To late nineteenth-century thinking, deforestation, while necessary for the progress of agriculture, brought less than desirable side effects. Concerns about climate change owing to bush clearance were aired in newspapers throughout the 1890s, and it was argued that the erosion caused by deforestation and consequent filling of rivers with gravel was leading to increasing flooding. The ravages of rabbits exacerbated the denuding of hill country being grazed by introduced stock. Conserving remnant forests and reforestation became an important issue for both farmers and the government. Holding up the examples of North Africa, Asia and North America as once-forested areas that were now suffering desertification, Prime Minister Julius Vogel introduced the New Zealand Forests Act in 1874 to allow for the creation and protection of state forests. By 1881 more than 2 million hectares had been set aside on upland slopes for the 'growth and preservation of timber' or 'climatic forest conservancy', and mountain reserves were established to protect rivers and streams.[40]

Ecologists, led by Walsh and brought into the mainstream by Cockayne, argued that deer were damaging the bush, making the very source of rivers and streams unstable. In the early 1920s two major publications brought erosion sharply into focus as a problem for the government. Cockayne's book *Vegetation of New Zealand*, published in 1921, made clear links between deer, forest degradation and erosion and flooding. In 1922 forester Allan Perham presented his report to the House of Representatives which argued that deer were causing significant damage. Damage to mountain pastures and upland forests would create problems for farming, increase the risk of flooding and cause problems for the government's hydroelectric schemes.

The government began to take notice. With increasing pressure from the Royal Forest and Bird Protection Society (created in its current form in 1923) and the newly formed government Forest Service (brought about by pressure from the New Zealand Forestry League, founded in 1916), the connections between deer, damage to forests and erosion became firmly fixed in the minds of those in power. It remained a powerful driver for wild-animal control well into the late twentieth century.

The prevailing logic was that deer reduced vegetation density. As vegetation helped hold soil together and slowed run-off, deer browsing must be responsible for the widespread scarring of slopes in the Southern Alps and the rivers of shingle flowing down from the mountains to the plains and the sea. Reducing (or eliminating) deer in the high country, then, would stabilise the hills and protect the lowlands from being overrun by gravel and floodwaters.

In the early 1950s, questions were raised about the efficacy of the deer-control programme. American biologist Thane Riney attempted to test and measure the relationships between deer numbers, vegetation and erosion. Cockayne had argued that deer would eventually modify forests to the point of destroying them but since the beginning of the deer-control campaigns in the 1930s no measurements had been taken of forest regeneration in areas where deer had been reduced. Measuring the numbers of deer or the extent of erosion 'had always seemed dauntingly difficult', but Riney was not restrained by years of New Zealand conservation orthodoxy. His methods for measuring deer numbers were deceptively simple. Along a sample line he counted deer droppings — a method that is still used today.[41] Along the same sample lines Riney measured the extent of vegetation cover compared with bare earth, repeatedly visiting the area to examine trends in coverage.

Riney's research on erosion showed beyond doubt that there was 'little overlap between the areas judged prone to erosion and those where the department shot most of their deer'. The focus of the deer-destruction campaigns had been areas with the highest populations of deer and the skin and tail bonuses paid ensured hunters spent their energies in places that yielded the highest tallies. These did not always correlate to areas where a reduction in deer numbers could have the greatest benefit to the land. It also did not explain why areas of the most severe erosion were not necessarily the habitats of the largest numbers of deer. Riney also argued that deer were not *the* problem, rather they were part of a wider ecological community that included a range of browsing and grubbing animals, as well as humans and their domesticated flocks and herds. These were not popular conclusions and Riney ended his stint in New Zealand working for the Forest Service because his relationship with the Department of Internal Affairs had become so strained.[42]

Despite Riney's work, animal-induced erosion persisted as a basic assumption in the research conducted by Forest Service ecologists. The Forest and Range Experiment Station (FRES) was established near Rangiora to survey plots of vegetation in five-yearly cycles, observing changes so as to calculate the level of deer control necessary. If the vegetation in plots was thinning then deer control needed to increase; when the bush showed signs of thickening up again, deer control was succeeding. But these conclusions all assumed a benchmark of the level of vegetative cover sufficient to prevent erosion — a benchmark that was never actually defined. Wildlife scientist Graeme Caughley suggests that there was reluctance within FRES to question what had been accepted as orthodoxy for so long in the Forest Service and what had been publicly stated as truth for 30 years. To question the idea that vegetation controlled serious erosion would also have undermined 'the protection forester's reasons for living', creating another reason not to worry the sore tooth of erosion.[43]

It does not seem all that unusual that a government department might sink significant resources into a policy without ever measuring whether or not it was meeting its objectives, and certainly no one publicly argued with the equation that because vegetation held the land together on coastlines and on farmlands, it must hold the land together in the mountains. Caughley suggests the strongest deterrent to querying the idea of protective vegetation was that there was no alternative theory of why some parts of New Zealand were erosion- and flood-prone and others weren't — that is, until plate tectonics and the discovery of the Alpine Fault.[44]

Above: As the commercial venison industry took off, photographic points were established throughout the Southern Alps to monitor vegetation recovery. These two photos taken at Rock Burn in Mount Aspiring National Park show the changes between the 1970s when the photopoint was established (top) and 1999 (above). By 2007, the regeneration of beech seedlings was so thick that the view from the photopoint was completely obscured.

For the first half of the twentieth century, similarities in rock formations, flora and fossil records on different continents were explained by some geologists by the idea of 'continental drift': that all the landmasses on earth had once been a super-continent, which had broken up and the pieces drifted apart. In the 1940s British geologist Arthur Holmes offered a refinement to the theory that explained how these massive movements had occurred. Even with Holmes's clarification the theory was not popular and took a decade to become accepted by a slim majority of the scientific community. Even then, many scientists (including Holmes himself) had doubts that this idea absolutely explained movements in the Earth's crust.

During World War Two and into the 1950s, oceanographers were discovering the remarkable landscape of the sea floor, with its canyons and mountain ranges. In 1960, core samples revealed that the sea floor immediately alongside massive splits fracturing the seabed was very young but got older further away from these splits. A series of scientific papers suggested that the seafloor was spreading, steadily moving outwards from these fissures. By 1964 prominent scientists generally agreed that the Earth's surface was made up of a series of plates, moving in relation to each other, diverging and colliding. The Earth's continents were passengers riding atop these plates of oceanic crust. In 1968 the old term 'continental drift' was replaced by the more accurate name 'plate tectonics'.[45]

New Zealand is at the meeting of the Australian and Pacific plates. When plates collide, the edge of the down-travelling plate is forced toward the Earth's hot core. It typically melts, giving rise to volcanic activity (as happens in the case of the Central North Island volcanic zone). The top plate rides over the lower, scraping off the upper layers of rock to form mountains. In New Zealand, the rate of uplift through the grinding together of tectonic plates has been very rapid in geological terms, but has been matched by erosion because of high rainfall. Rock is constantly being broken up by freezing temperatures and hot sunshine forcing its expansion and contraction, allowing water and ice to do their slow but sure demolition job. So despite millions of years of mountain-building the New Zealand ranges are less than 4000m above sea level. 'Without the might of erosion, the Southern Alps would be six times taller than they are today.'[46] With plate tectonics explaining the rise and fall of the Southern Alps, a century of orthodoxy was turned on its head and 'animal-induced erosion' was recast as 'deposition': the gravel outwash plains alongside the mountain chain had in fact originally been scraped off the sea floor, uplifted then carried by rain to form the lowlands.

> **We were tahr-hunting in the Rangitata, about 7 or 8000 feet up and you could see across to Mount Cook, it was a brilliant view . . . the astonishing thing was, there was this outcrop of rock and it was full of sea shells and things and that had been on the ocean floor at one stage many millions of years ago, up there at 7000 feet.**
> — Hunter Viv Collings [47]

It was not until 1986 that the final death knell of the justification for wild-animal control based on erosion sounded. One example of this changing science was presented at the annual conference of the New Zealand Ecological Society. Hydrologist Patrick Grant presented research findings that demonstrated that 'the accelerated erosion alleviation and consequent vegetation destruction in erosion periods . . . were associated with atmospheric warming and increases of major rainstorms and floods; they did not coincide with either colonisation or activities of humans or mammals'. Grant argued that browsing mammals had not contributed significantly to the development of the most severe areas of erosion. He also demonstrated that while vegetative cover did minimise normal soil erosion, it could not prevent the catastrophic erosion and flooding caused by unusually severe storms. However, his paper confirmed that browsing mammals did reduce the density of vegetation.[48]

The presentation was something of a bombshell. Recreational hunters were thrilled because deer could no longer be demonised; conservation groups, who had always argued for controlling browsing mammals in order to promote biodiversity rather than for erosion control, were vindicated by Grant's conclusions. By the mid-1990s, with erosion well and truly expunged from the justifications for pest control and the commercial venison industry's decimation of deer populations, the Department of Conservation's priorities were easy to see: $12 million per year on possum control, $5 million per year on goats, less than $1 million per year on deer control.[49]

## Shooting for the skipper

Until the acceptance of the science of tectonic plates, however, the attitude was that anything that could be done to stem the loss of vegetation from New Zealand's slopes had to be done, and that included declaring war on browsing mammals, most particularly deer. Following the Deer Menace Conference in 1930, the Deer Control Section of the Department of Internal Affairs was set up. Headed by Captain George Franklyn Yerex, the Deer Control Section was an unusual branch of the public service. Yerex literally mounted a campaign against deer, stringently vetting recruits to the service, and he became a legend among generations of hunters.

The creation of such a section was not at all surprising. Delegates at the conference represented a wide variety of conservation groups, farmers'

Above: Val Sanderson (left) was an enthusiastic hunter, a man with a deep sense of loyalty to his country and a fervent conservationist. A veteran of the South African War and businessman, Sanderson had supported the establishment of Kapiti Island as a reserve in the 1910s. When he returned from World War One (he had lied about his age, claiming to be younger than the 45 years cut-off for enlistment) he found nothing had been done to protect the island's bush from the goats and sheep. According to Ross Galbreath, 'Sanderson had a keen sense of duty and expected authorities to live up to their responsibilities. He lambasted the ministers and departments responsible for Kapiti and demanded that more be done to protect it.' In 1923, Sanderson founded the New Zealand Native Bird Protection Society and used his wide networks and individual mana to garner support for conservation. In 1935 the organisation was renamed the Forest and Bird Protection Society as it widened its mandate. Always the driving force behind the organisation, in 1933 Sanderson took over the presidency and held the position until his death in 1945.

## The American way

American scientists and commentators who worked in New Zealand had a very different perspective on the relationship between game mammals and the bush. In the late 1940s, John K Howard and H Wendell Endicott, both members of the Boone and Crockett Club, spent time in New Zealand. They were, in part, establishing what has become known as the Fulbright exchange programme, which was to promote 'educational and cultural programmes of benefit to the two countries'.

As keen hunters, the two men went to Fiordland and Mount Cook to hunt. Endicott's account of their experiences here was critical of what he saw as indiscriminate culling of a game asset. This account was published in The Listener in 1947 as 'Is Deer Extermination a Short-Sighted Policy?'.

Howard returned two years later as part of the first Fulbright exchange. He brought with him a wapiti expert, Olaus J Murie, and led a joint New Zealand–American expedition to Fiordland, with the aim of reporting on the adaptation of the American wapiti (originally donated by the Boone and Crockett Club) to the area. More than 60 people were involved: 'Almost every field scientist of note in the country was there . . . transport and supply personnel, hunters, cooks, radio operators and other field staff'.[51] The reports of the expedition all recommended to the government that its extermination policy on wapiti be reconsidered, given that moderate wapiti numbers posed no threat to the forests of the region.[52]

Thane Riney was an American biologist who had completed his studies under A Starker Leopold, the son of America's pioneering scientist, Aldo Leopold. Riney's research in New Zealand reflected American philosophies of wildlife management: that deer could be controlled through scientific and ecological principles. One of Riney's arguments was that there was a point at which deer populations would crash because of the lack of feed available — they would eat themselves out of house and home. For New Zealand wildlife workers and botanists this was unthinkable — what would deer destroy en route to their population crash?

Even before the term 'biodiversity' was coined, it was clear that botanists and wilderness advocates understood that New Zealand's forests and alpine regions were unique and vulnerable. While American biologists brought with them a level of professional training and techniques unknown in New Zealand, they were guided by fundamentally different ecological principles than local wildlife workers. The New Zealand ethos was that its ecology had evolved in the absence of mammals and its conservation demanded their removal.

## The Skipper

Frank Yerex has become a legend in the history of deer control in New Zealand. Born in 1893, he enlisted in the Territorial Force at the age of 17 and the New Zealand Expeditionary Force in 1915. Yerex served in Egypt and Palestine, being promoted to Captain in 1917, and returned to New Zealand in 1919. He was a fisheries officer at Taupo when the Deer Control Section was formed and he was appointed its head.[53]

There are many facets of his personality about which writers and biographers agree. Yerex was a natural leader, respected by his employees. He had high standards and, until he returned to active service in World War Two, ran the Deer Control operation virtually single-handedly. He researched areas thoroughly himself, spending as much time in the bush as his shooters did.

His commitment to the job was clear. Yerex's son, David, wrote that 'in 1931 Frank Yerex took his [young] family to live for almost a year on the edge of the bush at Makarora. From there, he and several of his recruits headed up into the Wilkin, the Young and the Haast region, into areas that in those days were marked on official maps as "Unexplored", checking on deer numbers and the state of the forests and open tops'.[54]

It was on the basis of this reconnaissance that Frank Yerex filed his first strategy as part of an annual report: 'deer-destruction operations could only be conducted successfully if carried out to a preconceived and comprehensive scheme, as sporadic efforts . . . would have the effect of scattering the deer and ultimately increasing the area of infestation . . . With a view to this principle, it was hoped to commence operations in the Makarora Valley . . . and to work in a north-westerly direction towards Mount Cook, working each valley in turn . . . '.

When ex-government culler Graeme Caughley first read this report 'in a musty departmental library' he was incredulous. 'He [Yerex] could not have had the remotest conception of how deer live or what South Island mountains are like; was the man mad? . . . I now see it differently. Yerex was rolling up an enemy flank across a desert landscape of the mind, careful to secure against enfilading fire as he went. Mountains in the way would be surmounted. They changed no principle of military science.'[55]

Yerex's commitment to his shooters was obvious and it is reputed that he knew them all by name. Certainly in the Internal Affairs files in Archives New Zealand, his hand-written letters to his hunters all address them by their Christian names. The loyalty he engendered is testament to his manner. In the early 1930s, Yerex sent his lower North Island hunters back into the field suddenly. His deputy at the time, Ken Francis, wrote that even though some of the hunters were desperate for leave and the winter was coming on, Yerex's main concern was to keep his men away from the attentions of the Economy Committee, which was charged with reducing the costs of the public service. Government shooters drinking in the bars of Wellington would have been fair game.[56]

Apart from the years Yerex was serving overseas during World War Two, he headed deer control from its inception in 1930 until his failing health, and perhaps the knowledge that 'his' operation was at an end, led to his decision to retire in 1956, shortly after deer control was transferred to the Forest Service. Many hunters and field officers who had served with him during these decades also retired at this time.

lobbies and acclimatisation societies, and were virtually unanimous in their agreement that deer were a problem that had to be controlled. The Minister of Internal Affairs, Philip de la Perrelle, opened the conference, stating, 'our aim is to obtain practical suggestions as to the best method of carrying out deer destruction . . . this is the only question which we will consider and I have no doubt that the speakers will confine themselves to this subject and that as the result of the views which will be expressed I will have all the facts before me thus enabling me to arrive at definite conclusions as to the future policy to be adopted'.[50] Delegates, perhaps with the exception of the slightly disgruntled acclimatisation societies, were also overwhelmingly in favour of a single authority to control deer. They believed trained and experienced hunters must be employed to do the job to avoid unnecessary animal suffering, disturbance to native birds and farm livestock. FE Hutchinson, a representative of the Canterbury Philosophical Institute, brought his American experience to the table, citing the government's full-time employment of many professional hunters to manage the overpopulation of deer in American forests.

The rather surprising outcome of the conference was that Internal Affairs got the job. The conference was in accord that because deer destruction was about saving forests, the Forest Service should be the department in charge. As W Stewart, the Commissioner of Lands and Chief Surveyor, put it, 'I would favour the State Forest Service in lieu of the Internal Affairs Department, because it is a practical problem and the Internal Affairs Department have not the field men or the experience necessary for control'.[57] Whatever power struggles went on behind the scenes, Internal Affairs got the job, however, and Yerex was appointed to run the campaign.

The 1930s was a good time to be mounting such an offensive. There was plenty of ammunition and .303 rifles left over from World War One, and the economic depression meant there was no shortage of men willing to do this kind of work. Few aspiring government shooters lasted more than one season; many barely lasted a month (see Chapter 3). Caughley puts the enthusiasm shown for the job down to 'the lure of high adventure, the chance for a man to try himself out on a job that had broken lesser men, and perhaps he would make enough to put together a deposit on that farm'.[58]

The government campaign looked impressive on paper. In the early seasons, the tallies were incredibly high, even with relatively few hunters — no more than 70 in the early years. Some daily tallies were remarkable: Archie Clarke shot 56 deer in a day in South Westland; three shooters working together in the Hunter Valley in Otago shot 138 deer in a day; Ken Francis and Bill Fairfield trapped a mob of deer on the Avalanche Glacier near Wanaka and shot 60 in 15 minutes.[59] On foot and without the advantages of modern equipment, Bert Barra shot 24,000 deer during his two-decade career in both islands.[60]

The numbers of deer killed in this first phase of government shooting (up to 1956, when the Forest Service took over animal control) are generally agreed to be in the order of 668,000 by Department of Internal Affairs shooters and more than 50,000 by Forest Service hunters, with private hunters probably shooting as many deer as all the government shooters put together.[61] Government hunters also shot more than 650,000 animals of other species — goats, tahr, chamois and pigs. The annual tallies over these years, however, increased steadily, and by the 1950s there was debate about why this might be. Some argued that the deer population was still growing, while Yerex continued to argue that it represented increased effectiveness on the part of the shooters and the re-employment of shooters after World War Two.

The virtual cessation of government shooting during World War Two meant that deer numbers recovered. In the 1950s, American biologist Thane Riney's research demonstrated that shooters were really no match for deer on the ground. Through the use of high observation platforms overlooking a fenced area, Riney showed that 'no matter how skilled or experienced the hunters were, many deer were eluding them'.[62] It is not clear that the deer destruction campaign had struck a blow for conservation.

## The modern era

David Yerex argues that almost as soon as the Forest Service took over deer control, the emphasis changed from killing as many deer as possible to 'a more scientific approach . . . The actual number of deer killed was not so important: the priority was to eliminate them from headwater catchments of key rivers, which comprised about one-fifth of the country infested by deer'.[63] One of the first actions taken by the service was to scrap the skin bonus. Tail bonuses were deemed to be sufficient and shooters were to get on with the real business of wild-animal control.

The Noxious Animals Act of 1956 declared all deer, tahr, chamois, wild goats and possums to be pests, finally lifting protection on possums and pitting recreational hunters, who still valued many of these species as assets, against conservationists and farmers. These divisions were highlighted sharply shortly afterwards by the first experiments with aerial drops of 1080 poison in 1958.

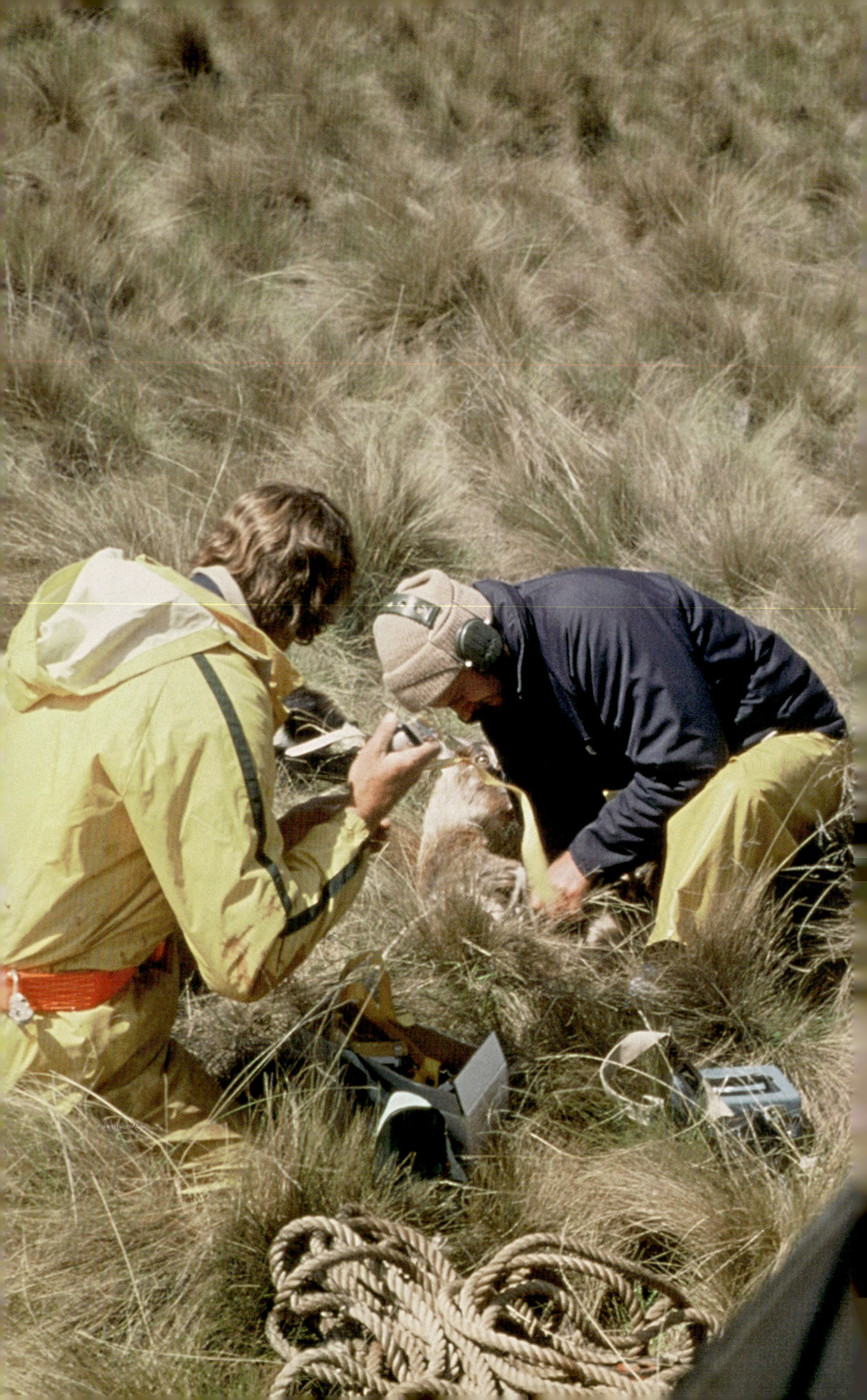

In October of that year, the Forest Service organised a conference on the use of 1080 poison (sodium monofluoroacetate) for wild-animal control. Various government departments were represented — Lands and Survey, Internal Affairs, Tourist and Publicity, Scientific and Industrial Research and Agriculture — as well as scientific, conservation and outdoors groups. The Royal Forest and Bird Protection Society, the Royal Society of New Zealand, Soil Conservation and Rivers Control Council, Federated Mountain Clubs, Federated Farmers and the New Zealand Deerstalkers' Association were all present. The Soil Conservation council's director, DA Campbell, pushed the

Opposite: Exploiting the gregarious nature of feral goats, some cullers capture and fit radio transmitter collars to goats that are then released to find and join mobs, unwittingly betraying their position to hunters. The mob is tracked and shot by hunters either on foot or using helicopters; the Judas goat is left unharmed to do its job again. Some play this role for many years and this method greatly increases the efficiency of goat culling. Here, Department of Conservation hunters fit a Judas collar to an unwilling recruit.

Above: 1080 poison was first used in New Zealand in 1958, to control possums. A conference on its use was held in October of that year, with government, acclimatisation societies, conservation groups and farmers represented. The positions articulated there have remained remarkably unchanged in over 50 years.

**Collecting and conserving** 275

animal-induced erosion argument, stating 'Extermination is the answer to the problem of high country conservation on our rivers . . . It is the safety of our river flats or the deer on the mountains — we cannot have both'.[64] The Rabbit Destruction Council endorsed 1080 as by far the most humane poison to kill rabbits, and Forest and Bird president Roy Nelson accepted that while some native birds would die from the poison, its use was necessary to eradicate noxious animals from the bush.

Prominent conservationist Lance McCaskill, at the conference representing the National Parks Authority, was cautious in his commitment to 1080, although unequivocal in his commitment to the eradication of noxious animals. 'It must be remembered that the protection of native fauna, particularly the native birds, is also a duty of the authority and the park board [and] before permitting the use of poisons to control exotic animals the possible effect on these native birds must be closely examined.'[65] Negative responses to the idea of using 1080 against deer were also communicated to the conference by some county councils concerned with its effect on birdlife, and from travel agents, who argued that tourists were dismayed by reports of poisoning deer because it would destroy hunting opportunities. A Dunedin travel agent told the conference, 'I cannot over emphasise the horror and amazement expressed by all travel people [at a travel conference in San Francisco]. They can hardly believe that we are poisoning one of our greatest natural assets.'[66]

Unsurprisingly, the Deerstalkers' Association was a lonely voice — but one with strong public support, as it turned out — categorically against the use of 1080. The association initiated a petition against 1080 which gathered thousands of signatures by the week, ending with more than 80,000 signatories by 1960. The use of 1080 went ahead but primarily against possums, especially after the confirmation in 1967 that possums were carriers of bovine tuberculosis. While techniques of administering the poison and the rates of application have changed dramatically since the 1960s, the reports of this conference demonstrate how little attitudes have changed in 50 years of debate about the use of 1080.

As outlined in Chapter 3, by the early 1960s the main players in deer-hunting were commercial venison-recovery operations. The opportunity to earn a very good living by shooting venison for sale provided a strong incentive to entrepreneurs and hunters alike. Aeroplanes and helicopters facilitated hunting to an extraordinary degree, and entrepreneurs such as Tim Wallis made venison-hunting efficient and more lucrative. It is fair to say that, despite the best intentions of government departments and the great skill and endurance of its shooters, the commercial venison operations did more for conservation — albeit only in the short term — than all the other efforts put together.

It is estimated that in the two decades up to 1984 up to 75 per cent of the deer were removed from some areas of Fiordland, and by 1990 similar declines in other areas were recorded.[67] In a significant understatement, the Forest Service's 1971 annual report acknowledged that 'high prices and consequent high [commercial] kill are believed to be masking a general reduction in animal populations; the quantity of venison will decline noticeably over the ensuing year'.[68] The commercial industry was the bane

Above: New Zealand's long relationship with American wildlife enthusiasts and scientists has included the introduction of wapiti to Fiordland by the Boone and Crockett Club in collaboration with the Department of Tourist and Health Resorts. In 1949, the first Fulbright scholars to visit New Zealand led the American–New Zealand Fiordland Expedition. It aimed to investigate how wapiti had adapted to this country's environment, and their effect on the bush. Here, C Lindsay and V Wood measure a wapiti cow.

of the Forest Service's attempts to control deer: the meat-hunters were unpredictable and unregulated, at least not by the Forest Service. They were, however, getting the job done.

By the time the heat went out of the commercial meat-hunting industry (when prices dropped, aviation regulations tightened and the 1977 Wild Animal Control Act was introduced), government shooting was also much reduced. There were very few hunters, full or part time, who had been able to resist the lure of the game-packer's cheque, and by the end of the 1970s Forest Service hunters found very few deer in areas where commercial hunters had operated. It was also becoming clear that, in some areas of the South Island and for the immediate future, deer were no longer the threat to native vegetation they once had been and that the damage being caused by possums far outweighed that of hoofed mammals. Because of this assessment, state

Above: During World War Two the number of government shooters dropped to 20. In the immediate post-war years, many cullers were men who had been too young to enlist. David Lyes (left) was only 22 years old when this photo of tahr-cullers in the Sealy Range was taken in February 1948. Three months later, he died in a fall in the same area.

resources were shifted markedly away from deer control, except in the case of specially targeted areas, and into possum control, mostly with the use of 1080 poison.

The sweeping social changes of the 1970s saw 'environmentalism' come to be equated with the saving of 'indigenous' flora and fauna, and with increasing challenges to the Forest Service and its continued logging of native forests. Representing a massive popular uptake of conservationist ideals, Forest and Bird managed to gather 264,907 signatures on a petition to save Lake Manapouri from being 'drowned' for hydroelectricity generation in 1970. The Commission for the Environment was formed in 1972 and the Waitangi Tribunal in 1975, both altering the ways New Zealanders saw 'their environment'.[69] A new generation of environmental activists, influenced by international movements such as the Sierra Club and Friends of the Earth, came to the fore in tackling the Forest Service on its policies, and many groups formed around a variety of environmental causes: wild rivers, endangered species, logging, fisheries and marine resources. All of this led to the promise by Labour's environmental spokesman in the 1984 election, Michael Cullen, of the establishment of a Ministry for the Environment and a single 'Environment and Conservation Council'. After sweeping to power, Labour implemented those promises and the Department of Conservation was formed in 1987, disestablishing and incorporating the Forest Service, large parts of the Lands and Survey department, the Wildlife Service of the Department of Internal Affairs and the DSIR.

Amid all this turmoil and redefinition of 'environment' and 'conservation' were recreational hunters. They were now caught between a punitive Wild Animal Control Act, greatly depleted deer stocks and urban-based social changes that, on the one hand, strengthened the forces in favour of eradicating introduced game but paradoxically reduced public acceptance of the use of firearms and killing animals. There was also a decline in the numbers of younger people taking up and sticking with hunting.

The lobby groups for recreational hunters, particularly the New Zealand Deerstalkers' Association, had argued since 1937 that recreational hunters were part of the deer solution, not the problem. The establishment of 10 Recreational Hunting Areas in the 1980s supposedly allowed scientists to test this idea. No commercial harvest of wildlife or government wild-animal control was carried out in these areas (unless it was shown that animal populations were not adequately controlled by recreational hunters), so all the data collected on hunting and animal populations represented the recreational hunting effort. The conclusion of these studies, as well as those carried out in forest parks, showed that recreational hunting was unlikely to reduce deer to the point where native vegetation could recover from decades of degradation by browsing. Recreational hunters shot too few deer for the vegetation to recover, and as the population of deer declined, recreational hunters stopped going to these areas because their chances of success were too low. Although

### Bird-watchers

*Bird-monitoring has long been a role of hunters, both formally and informally. Government shooters' daybooks were (and are) a record of bird sightings as well as tallies of animals shot. Ray Triall's 1940s daybook from Stewart Island provides a daily record of his bird sightings, including an unusual sight (the entry was underlined several times) of 'black teal ducks' (New Zealand scaup). More recently, and in the same vein, waterfowl biologist Murray Williams has used the diaries of duck-shooters to track longitudinal trends in bird populations and distribution. From the 1940s onwards, hunters' diaries record a steady increase in mallard populations in the lower North Island and the increasing rarity of native grey ducks. Hunters' diaries have provided evidence of a vast change in duck populations 'within a hunting lifetime'.[71] Formal arrangements between hunting groups and the Department of Conservation are also becoming more common. For example, the Fiordland Wapiti Foundation has assisted extensively in the stoat-trapping and whio (blue duck) monitoring programmes in the Glaisnock Wilderness Area.*

**I think probably my greatest memory of being out hunting with Dad is not so much stalking the game — although that was pretty exciting — but it was the bird life and the bush, which I just developed a huge appreciation for. He had a great passion for birds. — Jocelyn Rae**[72]

Opposite: The Department of Conservation and regional councils continue to employ hunters to control animal pests. The emphasis today is less on deer and more on possums and goats. Rick Abbott is shown here cutting the tail off a feral goat in Rimutaka Forest Park.

arguments were sometimes put forward that fewer deer increased the size and quality of trophy heads (because of increased available feed), repeated surveys of recreational hunters showed that meat was a much more important motivation than trophies, so success had to be reasonably frequent to warrant continued effort.[70]

The Department of Conservation has continued to employ hunters, as have regional councils and private conservation bodies. Goats and possums have been a much greater focus of such pest-control operations than deer. Hunters have also been employed to control pigs.

In general, ground-based and aerial hunting has been an important part of a range of measures for controlling introduced conservation pests, alongside the use of aerial poison drops. Poison, particularly 1080, has been used widely in New Zealand since the identification of possums as carriers of bovine tuberculosis in the late 1960s.

# Epilogue

The New Zealand we live in today is highly urbanised, yet many of us still long for the outdoors. We go on tramping trips or holidays at the beach that invoke a nostalgia for our own barefoot childhoods. 'Bach style' litters our lifestyle magazines. We love to cook, judging by the sales of cookbooks and barbecues and the number of cooking shows on television. We love our red meat slightly less than we did in the 1980s, but we still consume more than 50kg per person each year.[1] Some of us are lucky enough to live near a butcher who has managed to survive the onslaught of mass-produced, bulk-bought cheap supermarket meat, but generally it goes into our trolleys after the fruit and veg, and before the milk. Wherever we buy it, it is neatly cut, sliced, diced, marinaded, herb-crusted, minced, made into sausages. We are many steps removed from the process by which it is reared, killed and butchered.

We live in peace — war is a distant memory and we embrace our vaguely pacifist international political credentials. We consider ourselves lucky that our children's only experience of firearms is computer- or television-generated, though we might feel uneasy about how much of such violence they absorb. Every story on the news about crimes committed with firearms increases our mistrust of them (although they are used in fewer than 1.5 per cent of violent offences in New Zealand).[2] We are green and proud of it. Kids do conservation projects at school; we plant native trees in the city for urban kereru and tui; words such as 'biodiversity' and 'climate change' are part of our everyday speech.

Hunting is not part of this picture. Because of our increasingly urbanised lifestyle, hunting has become less commonplace. Most people have far fewer opportunities to hunt than did previous generations. Access to private land has become more restricted in the past 30 years and getting to deer country on Department of Conservation land takes more time than most people have and a good deal of exertion. Bird-hunting remains popular, with its opening-day rituals, but again, access to private land has become more difficult and the bags can be very small. Pig-hunters on the urban fringe and in rural areas still have a good chance of success as they head off on a 'walk' with their dogs, but pig-hunting is not for the inexperienced nor the faint-hearted.

While participation in hunting has declined from its heyday, interest in it remains high. Books and magazines dedicated to hunting are published in greater numbers now than ever before, and there are more hunting magazines available at the newsagents than on other outdoor activities. Game meat is increasingly popular (although much of this is farmed) and many restaurants, breweries and wineries take part in 'wild food challenges' and have game on the menu. Some restaurants still offer to cook hunters' birds for them during duck season.

Hunting has also declined as part of the government's conservation effort. There are still government shooters, but resources are much more concentrated on possum control, usually through poison. The Department of Conservation endeavours to prevent the establishment of new wild populations of deer in areas such as Taranaki and Northland, but control of possums, goats, stoats and rats is a greater priority.

Hunting does not seem to be part of this picture of twenty-first century New Zealand. Except that it is. Many of us are old enough to remember shooting rabbits with the .22 on our cousins' farm. Many of us had fathers, grandfathers or uncles who hunted; some of them worked for the Forest Service or were skin- or meat-hunters. Our grandmothers had a fur stole 'for good'. Perhaps you have inherited the family's bone-handled knives, or the piano with its ivory keys? Perhaps your father or grandfather was a pilot in World War Two, where his self-sealing fuel tanks were lined with New Zealand deer hides? Did your brother own a 'buckskin' jacket? Did you buy Al Brown and Steve Logan's *Hunger for the Wild*, or have you bought a wild venison salami at the deli?

Hunting is everywhere in New Zealand's past. That past is very recent and we remain connected to it through our families and whanau, our kitchens and communities, and through the history of the land itself.

# Endnotes

### Introduction
1. See Eric Pawson and Tom Brooking (eds.), *Environmental Histories of New Zealand*, for a range of authors' perspectives on New Zealand's environmental history. See also James Beattie and Paul Star, 'State forest conservation and the New Zealand landscape: Origins and influences, 1850–1914', in Tony Ballantyne and Judith Bennett (eds.), *Landscape/Community: Perspectives from New Zealand history*; David Young, *Our Islands, Our Selves: A history of conservation in New Zealand*; Paul Star, 'From Acclimatisation to Preservation: Colonists and the natural world in southern New Zealand, 1860–1894' (PhD thesis); Margaret McLure, *The Wonder Country*; Kirstie Ross, *Going Bush: New Zealanders and nature in the twentieth century*, page 4.
2. Tina Loo, *States of Nature: Conserving Canada's wildlife in the twentieth century*, page 6.
3. Louis S Warren, *The Hunter's Game: Poachers and conservationists in twentieth-century America*, pages 25, 27.

### Chapter 1
1. Lady Mary-Anne Barker, *A Year's Housekeeping in South Africa*, page 315; Barker, *Station Life in New Zealand*, page 136.
2. Newton McConochie, *You'll Learn No Harm from the Hills*, pages 26–7.
3. John MacKenzie, *Empire of Nature: Hunting, conservation and British imperialism*, pages 26ff.
4. MacKenzie, *Empire of Nature*, pages 116, 141. See also Claire Brennan, 'Imperial Game: A history of hunting, society, exotic species and the environment in New Zealand and Victoria, 1840–1901' (PhD thesis), page 43.
5. Charles Hursthouse, *New Zealand, the 'Britain of the South'*, pages 82, 83.
6. Paul Shepard, *English Reaction to the New Zealand Landscape before 1850*, page 3. Hursthouse, page 83.
7. John Bradshaw, *New Zealand As It Is*, 1883, in Evaan Aramakutu, 'Colonists and Colonials: Animals' protection legislation in New Zealand, 1861–1910' (MA thesis), page 70.
8. HF von Haast, *The Life and Times of Sir Julius von Haast: Explorer, geologist, museum builder*, page 379.
9. Dr David Munro, 1861, cited in WCR Sowman, *Meadow, Mountain, Forest and Stream: The provincial history of the Nelson Acclimatisation Society*, page 30.
10. Munro and Alfred Dommett, 1861, in Sowman, page 30.
11. LOH Tripp in *Wild Life Problems: The Question of Control. Recent articles by 'Mamaku' with replies from LOH Tripp*, page 9.
12. Hursthouse, pages 83–4.
13. Sir Robert Baden-Powell, *Scouting for Boys*, page 24.
14. John Deans to John Deans Snr, 10 November 1842, *Pioneers of Canterbury: Deans Letters, 1840–1854*, pages 49–50.
15. John Deans to Gavin Brackenridge, 16 January 1843, *Pioneers of Canterbury*, pages 57–58.
16. Ibid.
17. Rollo Arnold, *The Farthest Promised Land: English villagers, New Zealand immigrants of the 1870s*, page 29.
18. Donna Landry, *The Invention of the Countryside: Hunting, walking and ecology in English literature, 1671–1831*, page 3. See also MacKenzie, *Empire of Nature*.
19. Arnold, pages 210, 167, 195, 61, 51.
20. Robert Cameron, 'A history of the Camerons of Spring Hill, 1840–1900', 93–6/1.R3B6S4, WA, page 4.
21. Thomson W Leys (ed.), *Brett's Colonists' Guide & Cyclopaedia of Useful Knowledge*, page 181.
22. KA Wodzicki, *Introduced Mammals of New Zealand*, page 6; *New Zealand Parliamentary Debates* 14 August 1861, page 290.

23   OAS First Report 1865 cited in Paul Star, 'From Acclimatisation to Preservation: Colonists and the natural world in southern New Zealand, 1860–1894' (PhD thesis), page 80.
24   Bruce Ferguson, OHColl-0489/1, NLNZ.
25   RM McDowall, *Gamekeepers for the Nation*, pages 320–3.
26   Sowman, page 87, also cited in McDowall, page 325.
27   McDowall, pages 307–8.
28   Graeme Caughley, *The Deer Wars: The story of deer in New Zealand*, page 2.
29   Hursthouse, page 84.
30   Brad Coombes, 'Making "scenes of nature and sport" — resource and wildlife management in Te Urewera, 1895–1954', Waitangi Tribunal report, page 4.
31   Coombes, pages 43ff; H Vipond, 'Urewera National Park: Introduced mammals', 1965 cited in Coombes, page 11.
32   Coombes, page 32.
33   *Bay of Plenty Times*, 30 March 1882, cited in Coombes, page 32.
34   *Nature*, 18 July 1872 and *The Field*, 13 July 1872, both cited in Coombes, page 19.
35   Jim McAloon, 'Resource frontiers, environment, and settler capitalism, 1769–1860' in Eric Pawson and Tom Brooking (eds.), *Environmental Histories of New Zealand*, page 54.
36   Some of these comments are from EJ Wakefield (1845), Edward Shortland (1843) and Ernst Dieffenbach (1843). See CMH Clarke and RM Dzieciolowski, 'Feral pigs in the northern South Island, New Zealand: I. Origin, distribution and density', *Journal of the Royal Society of New Zealand*, vol 21, no 3, September 1991, pages 237–47; AH Clark, *The Invasion of New Zealand by People, Plants and Animals: the South Island*.
37   Robert Gillies cited in GM Thomson, *Wild Life in New Zealand, Part I: Mammals*, page 20.
38   Clark, page 251, Clarke and Dzieciolowski, page 242, Thomson, *Wild Life in New Zealand: Part I*, page 21.
39   A Hewson, 'Early days in the Ashburton County', CM ARC 1900.257.
40   Thomson, *Wild Life in New Zealand: Part I*, page 21.
41   Roberta McIntyre, *Whose high country? A history of the South Island high country of New Zealand*, page 51; Mervyn Addenbrooke, *Home from the Hill: My life story*, pages 81–2.
42   George Baker, 'Reminiscences of Early Kaiapoi, 1862', CM, ARC1989.34, Folder 675, page 4.
43   Carolyn King, *Immigrant Killers: Introduced predators and the conservation of birds in New Zealand*, page 75.
44   William Cullen cited in Jim McAloon, *Nelson: A regional history*, page 16.
45   Wodzicki, pages 154–68; Clark, page 258; King, pages 114–5.
46   Thomson, *Wild Life in New Zealand: Part I*, page 39; Hursthouse, pages 80–1.
47   Hursthouse, page 81.
48   James Ashworth, 'Recollections of "Harleston", Sefton, September 1918', CM ARC.61, Folder 599.
49   Chris Maclean, *Tararua: The story of a mountain range*, page 104.
50   EH Graham, 1944, cited in Wodzicki, page 177; JA Gibb and JEC Flux, 'Mammals' in Gordon R Williams (ed.), *A Natural History of New Zealand: An ecological survey*, page 352; *Wild Life Problems: The question of control*, 1930, page 13.
51   Haast, page 393; Wodzicki, pages 169–75.
52   William Dawbin, 'Diary' 28 November 1903, IMA. Dawbin calls the banded rail a 'land rail', but Walter Buller's *A History of the Birds of New Zealand* identifies a land rail as *Rallus philippensis*, now called a banded rail or moho-pereru (www.nzbirds.com).
53   Barker, *Station Life*, pages 110, 122–3, 128.
54   James Feldman, 'Treaty rights and pigeon poaching: alienation of Maori access to kereru, 1864–1960', Waitangi Tribunal report, pages 3–4.
55   Coombes, page 26.

56  NZASA Minute Book, 26 July 1904, FGNZ.
57  *Hawera & Normanby Star*, 21 May 1898, page 2.
58  *Evening Post*, 18 June 1904, page 14.
59  James Drummond, 'In touch with nature', *Taranaki Herald*, 19 December 1908, page 10.
60  *Evening Post*, 15 May 1907, page 2.
61  Feldman, pages 30–1.
62  *NZPD* 1908, vol 145, page 66, cited in Feldman, page 31.
63  *NZPD* 1910, vol 151, pages 260–1, cited in Feldman, page 31.
64  Feldman, page 33.
65  Feldman, page 19.
66  Hone Heke, *NZPD*, vol 110, page 407, cited in Feldman, page 19.
67  Feldman, page 20.
68  Details of Te Heuheu Tukino's petition to James Carroll in Feldman, pages 21–2.
69  Harry Ell, *NZPD*, 1908, cited in Feldman, page 27, Coombes, pages 173–4.
70  Coombes, page 1.
71  Hone Heke, *NZPD*, vol 96, 24 September 1896, pages 163, 178, cited in Coombes, page 66.
72  Coombes, pages 71–2.
73  *The Evening Post*, 30 March 1901, page 5. Feldman notes the paucity of archival records of prosecutions because many records were destroyed, hence a need to rely on newspaper reporting (page 43).
74  *The Evening Post*, 13 June 1912, page 3.
75  NZASA Minute Book, August 1912, September 1924.
76  Coombes, page 23.
77  *Wanganui Herald*, 16 August 1884, page 2; *West Coast Times*, 2 October 1884, page 3.
78  Drummond, 'In Touch with Nature'.
79  Major H Atkinson, 1867, cited in Feldman, page 5.
80  Hone Heke, *NZPD*, 1907, vol 142, page 786, cited in Feldman, page 23.
81  And it was not only Maori who used snaring as a hunting method. In 1878, 'Country Subscriber' informed readers of the *Otago Witness* (23 March 1878, page 14) :
   'There are different snares for pheasants and partridges. The commonest is a thin wire or horsehair noose placed over a shallow hole, into which a few grains of wheat or barley are placed; so that when the pheasant puts his head into the hole to pick up the grain, the feathers on the back of the neck ruffle up, and, catching the noose when the head is drawn back, the slipknot tightens, and the pheasant is strangled. Again, in snaring partridges, little nooses of thin wire are placed in known runs at different elevations from the ground, from one to four inches, so that the partridges, when running along, slip their heads into the noose, and are caught. A very good way of catching pheasants, and in fact most birds, is with corn stuck on very fine hooks, with their wire end tied to some stumpage.'
   Other reports of snaring in early twentieth-century newspapers were either stories of 'olden times' or from boys, such as 'Reggie' in the 'Letters from the Little Folk' column in the *Witness*. He wrote to 'Dot', 'I live near the bush, and I sometimes have some good fun climbing trees, running after rabbits and snaring birds'. For an example of 'In Olden Times' see 'Maori v. Pigeons', *Evening Post*, 8 July 1909, page 8; 'Letters from the Little Folk', *Otago Witness*, 24 September 1902, page 67.
82  Young, *Our Islands, Our Selves*, page 99. For arguments about settlers' attitudes to the bush see also Geoff Park, *Nga uruora: Groves of Life: Ecology and history in a New Zealand landscape*; Star, 'From acclimatisation to preservation'.
83  Gibb and Flux, page 352.
84  Judith A Johnston, 'The New Zealand Bush: Early assessments of vegetation', *New Zealand Geographer*, vol 37, no 1, 1981, page 19.
85  E Campbell, 1840, cited in Johnston, page 21.
86  Clark, *The Invasion of New Zealand*, page 25.

87  See for example AF Mark, 'Responses of indigenous vegetation to contrasting trends in utilization by red deer in two southwestern New Zealand national parks', *New Zealand Journal of Ecology*, 12, 1989, pages 103–12.
88  Reverend P Walsh, 'The effect of deer on the New Zealand bush', *Transactions of the New Zealand Institute*, vol XXV, 1892, page 436.
89  Norman Elder cited in Mavis Davidson, 'Up in the Clouds: Deer and the Tararuas', *VUW Tramping Club, 50th anniversary publication*, page 54.
90  Bert Barra, letter dated 10 February 1941, www.nzdeercullers.org.nz (accessed June 2008).
91  Kirk, 1896 and Aston, 1912, both cited in Wodzicki, page 162.
92  Davidson, 'Up in the Clouds', page 54.
93  Victor Zotov, cited in Wodzicki, page 163.
94  Gibb and Flux, page 357.
95  See Wodzicki, pages 162–3.
96  King, page 114.
97  Davidson, 'Up in the Clouds', page 56.
98  Zotov, cited in Wodzicki, pages 193–4; Davidson, 'Up in the Clouds', pages 54–5.
99  Allan Perham cited in Wodzicki, page 193.
100 Leonard Cockayne cited in Wodzicki, page 193.
101 Wodzicki, pages 32, 164, 172; AD Thomson, 'Mason, Ruth 1913–1990', *Dictionary of New Zealand Biography*, updated 22 June 2007, www.dnzb.govt.nz.
102 Perham, cited in Wodzicki, page 193.
103 Haast, page 393.
104 Wodzicki, page 172.

**Chapter 2**
1   See for example Janet Davidson, *The Pre-history of New Zealand*; Athol Anderson, *The Welcome of Strangers: An ethno-history of southern Maori AD1650–1850*; Carmen McLeod, 'Pondering Nature: An ethnography of duck hunting in southern New Zealand' (PhD thesis).
2   Richard McGovern-Wilson, Fiona Kirk, Ian Smith, 'Small bird remains', page 229, cited in McLeod, page 72.
3   Bishop Augustus Selwyn in McLeod, page 75.
4   Edward Shortland, 'Journal notes kept while in the Middle Island', 15 January 1844, MS-440131 Hocken Library.
5   WH Skinner in McLeod, page 75.
6   David Burton, *Two Hundred Years of New Zealand Food and Cookery*, page 10.
7   David H Johnson, 'Review of *Forest Lore of the Maori* by Elsdon Best', *Journal of Mammalogy*, vol 27, no 3, August 1946, page 285.
8   William White to John Gare Butler, 13 July 1823, in RJ Barton (ed.), *Earliest New Zealand*, page 282.
9   John Boultbee, 1826 in Lydia Wevers (ed.), *Travelling to New Zealand: An Oxford anthology*, page 17.
10  Cited in Thomson, *Wild Life in New Zealand*, page 21.
11  Burton, page 16.
12  Elizabeth McDiarmid, 'Reminiscences', c.1916, MS-0579 Hocken Library, pages 1–2.
13  John Bethell, 'Pioneering in the Waitakere Ranges', *Auckland-Waikato Historical Journal*, April 1968, page 3.
14  McDiarmid, page 2.
15  Jean Boswell cited in Burton, page 25.
16  Charles Heaphy, *Narratives of a Residence in Various Parts of New Zealand*, page 32.
17  Maclean, *Tararua*, page 93.
18  Charles Bannister wrote an article for the *Wairarapa Times-Age* (15 December 1939, page 17) called

'Mountain Traverse in the Eighties. In search of Hapuakorari. How a Food Shortage was Overcome'.
19   In 1892 Douglas reported the disappearance of many species on the Copland River. (John Pascoe [ed.], *Mr Explorer Douglas*, page 174.)
20   Pascoe, pages 118, 146.
21   Ibid, page 136.
22   Ibid, page 123.
23   Ibid, pages 81, 89.
24   William Swainson, cited in Burton, page 17.
25   McDiarmid, pages 1–2.
26   Ernst Dieffenbach cited in The Pouakani Report, Waitangi Tribunal, section 3.2.
27   *New Zealand Railways Magazine*, 1 August 1930, page 42.
28   Viv Collings, interviewed by Kate Hunter, 4 March 2007.
29   Cameron, 'A History of the Camerons of Spring Hill, 1840–1900', WA, page 34.
30   Philip Kenway cited in GC Petersen, *Forest Homes: Scandinavian settlement in New Zealand*, page 104.
31   Cameron, page 52.
32   Hubert Ostler, 'Bushwhacking', *Otaki Historical Society Journal*, vol 20, 1997, page 38.
33   Alfred Barker, 18 June 1851, cited in EJ Burke, 'Reminiscences of "Old Canterbury"', ARC1900.109, folder 775, CM.
34   Henry Woulden, cited in Wevers, page 33.
35   Arnold, page 285
36   Ibid, page 11.
37   George Campbell, *The Golden North: Growing up in the Northern Wairoa*, page 24.
38   Bill Hiku and Pat Toi, Maori Linemen Oral History Project, OHC-016303, NLNZ.
39   'Memo: Deer Destruction — Employees' Food Supplies', 18 August 1936, IA1 18/2, ANZ.
40   Mrs E Du Pontet and Mrs AJ McCallion (eds.), *Falling Leaves of Memory as Gathered by the Eastern Bay of Plenty Federation of Country Women's Institutes*, page 86.
41   McDiarmid, page 2.
42   Jean Boswell, *Dim Horizons*, page 26.
43   Ibid, pages 54–5.
44   May Brown, 'Early days on the Northern Wairoa River', MS-Papers-2517, ATL, pages 15–6.
45   Kathleen M Bourke, *The Tui's Call*, pages 6, 37, 98.
46   Jill Brewis, *Colonial Fare*, page 67, Sarah Higgins, 'Autobiography, c.1920', MS-Papers-1146, ATL.
47   Jack Bull, Oral Archive 31, WA.
48   McConochie, pages 20–1.
49   Campbell, page 25.
50   Reweti T Kohere, *The Autobiography of a Maori*, page 39.
51   Mrs Howard Jackson, *Annals of a New Zealand Family: The household of Gilbert Mair, early pioneer*, pages 130–1.
52   McConochie, page 45.
53   Manawatu Acclimatisation Society Minute Books, 1956, IMA.
54   Campbell, page 9.
55   Ibid, page 20.
56   J Downie, letter, 4 September 1887, MSS443 A, 4007, NPM.
57   David Marino, OHInt-0610-3, NLNZ.
58   Sonny Te Ahuru, Tongariro Forest Project, OHInt-0425/9, NLNZ.
59   Ibid.
60   Fred Richards, Tongariro Forest Oral History Project, OHInt 0425/7, NLNZ.
61   Leys, page 496.
62   AD Rennie, *Tui's Third Book of Commonsense Cookery*, page 95.

63 Alfred Newberry, letter to Arthur Newberry, 14 December 1865, MS-Papers-4212, ATL. Trounce had been shot in July.
64 *Timaru Herald*, 2 August 1875, page 4.
65 Coroner's inquest into death of Cuthbert Harold Walker, 1899/313, ANZ.
66 The case was reported in the *Wanganui Herald*, 16 May 1902, page 2.
67 Coroner's inquest into death of Percy Stephenson, 1902/460, ANZ.
68 McDiarmid, page 7.
69 Caughley, pages 96–7
70 JF, pers. comm., December 2008.
71 Joe Green, 'To hunt and return: Developing safe hunting practice', New Zealand Police, 2003, www.police.govt.nz/service/firearms/safehunting.pdf, accessed September 2008.
72 Manawatu Acclimatisation Society Minute Book, IMA.
73 NZASA Minute Book, FGNZ.
74 NZASA Minute Book, FGNZ.
75 Charles Carter, *Life & Recollections of a New Zealand Colonist*, pages 94–101, cited in Wevers, pages 59–60.
76 *North Otago Times*, 1 May 1882, page 2; *Tuapeka Times*, 10 May 1882, page 5.
77 Rowland Lopdell, Cape Expedition Oral History Project, OHInt 0328-10, NLNZ. See also Fergus Sutherland, 'Keeping Watch', *New Zealand Geographic*, 17, January–March 1993, pages 70–80.
78 Sutherland, 'Keeping Watch', page 73.
79 Lopdell.
80 Alistair Duthie, Cape Expedition Oral History Project, OHInt-0328-08, NLNZ.
81 George Bish, Cape Expedition Oral History Project, OHInt-0328-03, NLNZ.
82 Lopdell.
83 Cameron, page 45
84 Boswell, page 130.
85 TE Donne, *Red Deer Stalking in New Zealand*, pages 256–64.
86 Mrs Isobel Broad, *The New Zealand Exhibition Cookery Book*; *Colonial Everyday Cookery*.
87 Broad, page 49.
88 Maud Basham, *Aunt Daisy's New Cookery No.6*; *New Zealand Listener*, 20 June 1947; Katrine Mackay, *Practical Cookery Chats and Recipes*; Kathleen Johnstone, *Self-Help Recipes and Household Hints*; *Waiau Cookery Book*.
89 *New Zealand Fishing & Shooting Gazette*, 1 July 1931, page 15.
90 *Taupo Deerstalkers 50th Anniversary: A history of the Taupo branch of the New Zealand Deerstalkers' Association, 1857–2007*, pages 13–4.
91 Edward Jerningham Wakefield, cited in Louis E Ward, *Early Wellington*, pages 105–6.
92 Reverend J Millar Thomson, *Bush Boys of New Zealand*, page 183.
93 'Personal Equipment', IA 78/8, ANZ.
94 Jon Knight, interviewed in *The Venison Hunters*, Southcoast Productions, 2004.
95 Ken Francis, *Wildlife Ranger: My years in the New Zealand outdoors*, page 25.

**Chapter 3**
1 Brian Burdon, *Hunting for a Buck*, pages 53–5.
2 Arnold, page 176.
3 Sowman, page 34.
4 *Taranaki Herald*, 19 December 1908, page 10.
5 *Evening Post*, 3 April 1884, page 3.
6 NZASA Minute Books, August 1912, FGNZ.
7 NZASA Minute Books, September 1925, FGNZ.

8. NZASA Minute Books, October 1932, FGNZ; *Evening Post*, 6 September 1906, page 2.
9. *Otago Witness*, 20 August 1891, page 15.
10. 'Export of venison carcasses', IA1 48/19 Part 1, ANZ.
11. Henry Buchanan, OHInt-0419/03, NLNZ.
12. 'Venison markets in Europe and Canada', *The Dominion*, 30 October 1958, page 13.
13. Henry Buchanan.
14. Mike Bennett, *The Venison Hunters*, page 33.
15. Bennett, pages 68–70.
16. Caughley, pages 90–94; Bennett, pages 152–3.
17. Burdon, page 9.
18. Ibid, page 18.
19. David Yerex, *Deer, the New Zealand Story*, pages 92–3; Caughley also has a chapter on deer farming, pages 107–17.
20. Graham Nugent, 'The conservation role of commercial deer hunting', Forest Research Institute Contract Report, FEW 92/3, pages 17ff.
21. Bill Black, interviewed in 'The Venison Hunters', Southcoast Productions, 2004.
22. Cited in Star, page 206.
23. Young, page 144.
24. McDowall, page 116.
25. Jack Bull, Oral Archive 31, WA. It's unclear which Wiffin brother Jack was talking about: Arthur had been to the South African War, but Ernie was in the Wellington Acclimatisation Society.
26. Ibid.
27. Addenbrooke, page 82.
28. Yerex, pages 31, 33.
29. Ross Galbreath, *Working for Wildlife: A history of the New Zealand Wildlife Service*, page 43.
30. DW Stewart, *From Fur to Fashion: The background story to the establishment of the New Zealand fur industry*, pages 9–10, 31–2.
31. Wodzicki, page 146.
32. Thomson cited in Wodzicki, page 27.
33. Wodzicki, page 27.
34. Addenbrooke, pages 101–2; Ben Thorpe, QEII National Trust Project, OHInt-0864-10, NLNZ; John Riseborough interviewed by Jonathan Kennett, OHInt-0830/13, NLNZ; Brian Woodley, 'Huntin', Shootin' and Fishin': a special way of life', 2005, WA.
35. Francis, page 8.
36. One example of this, although not for commercial gain, was a muff Greta Hyde had made from a swan skin. In the mid-1870s Hyde's mother had been out riding on Cheviot station in Canterbury and had come on a sawmillers' camp. The two millers had been very hospitable and served tea, damper and seagulls' eggs. One of the men, Joe Valentine, was clearly quite taken with Hyde's mother, because a little later he presented her with a swan skin that he had shot and cured.

    'For many years my mother had no use for such a 'trophy' so it was sprinkled with pepper and sealed in a tin. About thirty years later, when our family had gone to Christchurch to live, I took the swan skin from storage and made it into a muff. Besides being a fashionable accessory during the early 1900s, the thick, soft down of that bird kept my hands warm on many occasions.'

    (Greta Hyde, 'Memories of Early Cheviot', page 12, ARC1991.62, CM.)
37. Star, pages 143–5.
38. Docherty cited in Sally Burrage, 'Exchange of native bird skins, skeletons and eggs by Canterbury Museum from 1869–1913', *Records of the Canterbury Museum*, vol 15, December 2001, page 1. Rowi were only officially recognised as a distinct species in 2003, so Docherty was clearly using the Maori term for these birds.

39   Leo Barnes, letters from J Haast, 216/86 folder 797, CM.
40   Haast, page 557.
41   'Memo', 1931, DIA, IA78 Box 8, ANZ.
42   IA1 48/1, ANZ.
43   1 September 1938, IA1 48/1.
44   23 November 1939, IA1 48/1.
45   There are many references to these uses of deer skins in shooters' reminiscences. During World War Two a system of double-layered fuel tanks was developed, with one layer being vulcanized rubber and the other leather. This system was also used during the Korean War. (Omaka Aviation Heritage Centre, Blenheim, pers. comm., 12 January 2009). In 1943, the US Fish and Wildlife Service also began to solicit hunters for deer hides for the production of military equipment. See for example www.pgc.state.pa.us.
46   IA1 48/1, ANZ.
47   This is confirmed in letters from the department in the 1930s that referred to 'straight out wage payments up to a certain amount, the balance being composed of bonus according to the ability of the hunter concerned'. 12 July 1937, IA1 48/1, ANZ.
48   Yerex, page 43.
49   Yerex, page 41.
50   'Memo', 13 April 1944, IA1 48/1.
51   Caughley, page 82.
52   Caughley, page 83.
53   Galbreath, *Working for Wildlife*, pages 28–9.
54   Norman Hardie, *On My Own Two Feet*, page 15.
55   Hardie, page 17.
56   Hardie, page 26.
57   GF Yerex, cited in Galbreath, *Working for Wildlife*, pages 25–6.
58   IA 87 Box 8.
59   Cited in Galbreath, *Working for Wildlife*, pages 22–3.
60   Harry Wong Jnr, pers. comm., 8 December 2008.
61   Frank Buckland, cited in Christopher Lever, *They Dined on Eland: The story of the Acclimatisation Societies*, page 45.
62   James Ng, *Windows on a Chinese Past: Volume 3*, page 241; Yerex, page 74.
63   Robert Preston Bain, 'Journal of an expedition to the West Coast for the purpose of surveying 1863–4', Folder 723, CM.
64   See Eric Pawson, 'The meanings of mountains' in Pawson and Brooking, pages 136–9.
65   Thomas, cited in McLeod, page 102.
66   Anonymous, 1905 cited in Philip Holden, *The Golden Years of Hunting*, page 87.
67   Donne, *Red Deer Stalking*, page 47.
68   Major Robert A Wilson, *My Stalking Memories*, pages 129–30; RA Wilson, 'Conrad Hodgkinson and Jim Muir: Two Great Men of the Outdoor', *NZFSG*, January 1950, pages 4–6.
69   EJC Wiffin, 'Red deer stalking in South Westland', MS-Papers-7071–1, ATL.
70   Ibid.
71   *The Cyclopedia of New Zealand*, 1905, pp 761–2.
72   Ross Galbreath, *Walter Buller: The Reluctant Conservationist*, pages 25–6.
73   *Grey River Argus*, 4 September 1882; F398, GR Macdonald Dictionary of Canterbury Biographies, CM.
74   See *Otago Witness*, 10 February 1877, page 5; Galbreath, *Walter Buller*, page 142; advertisements in *Taranaki Herald*, 26 June 1903; *Evening Post*, 30 July 1895; *New Zealand Post Office Directories*.
75   *Evening Post*, 24 January 1896, page 2.
76   Galbreath, *Walter Buller*, page 142.

77  McDiarmid, page 5.
78  'Taxidermists', IA1 W2578/92 46/36, ANZ.
79  *Otago Witness*, 27 September 1905.
80  Tangaroa, 'Gun Making', *New Zealand Fishing & Shooting Gazette*, 2 January 1931, page 8.
81  Ibid, page 9.
82  Viv Collings interviewed by Kate Hunter, 4 March 2007.
83  Ibid.
84  Galbreath, *Working for Wildlife*, page 43.
85  FJ Lucas, *Popeye Lucas of Queenstown*, page 63.
86  www.doc.govt.nz/conservation/historic/by-region/southland/clark-hut, accessed December 2008.
87  Harry Scott, OHC4957, NLNZ.
88  Ibid.
89  Ibid.
90  Ibid.
91  Grant Fitz-William interviewed by Kate Hunter, 3 July 2007.
92  Ibid.
93  Ibid.
94  Jocelyn Rae, interviewed by Kate Hunter, 3 July 2007.
95  Ibid.

## Chapter 4

1  Grant Fitz-William, interviewed by Kate Hunter, July 2007.
2  Robert Shearing in Holden, page 146.
3  Viv Collings, interviewed by Kate Hunter, March 2007.
4  Chris Cosslett, interviewed by Kate Hunter, July 2008.
5  KW Fraser, 'Status and conservation role of recreational hunting on conservation land', *Science for Conservation* No. 140, page 9; Murray Williams, 'In praise of diaries', *Fish & Game New Zealand*, 18, 2004, pages 16–26.
6  DG Simmons and PJ Devlin, 'The recreational hunter', *Lincoln University College of Agriculture Bulletin*, no 33, 1980, page 47. See also KH Groome, D Simmons and LD Clark, 'The Recreational Hunter: Central North Island study', *Lincoln College Bulletin*, no 38, 1983.
7  Alexander Bathgate, 1874, pages 84–5, cited in McLeod, page 101.
8  Thomas, cited in McLeod, pages 101–2.
9  Ibid, page 102.
10  Barker, *Station Life*, page 193.
11  Barker, *Station Amusements in New Zealand*, page 30.
12  McConochie, page 46.
13  Hursthouse, page 80.
14  Ostler, 1997.
15  Montagu Cradock and William M Walnutt, cited in Holden, pages 86, 203.
16  Barker, *Station Amusements*, page 48.
17  McDiarmid, page 2.
18  Philip Kenway cited in Petersen, page 104.
19  F Whitley, 'Shooting diary 1888–1925', MSX-3800, ATL.
20  Walter Day, OA683, WA.
21  Dave Marino, interviewed by Kate Hunter, 30 April 2007; Fred Richards and Sonny Te Ahuru, Tongariro Forest Project, OHColl-0425, NLNZ.
22  Cameron, page 27.
23  Ibid, page 28.

24  Chris Laidlaw in Bill Sewell (ed.), *Sons of the Fathers: New Zealand men write about their fathers*, pages 45–6.
25  Jocelyn Rae, interviewed by Kate Hunter, 3 July 2007.
26  Muriel Henderson, Southland Oral History Project, OHColl-0464, NLNZ.
27  See the catalogue at the National Film Archive for the wide variety of films of hunting made by professionals and amateurs, www.filmarchive.org.nz.
28  Rae, interviewed by Kate Hunter, 3 July 2007.
29  Donne, *Red Deer Stalking*, page 683; *The Sun* (Christchurch), 23 July–6 August 1927; Holden, pages 321–35; see www.brown.edu/Research/Breaking_Ground for information on Mercy Money-Coutts; D Bruce Banwell, *Wapiti in New Zealand: The story of the Fiordland herd*, page 40.
30  *New Zealand Illustrated Magazine*, Mar 1901, April 1901, cited in Star, pages 200–1.
31  *New Zealand Illustrated Tourist Guide*, 1925, pages 233–4.
32  Banwell, *Highland Stags of Otago*.
33  Ibid; Leatham cited in Donne, *Red Deer Stalking*, page 3.
34  Donne, *The Game Animals of New Zealand*, pages 3–4.
35  Ibid, pages 283–4.
36  'Memo', 3 September 1935, IA 1 48/15, ANZ.
37  Ibid.
38  'Memo', 11 Sept 1935, JWA Heenan, MS-Papers-1132/Folder 316, ATL.
39  Ibid.
40  Clipping in file, IA 1 48/15.
41  Bill Monk, OHC-11457, NLNZ.
42  Yerex, page 51.
43  MM Davidson and KW Fraser, 'Official hunting patterns, and trends in the proportions of sika (*Cervus Nippon*) and red deer (*C. elaphus scoticus*) in the Kaweka Range, New Zealand, 1958–1988', *New Zealand Journal of Ecology*, 15, 1, 1991, pages 36–7.
44  Edgar J Russ cited in Camerons Community Club and Les Wright (eds.), *Between Two Rivers: A history of the Camerons community, Grey District, West Coast, 1865–2006*, pages 68–9.
45  Ross, page 89.
46  Ross, page 91. See also Yerex, page 37, for track-cutting in the Tararuas.
47  Yerex, page 68.
48  www.doc.govt.nz/parks-and-recreation/places-to-visit/wellington/wairarapa/tararua-forest-park/features/history/
49  'Papers relating to game hunting', Riddiford Family Papers, MS-Papers-5714-046, ATL.
50  'Particulars from Patons Leasing Agency', 'Papers relating to game hunting', Riddiford Family Papers, ATL.
51  Herbert Hart, 'Diary', 12 June 1926, 08–91, WA.
52  Hart, 'Diary' 25 September 1926; Hart, 'Diary or copies of letters written during shooting trip to Rhodesia in 1926', MSX-3897, ATL.
53  Salisbury Hut Book, December 1937–May 1957, AG209, NPM.
54  Ibid.
55  Ibid.
56  Ibid, 17 April 1942.
57  Ibid, 1944.
58  Ibid, 1943.
59  Ibid, 1938.
60  Herbert Hart, 'Rhodesia in 1926'.
61  J Holmes and Harold Thomas are both mentioned as wapiti hunters by Banwell in *Wapiti in New Zealand*, page 60.

62  *New Zealand Herald*, 5 November 1925, page 11.
63  J Holmes, 'My 1930 African Hunt', *New Zealand Fishing & Shooting Gazette*, 1 June 1931, page 20.
64  These wonderful books and many hundreds like them are in the Dorothy Neale White Collection, NLNZ.
65  'Tangataroa', 'This Shooting Business', *New Zealand Fishing & Shooting Gazette*, 1 July 1931, pages 7–8.
66  Ibid, page 8.
67  Kelly's & Co. catalogue, 1920s, Eph A GUN 1902–1957, NLNZ.
68  Viv Collings interviewed by Kate Hunter, 4 March 2007.
69  Gun catalogues all in the ephemera collection, Eph A GUN 1902–1957, NLNZ.

## Chapter 5

1  Young, page 60.
2  Sally Gregory Kohlstedt, 'International exchange in the natural history enterprise', in RW Home and SG Kohlstedt (eds.), *International Science and National Scientific Identity*, pages 121–49.
3  Kohlstedt, page 124.
4  *Australasian* journalist cited in Haast, page 840.
5  Burrage, pages 2–3.
6  Walter Buller, cited in Ross Galbreath, *Walter Buller*, page 24.
7  Galbreath, *Walter Buller*, page 142.
8  Ibid.
9  Ibid, pages 143–45.
10 Ibid.
11 Ibid, page 143.
12 Haast, page 549.
13 Ibid, page 555; Correspondence with Leo Barnes, 1874, 216/86 Folder 797, CM.
14 Burrage, pages 1–2.
15 Haast, page 555.
16 Although this file is labelled 'chamois' there is a surprising amount about kiwis in it. IA78 5 1901/178/63 Part 1.
17 Walter Buller, 'On the proposed introduction of the Polecat into New Zealand', *Proceedings of the New Zealand Institute*, 9 (2), 1876, page 634.
18 See Star; King, page 60.
19 JD Enys, 'An account of the Maori manner of preserving the Skin of the Huia, *Heteralocha auctirostris*, Buller', *Transactions and Proceedings of the Royal Society of New Zealand*, vol 8, 1875, page 205.
20 Star, page 21.
21 Potts in *Nature*, 1872, cited in Star pages 142–3.
22 Star, page 163.
23 Potts, cited in Star, page 162.
24 Thomas Potts, *Out in the Open*, pages 195–6. See also Star, pages 162–3.
25 Paul Star and Lynne Lochhead, 'Children of the Burnt Bush: New Zealanders and the indigenous remnant, 1880–1930' in Pawson and Brooking, page 119. See also Star, 'From acclimatisation to preservation'.
26 Young, page 63.
27 Star and Lochhead, page 121. See also Beattie and Star, 'State forest conservation and the New Zealand landscape' in Ballantyne and Bennett (eds.).
28 Thomas Donne, cited in Star and Lochhead, page 127.
29 Young, page 76.
30 Potts, pages 285–8.
31 Aldo Leopold, cited in Loo, page 26.
32 Onslow, cited in Young, page 92.

33  See Loo; Warren; Beinart; Hughes.
34  McLeod, page 100.
35  Roberts, 1895, pages 52–3, cited in McLeod, page 100.
36  Cameron, page 49.
37  Brown, pages 15–6.
38  Charlie Douglas, cited in Young, page 80.
39  Young, page 88.
40  Graeme Wynn, 'Destruction under the guise of improvement? The forest 1840–1920' in Pawson and Brooking, page 113.
41  See Dave Forsyth et al., 'Estimating changes in deer abundance using faecal pellet indices', *Kararehe Kino: Vertebrate Pest Research*, vol 7, Dec 2005, pages 11–2.
42  Galbreath, *Working for Wildlife*, pages 70–1; Caughley, pages 70–1.
43  Caughley, page 73.
44  Ibid, pages 72–3.
45  Bill Bryson, *A Short History of Nearly Everything*, pages 161–3.
46  Alison Ballance, *Southern Alps: Nature and history of New Zealand's mountain world*, page 62.
47  Viv Collings, interviewed by Kate Hunter, 4 March 2007.
48  Yerex, pages 106–7; Patrick J Grant, 'A hydrologist's contribution to the debate on wild animal management', *New Zealand Journal of Ecology*, 12 (s), 1989, pages 165–9.
49  Yerex, page 107.
50  Deer Menace Conference, Christchurch, 7 May 1930, IA1 23/36/78, Part 1, ANZ.
51  Galbreath, *Working for Wildlife*, page 68.
52  AL Poole (ed.), *New Zealand-American Fiordland Expedition*; Galbreath, *Working for Wildlife*, pages 66–9.
53  Peter McKelvey, 'Yerex, George Franklyn 1893–1967', *Dictionary of New Zealand Biography*, www.dnzb.govt.nz
54  Yerex, pages 43–4.
55  DIA annual report, 1931, cited in and quote from Caughley, page 29.
56  Francis, page 54.
57  Dear Menace Conference, 1930.
58  Caughley, page 25.
59  Ibid, page 26.
60  DoC Wairarapa newsletter, 2000, cited on www.nzdeercullers.org.nz; Caughley estimates Barra shot 14,000 deer in the South Island alone (Caughley, page 42).
61  Yerex, page 48.
62  Galbreath, *Working for Wildlife*, pages 70–1.
63  Yerex, page 64.
64  'Economy in Danger from Deer', *New Zealand Herald*, 31 October 1958, page 31.
65  'Pests All Harmful', *Otago Daily Times*, 30 October 1958, page 5.
66  'Poisoning of Deer: violent reactions in US reported', *The Press*, 28 October 1958, page 10.
67  See for example AB Rose and K Platt, 'Montane and alpine grassland community ecology: recovery of northern Fiordland alpine grasslands after reduction in deer population', Forest Research Institute Report; Graham Nugent, 'The conservation role of commercial deer hunting'.
68  Caughley, page 104.
69  Young, pages 168–9.
70  See Nugent; Fraser and Speedy; Groome et al; Chris Cosslett, 'Deer, recreational hunting and indigenous biodiversity', Forest & Bird Environmental Report.
71  RH Triall, 'Diaries, 1925–1952', AG-816, Hocken Library; Murray Williams, 'In praise of diaries', pages 16–26.
72  Jocelyn Rae, interviewed by Kate Hunter, July 2007.

**Epilogue**
1   www.beef.org.nz/statistics, accessed January 2009.
2   Inspector Joe Green, 'Arms control strategies: debunking the myths', 2008, www.police.govt.nz, accessed January 2009.

# Illustration credits

Archives New Zealand: 41 (bottom), 52 (bottom), 67, 70 (left, right), 84, 129 (top), 130 (bottom), 133, 151, 155, 208, 217 (bottom), 261, 277, 278.
Alexander Turnbull Library: 32, 36, 38, 41 (top), 45, 55 (right), 59, 64, 78, 80, 86, 89, 91, 92, 94, 98, 103, 104, 105 (top), 114, 119, 126 (top right, bottom), 138, 143 (bottom), 150, 154, 164, 166 (left, right), 169, 171, 174, 178, 193 (left, right), 204, 206, 207, 212, 214, 220, 227 (top right), 230, 232, 241, 243, 244, 247, 248, 251, 254, 259.
Department of Conservation: 50, 130 (top), 143 (top), 144, 265, 274, 275.
Macmillan Brown Library: 52 (top).
National Library of Australia: 49, 63, 56–57.
Nelson Provincial Museum: 24, 35, 54 (top), 55 (left), 96, 126 (top left), 175, 176, 192, 195, 202, 223.
Te Papa Tongarewa: 120, 142, 146, 240.
Wairarapa Archive: 23, 213.
Private collections: Athol Geddes, 157 (bottom right); B and A Woodley, 100; D and V Collings, 177 (bottom), 198, 217 (top left, right); Dave Hansford, 281; Foster family, 20; Ian Buchan, 116, 157 (top), 165; J Fogden, 135 (top, bottom); JR Rolfe, 15; M Bartram, 227 (top left, bottom); Nancy Jordan, 268; QW (Joe) Hansen, 129 (bottom), 157 (bottom left), 190; R Cross, 177 (top); R Tankersley, 105 (bottom), 200, 201.

# Bibliography

*Abbreviations*

| | |
|---|---|
| ATL | Alexander Turnbull Library |
| CM | Canterbury Museum, Christchurch |
| FGNZ | Fish & Game New Zealand |
| HL | Hocken Library, Dunedin |
| IMA | Ian Matheson City Archives, Palmerston North |
| NLA | National Library of Australia |
| NLNZ | National Library of New Zealand |
| NPM | Nelson Provincial Museum |
| NZASA | New Zealand Acclimatisation Societies Association |
| NZPD | New Zealand Parliamentary Debates |
| WA | Wairarapa Archive, Masterton |

## Published sources

Addenbrooke, Mervyn, *Home from the Hill: My life story, ninety years of farm-working and hunting in the North Island*, Palmerston North, 1992.

Anderson, Athol, *The Welcome of Strangers: An ethno-history of southern Maori AD1650–1850*, Dunedin, 1998.

Arnold, Rollo, *The Farthest Promised Land: English villagers, New Zealand immigrants of the 1870s*, Wellington, 1981.

Baden-Powell, Sir Robert, *Scouting for Boys*, London, (1908) 1916.

Ballance, Alison, *Southern Alps: Nature and history of New Zealand's mountain world*, Auckland, 2007.

Banwell, D Bruce, *Highland Stags of Otago*, Wellington, 1968.

———, *Wapiti in New Zealand: The story of the Fiordland herd*, Wellington, 1966.

Barker, Lady Mary-Anne, *A Year's Housekeeping in South Africa*, London, 1879.

———, *Station Amusements in New Zealand*, London, 1873.

———, *Station Life in New Zealand: with introduction and notes by Betty Gilderdale*, Auckland, 2000.

Barton, RJ (ed.), *Earliest New Zealand*, Masterton, 1927.

Basham, Maud, *Aunt Daisy's New Cookery No.6*, Christchurch, 1947.

Beattie, James and Paul Star, 'State forest conservation and the New Zealand landscape: Origins and influences, 1850–1914' in Tony Ballantyne and Judith Bennett (eds.), *Landscape/Community: Perspectives from New Zealand history*, Dunedin, 2005.

Beinart, William and Lottie Hughes, *Environment and Empire*, Oxford, 2007.
Bennett, Mike, *The Venison Hunters*, Wellington, 1979.
Bethell, John, 'Pioneering in the Waitakere Ranges', *Auckland-Waikato Historical Journal*, 12 April 1968, pages 3–5.
Boswell, Jean, *Dim Horizons*, Wellington, 1956.
Bourke, Kathleen M, *The Tui's Call*, Napier, ca. 1970.
Brewis, Jill, *Colonial Fare*, Auckland, 1982.
Broad, Mrs Isobel, *The New Zealand Exhibition Cookery Book*, Nelson, 1889.
Bryson, Bill, *A Short History of Nearly Everything*, London, 2003.
Buller, Walter, 'On the proposed introduction of the Polecat into New Zealand', *Transactions and Proceedings of the New Zealand Institute*, 9 (2), 1876, pages 634–5.
Burdon, Brian, *Hunting for a Buck*, Auckland, 1994.
Burrage, Sally, 'Exchange of native bird skins, skeletons and eggs by Canterbury Museum from 1869–1913', *Records of the Canterbury Museum*, vol.15, December 2001, pages 1–7.
Burton, David, *Two Hundred Years of New Zealand Food and Cookery*, Wellington, 1982.
Camerons Community Club and Les Wright (eds.), *Between Two Rivers: A history of the Camerons community, Grey District, West Coast, 1865–2006*, Westland, 2006.
Campbell, George, *The Golden North: Growing up in the Northern Wairoa*, Auckland, 1963.
Carle, CS, *Forty Mile Bush: A tribute to the pioneers*, Pahiatua, 1980.
Caughley, Graeme *The Deer Wars: The story of deer in New Zealand*, Auckland, 1983.
Clark, AH, *The Invasion of New Zealand by People, Plants and Animals*, New Brunswick, 1949.
Clarke, CMH and RM Dzieciolowski, 'Feral pigs in the northern South Island, New Zealand. I: Origins, distribution and density', *Journal of the Royal Society of New Zealand*, 21 (3), 1991, pages 237–47.
*Colonial Everyday Cookery*, Christchurch, 1901.
Cosslett, Chris, 'Deer, recreational hunting and indigenous biodiversity', Forest & Bird Environmental Report, 1998.
Davidson, Janet, *The Pre-history of New Zealand*, Auckland, 1984.
Davidson, Mavis, 'Deer in the Tararua Story', *Tararua*, 1960.
———, 'Up in the Clouds: Deer and the Tararuas', *VUW Tramping Club 50th anniversary publication*, Wellington, 1971.
Davidson, MM and KW Fraser, 'Official hunting patterns, and trends in the proportions of sika (*Cervus Nippon*) and red deer (*C. elaphus scoticus*) in the Kaweka Range, New Zealand, 1958–1988', *New Zealand Journal of Ecology*, 15 (1), 1991, pages 31–40.
Donne, TE, *Red Deer Stalking in New Zealand*, London, 1924.

———, *The Game Animals of New Zealand*, London, 1924.

Du Pontet, Mrs D and McCallion, Mrs AJ (eds.), *Falling Leaves of Memory as Gathered by the Eastern Bay of Plenty Federation of Country Women's Institutes*, Opotiki, 1963.

Enys, JD, 'An account of the Maori manner of preserving the Skin of the Huia, *Heteralocha auctirostris*, Buller', *Transactions and Proceedings of the Royal Society of New Zealand*, vol 8, 1875, pages 204–5.

Forest & Bird Protection Society, *Damage to Native Forests*, Wellington, 1935.

Forsyth, Dave et al., 'Estimating changes in deer abundance using faecal pellet indices', *Kararehe Kino: Vertebrate Pest Research*, volume 7, Dec 2005, pages 11–2.

Francis, Ken, *Wildlife Ranger: My years in the New Zealand outdoors*, Christchurch, 1983.

Fraser, KW, 'Status and conservation role of recreational hunting on conservation land', *Science for Conservation* No. 140, Department of Conservation, Wellington, 2000.

Fraser, KW and CJ Speedy, 'Can recreational hunting pressure help to limit the impacts of sika deer in the Kaimanawa Recreational Hunting Area?', *Target Taupo*, no 23, November, 1996, pages 3–10.

Galbreath, Ross, *Walter Buller: The reluctant conservationist*, Wellington, 1989.

———, *Working for Wildlife: A history of the New Zealand Wildlife Service*, Wellington, 1993.

Gibb, JA and JEC Flux, 'Mammals' in Gordon R Williams (ed.), *A Natural History of New Zealand: An ecological survey*, Wellington, 1973.

Grant, Patrick J, 'A hydrologist's contribution to the debate on wild animal management', *New Zealand Journal of Ecology*, 12 (s), 1989, pages 165–9.

Groome, KH, D Simmons and LD Clark, 'The Recreational Hunter: Central North Island study', *Lincoln College Bulletin*, no. 38, 1983.

Haast, HF von, *The Life and Times of Sir Julius von Haast: Explorer, geologist, museum builder*, Wellington, 1948.

Hardie, Norman, *On My Own Two Feet*, Christchurch, 2006.

Heaphy, Charles, *Narratives of a Residence in Various Parts of New Zealand*, reprint Christchurch, 1998 (1842).

Hill, Richard S, *State Authority, Indigenous Autonomy: Crown-Maori relationships in New Zealand/Aotearoa, 1900–1950*, Wellington, 2004.

Holden, Philip, *The Golden Years of Hunting*, Auckland, 1983.

*Hunting and Fishing in Marlborough: A history of the Marlborough Acclimatisation Society, 1873–1980*, Blenheim, 1980.

Hursthouse, Charles, *New Zealand, the 'Britain of the South'*, London, 1861.

Jackson, Mrs Howard, *Annals of a New Zealand Family: The household of Gilbert Mair, early pioneer*, Dunedin, 1935.

Johnson, David H, 'Review of *Forest Lore of the Maori* by Elsdon Best', *Journal of*

*Mammalogy*, 27 (3), August 1946, pages 284–5.

Johnston, Judith A, 'The New Zealand bush: Early assessments of vegetation', *New Zealand Geographer*, 37 (1), 1981, pages 19–24.

Johnstone, Kathleen, *Self-Help Recipes and Household Hints*, Wellington, 1932.

Kelly, Michael, 'Wild Animal Control Huts: A National Heritage Identification Study for Department of Conservation', Wellington, 2007.

King, Carolyn, *Immigrant Killers: Introduced predators and the conservation of birds in New Zealand*, Auckland, 1984.

Kohere, Reweti T, *The Autobiography of a Maori*, Wellington, 1951.

Kohlstedt, Sally Gregory, 'International exchange in the natural history enterprise', in RW Home and SG Kohlstedt (eds.), *International Science and National Scientific Identity*, Dordrecht, 1991.

Landry, Donna, *The Invention of the Countryside: Hunting, walking and ecology in English literature, 1671–1831*, Hampshire, 2001.

Lever, Christopher, *They Dined on Eland: The story of the Acclimatisation Societies*, London, 1992.

Leys, Thomas W (ed.), *Brett's Colonists' Guide and Cyclopaedia of Useful Knowledge*, Auckland, 1883.

Loo, Tina, *States of Nature: Conserving Canada's wildlife in the twentieth century*, Vancouver, 2006.

Lucas, FJ, *Popeye Lucas of Queenstown*, Dunedin, 1968.

Mackay, Katrine, *Practical Cookery Chats and Recipes*, Christchurch, 1929.

MacKenzie, John, *Empire of Nature: Hunting, conservation and British imperialism*, Manchester, 1988

Maclean, Chris, *Tararua: The story of a mountain range*, Wellington, 1994.

Mark, AF, 'Responses of indigenous vegetation to contrasting trends in utilization by red deer in two southwestern New Zealand national parks', *New Zealand Journal of Ecology*, 12, 1989, pp.103–12.

McAloon, Jim, *Nelson: A regional history*, Whatamango Bay, 1997.

McConochie, Newton, *You'll Learn No Harm from the Hills*, Auckland, (1965) 1987.

McDowall, RM, *Gamekeepers for the Nation*, Christchurch, 1994.

McIntyre, Roberta, *Whose high country? A history of the South Island high country of New Zealand*, Auckland, 2008.

McLure, Margaret, *The Wonder Country*, Auckland, 2004.

Nelson, Roy, *Deer and Resulting Devastation in New Zealand: a review of the concern and evidence presented over the last 100 years*, Wellington, 1979.

*New Zealand Illustrated Tourist Guide*, 1925.

*New Zealand Parliamentary Debates*

Ng, James, *Windows on a Chinese Past: Volume 3*, Dunedin, 1999.

Nugent, G, 'The conservation role of commercial deer hunting', Forest Research Institute Contract Report, 92/3, Christchurch, 1992.

Ostler, Hubert, 'Bushwhacking', *Otaki Historical Society Journal*, vol. 20, 1997, pages 36–9.

Park, Geoff, *Nga Uruora: The Groves of Life: Ecology and History in a New Zealand landscape*, Wellington, 1995.

Pascoe, John (ed.), *Mr Explorer Douglas*, Wellington, 1957.

Pawson, Eric and Tom Brooking (eds.), *Environmental Histories of New Zealand*, Melbourne, 2002.

Petersen, GC, *Forest Homes: Scandinavian settlement in New Zealand*, Wellington, 1956.

*Pioneers of Canterbury: Deans Letters, 1840–1854*, Wellington, 1937.

AL Poole (ed.), *New Zealand-American Fiordland Expedition*, Wellington, 1951.

Potts, Thomas, *Out in the Open*, Christchurch, 1882.

Rennie, AD, *Tui's Third Book of Commonsense Cookery*, Wellington, ca. 1950.

Rose, AB and K Platt, 'Montane and alpine grassland community ecology: recovery of northern Fiordland alpine grasslands after reduction in deer population', Forest Research Institute Report, Christchurch, 1988.

Ross, Kirstie, *Going Bush: New Zealanders and nature in the twentieth century*, Auckland, 2008.

Sewell, Bill (ed.), *Sons of the fathers: New Zealand men write about their fathers*, North Shore City, 1997.

Shepard, Paul, *English Reaction to the New Zealand Landscape before 1850*, Pacific Viewpoint Monograph No. 4, Wellington, 1969.

Simmons, DG and PJ Devlin, 'The recreational hunter', *Lincoln University College of Agriculture Bulletin*, no. 33, 1980.

Sowman, WCR, *Meadow, Mountain, Forest and Stream: The provincial history of the Nelson Acclimatisation Society*, Nelson, 1981.

Stewart, DW, *From Fur to Fashion: The background story to the establishment of the New Zealand fur industry*, self-published, Dunedin, 1991.

Sutherland, Fergus, 'Keeping Watch', *New Zealand Geographic,* issue 17, January–March 1993, pages 70–80.

*Taupo Deerstalkers 50th anniversary: A history of the Taupo branch of the New Zealand Deerstalkers' Association, 1857–2007*, Taupo, 2007.

*The Cyclopedia of New Zealand*, Wellington, 1905.

Thom, David, *Heritage: The parks of the people*, Auckland, 1987.

Thomson, GM, *The Naturalisation of Animals and Plants in New Zealand*, Cambridge, 1922.

———, *Wild Life in New Zealand, Part I: Mammals*, Wellington 1921.

———, *Wild Life in New Zealand, Part II: Introduced Birds and Fishes*, Wellington, 1926.
Thomson, J Millar (Reverend), *Bush Boys of New Zealand*, London, 1905.
*Waiau Cookery Book*, Christchurch, 1933.
Walsh, P (Reverend), 'The effect of deer on the New Zealand bush', *Transactions of the New Zealand Institute*, vol. XXV, 1892, pages 435–9.
Ward, Louis E, *Early Wellington*, Wellington, 1928.
Warren, Loius S, *The Hunter's Game: Poachers and conservationists in twentieth-century America*, New Haven, 1997.
Wevers, Lydia (ed.), *Travelling to New Zealand: An Oxford anthology*, Auckland, 2000.
*Wild Life problems: the question of control. Recent articles by 'Mamaku' with replies from LOH Tripp*, Wellington, 1930.
Williams, Murray, 'In praise of diaries', *Fish & Game New Zealand*, 18, 2004, pages 16–26.
Wilson, RA, 'Conrad Hodgkinson and Jim Muir: Two Great Men of the Outdoor', *NZFSG*, January 1950.
———, *My Stalking Memories*, Wellington, (1961) 1978.
Wodzicki, KA, *Introduced Mammals of New Zealand*, Wellington, 1950.
Yerex, David, *Deer, the New Zealand Story*, Christchurch, 2001.
Young, David, *Our Islands, Our Selves: A history of conservation in New Zealand* Dunedin, 2004.


## Newspapers and magazines
*Bay of Plenty Times*
*The Dominion*
*The Evening Post*
*The Field*
*Grey River Argus*
*Hawera and Normanby Star*
*New Zealand Fishing & Shooting Gazette*
*New Zealand Herald*
*New Zealand Illustrated Magazine*
*New Zealand Listener*
*New Zealand Railways Magazine*
*North Otago Times*
*Otago Witness*
*The Press*
*The Sun*

*Taranaki Herald*
*Timaru Herald*
*Tuapeka Times*
*Wairarapa Times-Age*
*Wanganui Herald*
*West Coast Times*

**Unpublished manuscripts**

Ashworth, James, 'Recollections of "Harleston", Sefton, September 1918', ARC 1900.61, Folder 599, CM.

Bain, Robert Preston, 'Journal of an expedition to the West Coast for the purpose of surveying, 1863–4', Folder 723, CM.

Baker, George, 'Reminiscences of early Kaiapoi, 1862', ARC1989.34 Folder 675, CM.

Barnes, Leo, Letters from Julius von Haast, 1873–5, 216/86 Folder 797, CM.

Brown, May, 'Early days on the Northern Wairoa River', MS-Papers-2517, ATL.

Burke, EJ, 'Reminiscences of "Old Canterbury"', ARC1900.109 Folder 775, CM.

Cameron, Robert 'A history of the Camerons of Spring Hill, 1840–1900', 93-6/1. R3B6S4, WA.

Comyns, Mary Adeline, 'Life with Father and friends', 140/78 Folder 700, CM.

Dawber, Robert, 'Robert and Rebecca Dawber', 251/74, CM.

Dawbin, William, 'Diary', Series 1, Box 1, IMA.

Downie, J, letter, 4 September 1887, MSS443 A, 4007, NPM.

GR Macdonald Dictionary of Canterbury Biographies, CM.

Hart, Herbert, 'Diary or copies of letters written during shooting trip to Rhodesia in 1926', MSX-3897, ATL.

Hart, Herbert, 'Diary', 08-91, WA.

Heenan, JWA, MS-Papers-1132/Folder 316, ATL.

Hewson, A, 'Early days in the Ashburton County', ARC1900.257, CM.

Higgins, Sarah, 'Autobiography, c.1920', MS-Papers 1146, ATL.

Hyde, Greta, 'Memories of Early Cheviot', ARC1991.62, CM.

Manawatu Acclimatisation Society Minute Books, IMA.

McDiarmid, Elizabeth, 'Reminiscences', ca. 1916, MS-0579, HL.

New Zealand Acclimatisation Societies Association Minute Books, FGNZ.

Alfred Newberry, letter to Arthur Newberry, 14 December 1865, MS-Papers-4212, ATL.

Riddiford Family Papers, MS-Papers-5714-046, ATL.

Salisbury Hut Book, December 1937–May 1957, AG209, NPM.

Shortland, Edward, 'Journal notes kept while in the Middle Island', 15 January 1844, MS-0024, HL.
Stahl (née Foster), Eleanor, 'Recollections of Grandmother Lucy Foster (née Grierson) and Reginald Foster', ARC1900.437, CM.
Triall, RH, 'Diaries, 1925-1952', AG-816, HL.
Whitley, F, 'Shooting diary', MSX-3800, ATL.
Wiffin, EJC, 'Red deer stalking in South Westland', MS Papers-7070-1, ATL.
Woodley, Brian, *Huntin', Shootin', Fishing': A special way of life*, self-published, WA.

## Theses

Aramakutu, Evaan, 'Colonists and Colonials: Animals' protection legislation in New Zealand, 1861–1910', MA thesis, Massey University, 1997.
Brennan, Claire, 'Imperial Game: A history of hunting, society, exotic species and the environment in New Zealand and Victoria, 1840–1901', PhD thesis, University of Melbourne, 2004.
McLeod, Carmen, 'Pondering Nature: An ethnography of duck hunting in southern New Zealand', PhD thesis, University of Otago, 2004.
Star, Paul, 'From Acclimatisation to Preservation: Colonists and the natural world in southern New Zealand, 1860–1894', PhD thesis, University of Otago, 1997.

## Waitangi Tribunal reports

Coombes, Brad, 'Making "scenes of nature and sport" — resource and wildlife management in Te Urewera, 1895–1954', Wellington, 2003.
Feldman, James, 'Treaty rights and pigeon poaching: alienation of Maori access to kereru, 1864–1960', Wellington, 2001.
Marr, Cathy, Robin Hodge and Ben White, 'Crown Laws, Policies and Practices in Relation to Flora and Fauna, 1840–1912', Wellington, 2001.
Park, Geoff, 'Effective Exclusion? An exploratory overview of Crown actions and Maori responses concerning indigenous flora and fauna, 1912–1983', Wellington, 2001.
The Pouakani Report, Wellington, 1993.

## Archives New Zealand

Chamois IA78 5 1901/178/63 Part 1.
Coroners' Inquests, Reports, Indexes and Registers.
Deer Menace Conference, Christchurch, 7 May 1930, IA1 23/36/78, Part 1.

Department of Internal Affairs files relating to personnel of the Deer Control Section:
IA 1 18 Box 2, IA 1 48 Box 1, IA 1 48 Box 2/1, IA 1 48 Box 2/2, IA 1 48 Box 15, IA 78 Box 5, IA 78 Box 8.
Export of venison carcasses, IA1 48 Box 19 Part 1.
Taxidermists, IA1 W2578/92 46/36.
Inquests.

## Photographs and albums
Brown, Thomas W, Album 1900–1920, PA1-o-075, ATL.
Furkert, F, Albums, PA1-o-078, ATL.
Hart, Herbert, Negatives of hunting in Rhodesia, PAColl 1197, ATL.
Hart, Herbert, A wapiti hunt on the West Coast [Fiordland], PA1-o-714, ATL.
Iorns, Bennett, Photographs, 04-159/3.R7B2S8, WA.
Wallace, Gavin, Album of family, friends and holidays, PA1-f-182, ATL.

## Oral histories
*National Library of New Zealand*
Ben Thorpe, interviewed by Shona McCahon, 2007, QEII National Trust Project, OHInt-0864-10.
Bill Hadfield, 1998, OHInt-0417/1.
Bill Monk, interviewed 1992, OHC-011457
Bruce Ferguson, interviewed by Carol Dawber, 2000, OHColl-0489/1.
David Marino, interviewed by Michael Walsh, 1996, OHInt-0610-3.
Henry Buchanan, interviewed 1995–6, OHInt-0419/03.
John Riseborough, interviewed by Jonathan Kennett, Otari Bush Project, OHInt 0830/13.
Muriel Henderson, interviewed by Beth Cairns, 1988, Southland Oral History Project, OHInt-0464/08.
Ted Buchanan, 1996, OHInt-0419/02.
*Arthur's Pass Oral History Project, OHColl-0049:*
Harry Scott, interviewed by Kay Holder, 1992, OHInt-0049/7.
Ray Cleland, OHInt-0049/3.
*Cape Expedition Oral History Project, OHColl-0328:*
Alistair Duthie, interviewed by Fergus Sutherland, 1991, OHInt-0328-08.
George Bish, interviewed by Fergus Sutherland, 1991, OHInt-0328-03.
Rowland Lopdell, interviewed by Fergus Sutherland, 1991, OHInt 0328-10.

*Maori Linemen Oral History Project, OHC-016303.*
    Pat Toi, interviewed by David Young.
    William (Bill) Hiku, interviewed by David Young.
*Tongariro Forest Oral History Project, OHColl-0425:*
    Fred Richards, interviewed by Jonathan Kennett, 1998, OHInt 0425/7.
    Kevin Smith, 1998, OHInt-0425/8.
    Sonny Te Ahuru & Kepa Patena, interviewed by Jonathan Kennett, October 1998, OHInt-0425/9.

*Wairarapa Archive, Masterton*
Adi Paku
Albert Speedy
Duncan McPhee
Jack Bull, interviewed by Alison Thompson, 1991
Kuini Te Tau
Norman Bull
Walter Day

*Interviewed by author*
Chris Cosslett
Dave Marino
Grant Fitz-William
Jocelyn Rae
Viv Collings

## Personal communications

Wong, Harry Jnr, 8 December 2008
Omaka Aviation Heritage Centre, Blenheim, 12 January 2009.

## Websites

Clark Hut, www.doc.govt.nz/conservation/historic/by-region/southland/clark-hut/
Galbreath, Ross, 'Sanderson, Ernest Valentine 1866–1945', *Dictionary of New Zealand Biography*, www.dnzb.govt.nz
Green, Joe, 'To hunt and return: Developing safe hunting practice', New Zealand

Police, 2003, www.police.govt.nz/service/firearms/safehunting.pdf
McKelvey, Peter, 'Yerex, George Franklyn 1893–1967', *Dictionary of New Zealand Biography*, www.dnzb.govt.nz
Thomson, AD, 'Mason, Ruth 1913–1990'. *Dictionary of New Zealand Biography*, updated 22 June 2007, www.dnzb.govt.nz
www.brown.edu/Research/Breaking_Ground
www.doc.govt.nz/parks-and-recreation/places-to-visit/wellington/wairarapa/tararua-forest-park/features/history/
www.filmarchive.org.nz
www.nzdeercullers.org.nz
www.victorianartinbritain.co.uk/biog/landseer.htm

**Film**

*The Venison Hunters*, Southcoast Productions, 2004.

**Ephemera and objects**

Cigarette Cards, Eph A PICTURE CARDS, Wills Sport, c.1927, ATL.
Eph HUNTING, ATL.
Eph TOURISM, ATL.
Gun catalogues, Eph A GUN 1902-1957, ATL.

# Index

Abbott, Rick  280
Abel Tasman National Park  71
accidents  109–11, 176, 258
acclimatisation  22, 38, 46–7, 107, 210, 258
  Maori rights discontent  58
  records  12, 48
  society meetings  58, 103, 228
acclimatisation societies  19, 31, 33, 43–4, 47, 51, 56–8, 65, 73, 112, 119, 127–8, 142–3, 145–6, 173, 196
Acland, John  48
Adam, Alex  197
Adam, James  197
Adams, Earnest  205
Addenbrooke, Mervyn  145, 147
advertisements  13, 131, 211–12
  chamois  209–12
  deer-stalking  209–12
  gun catalogues  231, 233–4, 242
aerial hunting industry  130, 154, 218, 276, 279
Africa  37, 39, 54, 135, 219–20, 230
agriculture  20, 33, 66, 71, 77–8, 134, 140, 144, 247, 262
aircraft  127, 130, 134, 136–7, 178, 179 — see also helicopters and specific types
  helicopters  111, 121, 127, 129–30, 134, 137–8, 140, 184, 224, 275–6
Akatarawa Forest  199
Akitu  84–5
Alaska  135
Albert Burn  180
Albury estate  246
Allom, Thomas  56
Alpine Fault  264
American–New Zealand Fiordland Expedition (1949)  269, 277
ammunition  48, 85–5, 90, 98–9, 115, 128, 145, 152, 154, 162–3, 179, 203, 209, 231, 234, 272
Anderson, E  59
angora goats  50
animals — see specific types
Animals Protection Act (1895)  60–2, 65
Antipodes Islands  51
antlers  127, 146, 152, 164, 166, 176, 205–6, 209–10
Aoroa  93, 99
Arawhata Valley  158
Arch, Joseph  42
Arete  84
arsenic  172, 174, 239
Arundel  174
Ashworth, James  50
Asia  22, 44, 230, 262
Atkinson, Rt Hon Sir Harry  65
attitudes to hunting, colonists' and settlers'  19–21, 27, 31, 33, 66, 229, 241, 261
Auckland  58, 64, 87, 112, 128, 181, 222–3
Auckland Acclimatisation Society  62
Auckland Islands  114–5, 246
Audubon Society  258
Aunt Daisy's New Cookery No. 6  119
Auster aircraft  136
Australia  46, 110, 219, 221, 259

Avalanche Glacier  273
Avery, AW  173, 246
Avoca  97

bacon  113, 117, 199, 215
Baden–Powell, Robert  39
Bain, Robert  167
Baker, C  112
Ballantyne, RM  229
Balloon Hut  222–3, 225
banded rail  55
Bangweolo Swamp  226
Banks, Joseph  242
Bannister, Charles  82, 84–5
Bannister, John  82
Banwell, Bruce  209
Barker, Alfred  91
Barker, Lady Mary–Anne  34, 55, 194, 196
Barnes, Leo  149, 246
Barra, Bert  69, 155, 158, 273
Barraud, Charles  62
Bathgate, Alexander  194
bats  19, 80–1
Bay of Islands  81, 168
Bay of Plenty Acclimatisation Society  60
Bay of Plenty Times  46
Beatson, Ruth  222
Beattie, James  19, 101
beech forests  157, 159, 256, 265
beef  81, 88, 115, 184, 197
beer  125, 137
Bell, Donald  180
bellbirds  60
Bennett, Mike  136, 138, 152
Best, Elsdon  79
Bethell, John  82
'Bicycle Rifle'  232
big-game hunting  37, 220–1, 226, 229
biodiversity, promotion of  267, 269, 285
biologists  51, 69, 114
bird-hunting  19, 78, 193–4, 229, 258
bird skins  146, 149–50, 239, 245, 247, 258
birds — see specific types
Birmingham Small Arms Co.  252
Bish, George  115
Bishop, Brenda  223
bivouacs  209, 218
Black, Bill  141, 179
Black Hills  55
black swan  194
black teal  280
blackberries  50, 102
blackbird  43
Blackwood's Magazine  209
Blenheim  24
Blue Lookout  191
blue mountain duck  195, 257
Blue Mountains  191
Bluff  146, 260
boats  81, 94, 102, 109, 141
bones  108, 112, 245
bonuses, government shooters'  144, 150, 153–4, 156, 158, 161–2, 169, 180
Boone and Crockett Club  259, 269, 277

Boswell, Jean  95, 115
botanists  68–9, 71–3, 235, 239, 254, 262, 269
Boughton, Russell  156
Boultbee, John  81
bounties  17, 25, 29, 75, 86, 123, 127, 138, 142–6, 150, 152, 156, 180, 187, 193, 237
Bourke, Harry  97–8, 166
Bourke, Kathleen  97
bovine tuberculosis  276, 281
Boyle base camp  159
Brackenridge, Gavin  39
Bradshaw, John  37
Brander & Potts Co.  252
bread  82, 84, 86–7, 93–5, 113, 249
Brees, Samuel  56
Brereton, Denis and Patricia  222
Brett's Colonists' Guide  42, 107
Britain  22, 25, 31, 35–7, 42–4, 46, 56, 77, 127, 172, 189, 209, 219–20, 231, 259
Broad, Isobel  88
Brocklesby, Joseph  92
Brooking, Tom  19
Brougham  120
Brown, Koi  97
Brunner, Thomas  167
Bryce, John  113
Buchan, Ian  157, 159
Buchanan, Henry  132, 134, 136
buckskin jackets  286
buffalo  221, 226
Bull, Jack  99, 145
Bull, Norm  201
Buller, Walter  245–6, 250, 252
Buller Gorge  93
bullets  84, 110, 153, 210
Burdon, Brian and Carol  125, 139
Burke River  158
bush  13, 20–1, 25, 66–9, 81–2, 93–5, 99, 106, 181–3, 191, 197–200, 202–3, 216–18, 255, 269–70
  airstrips  136
  browsers  26, 239, 254
  burn-offs  260
  clearing  90, 94, 262
  contractors  97, 145, 196, 213, 235
  food  87–8
  huts  218
  skills  167, 191
  workers  13, 68, 77, 81, 88, 120, 197, 259
  wrens  246
Bush Boys of New Zealand  229
bushcraft  36, 39, 162
butchers  26, 73, 77, 121, 127–8, 131, 285
Butler, Rev. John  81
butter  82, 102, 107, 113, 115, 160

Caithness  172
California  44, 132
Cameron, Robert  88, 113, 202, 260
camp cooking  116-7, 168–70
Campbell, DA  273
Campbell, E  102
Campbell, George  93, 99, 101
Campbell, Peter  140
Campbell Island  115

314   Hunting

camping  84, 183, 189, 191
camps  85, 88, 90, 93–4, 104, 109, 115, 121, 136–8, 156–7, 162, 164, 170, 179, 183, 221
Canada  19, 21, 56, 73, 135, 147, 258
Canterbury Acclimatisation Society  252
Canterbury Museum  38, 149, 172, 241, 245, 252
Canterbury Philosophical Institute  272
Canterbury region  34, 38, 48, 50, 91, 153, 196
Cape Campbell  246
Cape Kidnappers  47
Carroll, James MP  46, 62
Carter, Charles  113
Cascade Valley  158
catalogues, gun  231, 233–4, 242
cats  44, 54, 249, 259–61
cattle  42, 47, 49–51, 67–8, 81, 84, 99, 102–3, 106, 114–15, 127, 208
Cattle Ridge  51
Caughley, Graeme  111, 158–9, 231, 264, 271–2
Cecil Peak  182
Central Otago Railway  81
Cessna aircraft  136–7
Chambeshi River  226
chamois  13, 19, 21–2, 38, 52–3, 67, 72, 205, 211–13, 235, 241–2, 249, 255, 259, 261–2, 273
Chapman, M.  222–3
Chatham Islands  114, 260
Cheeseman, TF  59
children  11, 46, 92, 95, 97, 99–101, 106, 108, 137, 148, 176, 180, 202–4, 213, 229, 235
China, exports to  152, 166
Chinese merchants  25, 127, 164, 166–7, 176
Chisolm, Bill  180
Christchurch  93, 138, 173, 245
*Christchurch Sun*  207
cigarette cards  13, 193
Clark Hut  179
Clarke, Archie  155, 272
Clarke, Jack  199
class differences  27, 31, 193
climate change  262, 285
Clingin, W.  153
closed seasons  13, 60–2, 115, 250, 258, 261
Cloudy Bay  79
coast-watchers  114–15
Cobb & Co  24
Cobb Valley  222
Cockayne, Leonard  72, 239, 260, 263
Coldstream  48
Coleman, Hector B  222
Colenso, William  42
collectors and traders  22, 239, 241, 246, 249, 252
Collier, Joan  223
Collings & Brady Gunsmiths  176–7
Collings, Din  176–8
Collings, Viv  88, 178, 191, 213, 217, 234, 267
Collins, Michael  110
Colonial Ammunition Company  234
*Colonial Everyday Cookery*  118

Colonial Museum  149, 242, 253
Colonial Secretary  42, 57, 60
colonists' and settlers' attitudes to hunting  19–21, 27, 31, 33, 66, 229, 241, 261
Conrad, William  131
conservation  11–13, 21, 25–6, 73, 181, 184, 228, 239, 242, 247, 254–5, 268, 273, 275–6, 279–80, 286
conservation movement  13, 21, 26, 60, 64, 66, 87, 235, 241, 253, 258
conservationists  25, 27, 33, 60, 62, 65–6, 255, 267–8, 273, 275
construction work  65, 216–18
Cook, Captain James  47
cookbooks  118, 231, 285
*Cooking With New Zealand Game*  119
Coombes, Brad  46, 62, 64
*Country Life*  228
Cow Saddle  51
Cox, Henry  127
Cradock, Montagu  167
cranes, white  149, 246
Crawford, Peter  173
Crete  207
Cromwell  136
Crump, Barry  163, 230–1
Cullen, Hon. Michael  279
Cullen, William  49
cullers  121, 145, 146, 155, 156–7, 160, 162, 168, 179, 180, 216, 269, 275, 278
 pig  145
Curral, John  110
cushats  40

damage, ecological  12, 49, 66, 68–71, 210, 260, 263
Danderson, Jocelyn  70
Dannefaerd, Sigvard  173
Dargaville  97, 115, 245, 260
Davidson, Mavis  69–70, 71
Davidson, Ted  155, 180
Dawbin, William  55
Day, Walter  201
daybooks  163, 280
Deans, John  39–40
deaths  12, 79, 95, 101, 108–9, 111, 148, 179, 226
decoys  109, 232, 234
deer  38–9, 53, 66–73, 127–32, 136–8, 140–1, 146, 153–4, 160–4, 180–1, 183–4, 209–13, 222–5, 241–2, 261–4, 267–73, 280–1
 carcasses  127–8, 130, 132, 134, 136, 140, 179, 183
 control  142, 150, 155–6, 159, 161, 263–4, 267, 270–1, 273, 277
 culling  69, 82, 93, 146, 153, 155–6, 168, 180, 269
 destruction campaigns  93, 152, 209–10, 228, 267, 272–8
 farming  183
 heads  172, 207, 210
 hinds  128, 139, 141, 160, 210, 215
 hunting  13, 39, 44, 46, 125, 134, 140, 152, 161, 164, 168, 172, 184, 196, 206, 211, 213, 228, 233, 259, 276
 leather  120, 153, 296

 liberation of  44, 67
 numbers  154, 212, 263–4, 269–70, 272, 280
 products  164, 167
 red deer  22, 38, 41, 44, 46, 51, 128, 135, 168, 208–9, 225
 skins  82, 86, 132, 150, 152–4, 162, 204, 216, 224
 species  22, 44, 228
 stags  54, 125, 138, 141, 146, 160, 189, 196, 200, 206, 209–10, 219, 225
 tails  146, 164, 166
 velvet  26, 166
Deer Control Section, Department of Internal Affairs  13, 25, 152, 156, 158–9, 179–80, 200, 210–11, 242, 267, 270
Deer Menace Conference (1930)  267
*Deer Wars*  158
Deerstalkers' Association — see New Zealand Deerstalkers' Association
Deerstalkers' Ball  120
deforestation  250, 262
Denniston, Jack  170
Department of Agriculture  144
Department of Conservation  25, 181, 185, 242, 267, 275, 279, 286
Department of Industry and Commerce  210
Department of Internal Affairs  13, 25, 60, 71, 93–4, 120, 131–2, 146, 152–3, 156, 160–3, 210–11, 218, 255, 267–8, 271–3
 Deer Control Section  13, 25, 152, 156, 158–9, 179–80, 200, 210–11, 242, 267, 270
Department of Scientific and Industrial Research  72, 273, 279
Department of Tourist and Health Resorts  51, 53, 189, 207–8, 210–11, 249, 255, 259, 277
Dicks, Dave  198–9
Dickson, Lindsay  179
Dieffenbach, Ernst  87, 167, 242, 253
Docherty, William  149–50, 246, 252
Dominie aircraft  179
Dominion Timber Company  104
Donald, Margaret  207
Donald, Vivian  168, 220–1, 226
Donne, Thomas  116, 168, 207–10, 249, 255, 259
Douglas, Charlie  82, 86, 136, 259, 261
Downie, J.  102
dried foods  166
Drummond, James  58, 65
DSIR *see* Department of Science and Industrial Research
Duck-shooting  108, 167, 194, 202, 204, 228, 286
ducks  37, 42, 58, 64, 79, 86–7, 101, 108, 112, 119, 127–8, 131, 150, 166–7, 194, 204
 black teal  280
 blue  84, 195, 257, 280
 mallard  22, 44, 91, 280
 grey  44, 280
 paradise  79, 88, 194
 teal  119, 194

**Index 315**

Duncan, George  197
Dunedin  40, 48, 115, 146–8, 173, 179, 232, 276
Dusky Sound  47, 208
Duthie, Alistair  115

East Coast Railway  97
ecological damage  12, 22, 49, 66, 68–71, 210, 260, 263
ecologists  12, 66, 239, 263
ecology  21, 26, 68, 247, 250, 252–3, 260, 269
educated classes  37
eels  42, 49, 85–6, 113, 119
egg stealing  64, 112
eggs  49, 64, 81, 112, 149, 215, 226, 239, 246, 253, 260
Egmont National Park  72
Egypt  168, 270
Elder, Norman  69
Ell, Harry MP  61
Elliott, George  44
Elliott, Joe  93
Ellis, Edward S.  229
Enderby Island  115
Endicott, Wendell  228, 269
England  38, 40–4, 51, 55, 90–3, 113, 148, 154, 197, 211
Environment and Conservation Council  279
environmental issues  19, 73, 197, 207, 253, 260
  browsing mammals  66–7
  cattle  67
  countryside damage  71–3
  recreational hunters  66, 280–1
Enys, John  149, 250, 252
erosion  26, 71–2, 146, 241, 255, 261–6
  animal-induced  250, 264, 267, 273
  fears  262–7
Esson, Lt. Col. J.J  199
'estate creation'  31, 37, 46, 49
Europe  44, 159, 245, 249
exotic species  42–3, 46–7, 260
expeditions  36, 47, 71, 95, 100, 191, 203, 205, 252, 261, 269
explorers  14, 25, 49, 67, 77–8, 82, 87, 113, 242
exports  44, 132, 134, 147, 152, 166–7
Eyre, Lieutenant–Governor Edward  167

Fairfield, Bill  273
falcons  143, 252
families  11–13, 20, 25, 31, 39–40, 49, 77, 90–1, 94–5, 97–103, 121, 139, 198–200, 203, 213–14, 286
farmers  27, 34, 42, 198, 213, 241, 252, 262, 268, 273, 275
feathers  17, 29, 75, 107, 115, 123, 127, 142, 149, 187, 237, 258, 283
Federated Farmers *see* New Zealand Federated Farmers
Federated Mountain Clubs  275
Feldman, James  57, 61
feral goats  46, 50, 235, 275, 280
feral pigs  46, 48
Ferguson, Bruce  43
ferns  72, 120, 252
ferrets  43, 46, 234, 250, 261
*Field, The*  228
field officers  155, 159–60, 163, 180, 271
Findlater, Jock  160–1

Fiordland National Park  212
Fiordland region  141, 157–8, 168–9, 179, 208–9, 212, 228, 252, 255, 259, 269, 276–7
Fiordland Wapiti Foundation  280
First Island  215
fish  31, 49, 60, 62, 81, 86–7, 92, 95, 114, 119, 134, 173
*Fish & Game*  229
Fish & Game New Zealand  82, 229
fishing  40, 42, 78, 131, 167, 189, 200, 212–13, 228, 230
*Fishing & Shooting Gazette*  175
Fitz-William, Grant  181–2, 184, 189
Flagstaff Hill  48
flaxes  72, 101, 257
floods  159, 199, 267
Foa, Edouard  230
Fogden, John  135
food  14, 19, 22, 25, 31, 39, 47, 48, 50, 56, 59–60, 65, 72–3, 77–9, 81–2, 86–7, 92–3, 97–9, 102, 134, 258
  dried  166
Forest and Bird Protection Society
  — *see* Royal Forest and Bird Protection Society
Forest and Range Experiment Station  264
*Forest Lore of the Maori*  79
Forest Service  13, 25, 46, 53, 150, 154–8, 161, 164, 179–82, 214, 217–18, 231, 261, 264, 271–3, 276–9, 286
forests  12–13, 31, 34, 43, 46, 53, 61–2, 66, 67, 68, 69, 70–1, 72, 73, 103, 210, 254, 255, 260, 262, 263, 269–70
Forests Act (1874)  255
Forsyth, Malcolm  134, 136
Fox, William  42, 78, 149
Foxton  42
Francis, Ken  148, 271, 272
Fraser, Ron  179
FRES *see* Forest and Range Experiment Station
fresh–water crayfish  85
Fuller, Frederick  172, 241
fur  53, 107, 115, 127, 142, 146–7, 286
fur trade  13, 26, 33, 43, 115, 142, 146–7, 149, 154, 173
Furkert, Fred  205, 212, 229
furriers  25, 127, 142

Galbreath, Ross  12–13, 21, 172–3, 245, 268
game  37–9, 41–3, 45–7, 49, 55–7, 59–61, 65–7, 69, 77, 81–2, 93–5, 107, 112–13, 127–8, 194–6, 256–8
game animals  21, 25, 37, 39, 43, 46, 51, 53, 61, 66, 70, 210, 233, 262
*Game Animals of New Zealand*  209
game birds  12, 22, 42–4, 47, 118, 128, 173, 219
game laws  37, 40, 42–3, 56, 62
game meat  25–6, 107, 115, 127, 132, 140, 154
game recipes  118–9
gamekeepers  39
George Sound  178
Gillies, Robert  48
Gisborne  109, 152
Glaisnock Wilderness Area  280
goat culling  102, 275

goats  21, 42, 47, 50, 53, 67–70, 72, 81, 98, 102, 106, 113, 139, 202, 267, 281
  angora  50
  browsers  68–9, 71
  browsing mammals  67–8
  conservation  281
gold  84, 215, 257
gold prospectors  77, 82, 152
Golden Bay  182, 184
Golden Downs  155
*Good Keen Man*  163, 230–1
Goodwin, George  40
government forest rangers  148
government huts  218
government shooters  13, 25, 53, 93, 120, 127, 144, 146, 150, 152–3, 155, 159–61, 164, 181, 216, 222, 231
  bonuses  150, 156, 158, 161–2, 169
  off-season  235
  support  130
Grant, Patrick  267
grasslands  49, 53, 71, 221, 232
Great Depression  99, 181, 226, 233, 272
Great Island  70
Grebe Valley  179
Green, Harry  110
Green, Thomas  40
greenstone  182
Gregg, Arthur  212
Grey, Sir George (Governor)  252
Grey, Zane  168–9
grey ducks  79, 91, 194
Greymouth  134
ground hunters  137–8
grouse  35, 39, 219
Grumman Widgeon aircraft  178
guides  25, 53, 78–9, 87, 116, 127, 168–70, 172, 206, 209, 212, 221, 231, 259
*Gun and Game*  228
gun catalogues  231, 233–4, 242
Gunn, Davey  158
guns  12, 65, 82, 85, 87–8, 93, 95, 99–102, 108–9, 113, 120, 152, 182, 194, 199, 209
'gunshipping'  130, 134, 138
gunsmiths  25, 127, 164, 175–6, 178, 234
Gutschlag, Russell  140
gutters  140–1

Haast, Julius von  37–8, 53, 136, 149–50, 239, 241, 245–7, 249, 252
Haast region  44, 138, 158, 270
Halford, J  222
Halfway Bay  182
Hammond & Turner catalogues  176, 233
Hanga Ohia Tangata  84
Hanmer  180
Hapukorari  84
Hardie, Jack  159–61
Hardie, Norman  155, 159–61
Harper, AP (Arthur)  144
Harper, Leonard  167
Harper Pass  218
Harper's Bluff  170
Harrods, London  132
Hart, Herbert  168–9, 220–1, 226
Harwood, Richard  42
Hastie, James  131

Haurangi Forest Park  157
Hawea Flat  168
Hawera  128
Hawke's Bay Acclimatisation Society  57, 62
Hawke's Bay region  208, 214
hawks  145, 262
heads, mounted  13–14, 209
Heaphy, Charles  82, 167, 253
Hector, James  149, 239, 242, 245, 252
Heenan, Joseph MP  152
Heke, Hone  60–1, 65
helicopters  121, 127, 129–30, 138, 140, 224, 276–7
  accidents  111
  hunting  134, 137, 140
  pilots  184
  operators  135
  recoveries  137
  super-charged  140
Hell's Gate  69
Henderson, Muriel  204
Henry, Richard  253
Hens, William  108
Hermitage, Mt Cook  255
Herrick, E.R.  208
Hewitt, Bill  179
Hickford, Arthur  249
Higgins, Sarah  98
high-country regions  48, 158, 179, 184, 205, 262–3
hihi (stitchbird)  60
Hiku, Bill  93
Hinakura  199
hinau berries  95
hinds — see deer
historians  12–13, 21, 23, 26, 254
*History of the Birds of New Zealand*  239, 245
Hochstetter, Dr Ferdinand von  48
Hodgkinson, Con  169–70
Hokianga  58, 94
Hokitika  217
Hole, GG  224
Holland, Peter  19
Hollyford River  158
Holmes, Arthur  266
Holmes, J  226
Hopkins Valley  261
horns  54, 98, 102–3, 205, 209, 221
horses  34, 94, 103, 109, 113, 170, 182–3, 199, 218
hotels  13, 58, 107, 112, 121, 127–8, 131
household provisions  14, 58, 73, 84–5, 185, 193
Howard, John K  269
Hughes helicopters  140, 224
huia  55, 85, 173, 246, 250, 258
Humphreys, George  169–70
*Hunger for the Wild*  286
'hunter-pilots'  130
Hunter Valley  272
hunting deaths  12, 79, 95, 101, 108–9, 111, 148, 179, 226
hunting rights, Maori  33, 56–8, 60–2, 64, 180
Hursthouse, Charles  31, 37, 39, 43, 46, 73, 195–6, 234
Hurunui  82
hut books  13, 222, 224–5
Hutchinson, FE  272
huts  14, 82, 92, 121, 136–7, 156–8, 160, 162, 183, 189, 197, 214, 216–17, 222–5
  club  218
  construction of  217–18
  early bush  218
  high-altitude  179
  shared  21, 235
  shepherds'  55
Hutt Valley  198–9

ice  111, 121, 145, 266
immigrants  14, 31, 35, 38, 40, 43, 94, 194
imports  25, 42, 44, 47
income earning  125–85
India  35, 37, 39, 54, 180, 209, 219, 221, 230
industries, creation of  31, 43, 127, 132, 135–6, 140, 142, 176, 210, 219
Iorns, Ben  205
ivory  14
iwi  56, 61, 73

Jackson Bay  150, 158, 246
Jacobs, AJ (John)  173
James, Thomas  60
Johnson, Harry  229
Johnstone, Kathleen  119
Jones, MJ  173
Jones, Yvonne  222

Kahurangi National Park  180
Kaiapoi  49
Kaihau, Henare MP  60
Kaimai Ranges  181
Kaituna  51
kaka  49, 57, 85, 97, 99, 110, 150, 198, 257
kakapo  49, 60, 81, 86, 150, 246, 249
kamahi  72
Kane, Jim  179
Kapiti Island  50, 249, 260, 268
Karamea  88
karamu  72, 256
kauri gum  95, 97
Kaweka Ranges  214
kea  136, 143–4, 262
Kemp, Isobel  94
Kemp, Les  138
Kennedy, Alexander Esq.  49
Kenway, Philip  197
kereru  33, 37, 49, 56–8, 61–2, 65–6, 86, 101, 113, 128, 131, 134, 173, 257— see also pigeons
Kermadec Islands  70
kiekie vines  97
King, John  173
Kipling, Rudyard  229
Kirk, Audrey  223
Kirk, Thomas  149, 252
Kirkpatrick & Co.  127, 131
kiwi  52, 60, 81, 149–50, 246, 252
  captive  249
  eggs  246
  hunters  249
  skins  146, 149, 242
  spotted  246
  trapped  249
Knight, Jon  121
knives  14, 25, 120–1, 215, 234
koheperoa  245
kokako  60, 101, 253
konini berries  256
kotuku  149, 246
Lake Manapouri  279

Lake McKerrow  158
Lake Sumner  160
Lake Taupo  61, 87, 120, 249, 270
Lake Waikaremoana  61, 163
Lake Wanaka  156
Lambert Glacier  191
Lance, James Dupré  34
land girls  97
Landsborough Valley  170
Landseer, Sir Edwin  33
Lasenby, Jack  163
Latymer, Lord and Lady  168, 170
Leatham, AE  209
Lee, Edward  110
Leopold, Aldo  258, 269
Lewis Pass  159
Leys, Thomson W  42, 155
Liardet, Hector and St Clair  173
liberations, exotic animals  46, 48, 51, 53, 70
licence fees  57, 211
licences  53, 57–8, 101, 127–8, 131–2, 206, 208, 212–13, 258–9
Lindauer, Gottfried  246
Lindsay, Michael  219
lions  37, 221, 226, 230, 245
Little Barrier Island  258
logging  14, 181, 279
Longbeach  48
Loo, Tina  21
Lopdell, Rowland  114–5
Luangwa Valley  221, 226
Luapula River  221
Lucas, FJ (Popeye)  179
Lyes, Percy  208

Macauley Island  70
Mackay, Katrine  119
mail  136, 159–61
Mair, Gilbert  229
Mair, Lavinia  100–1
Makarora Valley  156, 270
Makawhai Stream  62
mallard ducks  22, 44, 91, 280
mammals, introduction of  19, 70, 235, 267, 269
Manapouri  168
Manawatu  100–1
Manawatu Acclimatisation Society  101, 112
Mangakino  181
Maori  12, 23, 25, 33, 42–3, 48–9, 56–62, 64–5, 73, 77–80, 87, 97–8, 112–13, 128, 167–8, 249–50
  acclimatisation societies  58, 267
  councils  62
  employment  84, 87, 97, 101, 167
  hunting rights  33, 56–8, 60–2, 64, 180
  MPs  60
Marino, David  102, 202
markets  131–2, 134, 141, 153, 224, 246, 249
Marlborough region  98, 210
Marsh, George Perkins  253
Martinborough  172
Martins Bay  158
Marton  173, 246
Mason, Ruth  72, 160
Masterton  173, 201, 206
Matatua district  61
Matiri  180
maumi  79
McCarthy Co.  176, 231–2

Index  317

McCaskill, Lance  276
McClaren, W  222
McConochie, Newton  34, 99, 101, 195
McCormick, Jack  199
McDiarmid, Elizabeth  82, 87, 95, 110
McDiarmid, Francis  82, 197
McDonald, Barbara  229
McGillivray, Roderick  168
McKinnon, Alic  226
McNair, Jack  160
Mead, Jack  155, 158
meat  11, 24–5, 82, 93–4, 97, 99–100, 106–7, 115, 121, 127, 131–2, 134, 136–9, 156–7, 203, 221
medicines  166–7
Milford Sound  81, 252
Millais, John Everett  34
milliners  127, 142
miners  48, 81, 215
missionaries  48, 50, 81, 87
Mitre Peak  85
moa bones  241
Moeraki Valley  156
Mohaka River  97, 214
Mokau River  104
Molesworth Station  180
*Monarch of the Glen*  196
Moncrieff, Perrine  34
Money-Coutts, Mercy  207
Monk, Bill  213
moose  208, 211, 229, 233
moreporks  85, 143, 145
Motueka  222
mounted heads  13–14, 209
Mt Arthur  222, 224
Mt Cook  52–3, 72, 249, 255, 267, 270
Mt Crawford  179
Mt Hector  217
Mt Luna  88
Mt Matthews  69
Mt Nicholas Station  182
Mt Peel  48
Mt White Station  41
muffs  14, 146, 149, 246
Muir, Jim  168–9, 208
Munro, Alex  155
Munro, David  81
Murchison  224
Murie, Olaus J  269
Murrell, Leslie  168–9, 207
museums  26, 173, 175, 241–2, 245, 247, 249, 252
mustelids  43, 261–2
musterers, high-country  138

Naked Possum Tannery Co.  184
national parks  218, 235, 255, 258, 262
National Parks Authority  276
native birds  21, 25, 31, 37, 43, 47, 56–7, 60–2, 66, 73, 82, 128, 143–5, 254, 261–2, 276
  skins  241, 245
native game  21, 33, 57–8, 60, 62, 64, 66, 128, 250
native game licence fees  57, 211
naturalist collectors  242–54
naturalists  12, 22, 73, 146, 229, 239, 242, 245, 250, 252, 259, 261
Nelson  24, 34–5, 39, 43–4, 48–9, 93, 101, 131, 210, 222, 260
Nelson Acclimatisation Society  38, 44, 127
Nelson Lakes  53
New Zealand Acclimatisation Societies Association  58
New Zealand and Australian Cable System  197
*New Zealand Beech Forest*  72
New Zealand Deerstalkers' Association  120, 167, 214, 275, 276, 279
New Zealand Department of Tourist and Health Resorts  259
New Zealand Ecological Society  267
*New Zealand Exhibition Cookery Book*  88, 118
New Zealand Expeditionary Force  270
New Zealand Federated Farmers  275
*New Zealand Fishing and Shooting Gazette*  119, 226, 229
New Zealand Forestry League  263
New Zealand Forests Act (1874)  262
*New Zealand Gazette*  61
*New Zealand Graphic*  228
*New Zealand Illustrated Magazine*  228
*New Zealand Illustrated Tourist Guide*  209
New Zealand Institute  68–9, 262
*New Zealand Listener*  228
New Zealand Native Bird Protection Society  268
New Zealand Railways  249
*New Zealand Railways Magazine*  228
*New Zealand Rod and Gun*  229
Newberry, Alfred  108
newspapers  62, 65, 113, 118, 137, 152, 161, 206, 262
Newton Flat  93
Ngati Porou  100
Ngati Tuwharetoa  61
North Island  46–7, 61, 69, 94, 102, 104, 135, 145, 147, 159
North Mitre Creek  85
Northland  93, 99–100, 286
noxious animals  273, 276
Noxious Animals Act (1956)  242, 273

Okarito  149, 246
Okuru  131
Oldham, Daniel  229
Oldham, John  128
Oliver, Rev. WC  208
Ollerenshaw, HJ  155
*On the Trail of the Moose*  229
onions  99, 224, 226
Onslow, Sir William (Governor-General)  258
'Opossum Regulations'  147
ornithologists  21, 80, 149, 239, 250, 253
Orongorongo Valley  72, 198, 205
Ostler, Sir Hubert  90, 196
Otago Acclimatisation Society  43
Otago Mounted Rifles  168
Otago region  48, 78, 81, 112, 146–7, 167, 194, 209, 272
Otaki  147, 196
Otorohanga  58–9
Owhango  104

packhorses  134, 183
Paekakariki  201
Pakawau  43
Palliser Bay  56
paradise ducks  79, 88, 194
Parariki  157
Parihaka  246
Parry, Hon. Bill  216
partridges  39, 219
Pawson, Eric  19
Pegely's Sports Shop  215
Pelorus Sound  50
Perham, Allan  71–2, 210, 263
perks  88–102
Perrelle, Philip de la  272
pest eradication  51, 214, 276
pests  142–3, 182, 262, 273
pheasants  22, 43–4, 49, 73, 88, 92–3, 97, 143, 145, 174, 209
Philp, R.  131–2
pig hunting  40, 48, 59, 82, 85, 88, 90, 93, 95, 97, 101, 109, 113, 121, 145, 167–8, 193, 195–7, 201–2
pigeons  40, 42, 56, 58–60, 65, 78, 82, 85–7, 95, 99–101, 110, 115, 118, 131, 203, 256 — see also keruru
pigs  13, 21, 34, 38, 47–50, 56, 81–2, 87–8, 90, 92–3, 101–2, 114, 145, 195–6, 201, 209
Pike Valley  158
pilots  26, 111, 121, 127, 130, 135–6, 140, 153–4, 178–9, 286
Piopio  59
Pirongia  246
planes see aircraft
plate tectonics  264–6
poaching  21, 40, 56, 58, 60, 64–5, 128, 141, 148, 181
Pohio, John Solomon  60
poisons  148, 154, 214, 273, 273–7, 281, 286
police  39, 59, 108–9, 112
pork  48, 73, 81–2, 92, 99, 117, 119–20, 163
Port Chalmers  127
porters  25, 168, 170, 221
possum leather  184
possum skins  144, 147, 182, 184
possums  21, 33, 53, 67, 70, 72, 144, 147–8, 154, 182, 235, 242, 262, 273, 276–7, 279–80
potatoes  87, 94–5, 99, 113, 249
Potts, Thomas  144, 149, 239, 245, 249–50, 252–3, 255–6
Poulter River  41, 180
*Practical Cookery Chats and Recipes*  118
predators  12, 22–3, 49, 52, 66, 73, 239, 249–50, 252, 254, 262
Preservation Inlet  87
private shooters bounty  150, 152
prohibition, sale of game  60, 65, 112, 131
prosecutions  56, 58, 60, 65
Protection of Certain Animals Act Amendment Act (1866)  57
provisions  11, 14, 22, 73, 77, 84–5, 98, 101, 185, 193–4
Pudding Hill  48
pukeko  42, 118, 119, 194
Purau  51

quail  22, 40, 43–4, 47, 58, 118, 127, 131, 145, 209, 257, 260
Queen Charlotte Sound  47, 167
Queen Victoria  33
Queenstown  181–2, 184

Rabbit Destruction Council  276
rabbit shooting  81, 180, 203, 286
rabbit skins  142, 147
rabbits  12, 40, 42, 115, 118–19, 127, 131, 139, 142, 146–7, 202, 219,

**318  Hunting**

262, 276
Rae, Jocelyn  182, 203, 205, 280
Raetihi Block  65
Rakaia River  108
Ram Island  110
Randall, James  92
rangers, government forest  148
Rangihoua  81
*Ranginui*  141
Rangiora  264
Rangitata  252, 267
rata  72
rations, government-issued  82
rats  44, 46, 80, 91, 259–60, 286
recipes  118–19
recreational hunting  26, 139–40, 193–4, 197, 199, 205, 214–15, 217–18, 220, 222, 234–5, 256, 267, 273, 279
  birds  19, 78, 193–4, 229, 258
  deer  13, 46, 125, 134, 140, 152, 161, 164, 172, 184, 196, 211, 276, 279
  environmental issues  279
  huts and track networks  217–18
  pigs  40, 48, 59, 82, 85, 88, 90, 93, 95, 97, 101, 109, 167–8, 193, 195–7, 201–2
  shooting for the pot  193–4
red deer — see deer
red wattlebird  246
Reikorangi Basin  213
Resolution Island  250, 253
restaurants  12, 112, 127–8, 286
retailing — see shops and shopping
Richards, Fred  104, 106, 202
Richards Cave  222
Riddiford, Daniel  219
Rider Haggard, Sir Henry  229
rifles  21, 25, 34, 48, 87–8, 98, 104, 114, 121, 136, 154, 159–60, 162–3, 182, 215–16, 231–4
Rimutaka Forest Park  280
Riney, Thane  263–4, 269, 273
Riseborough, John  147
Ritter, John  108
roa  150, 246
Roberts, W.  260
Robson, Charles  246
Roosevelt, Theodore  36, 229, 239, 259
Ross, Hugh  131
Ross, John McLeod  172
Rotorua region  61, 249
Routeburn Station  153
Royal Forest and Bird Protection Society  144, 239, 263, 268, 275
Royal Society of New Zealand  275
Ruamahanga  145
rucksacks  231, 234
Rutland, Cyril  104

sale of game, prohibition  60, 65, 112, 131
Salisbury  222–5
salmon  117, 212, 219
Sanderson, Val  268
sawmills  65, 215
scientists  22, 242, 260, 265, 277, 279
Scotland  39–40, 44, 51, 172, 219
Scott, Allan  229
Scott, Harry  155, 179–80
Seaforth River  208
Sealy Range  278
Seddon, Richard  62
*Self–Help Recipes and Household Hints*

119
Selous, F.C.  229
Selwyn, Bishop George Augustus  79
settlers  14, 19, 25, 31, 42, 48–9, 59, 77–8, 82, 87, 90, 193, 254–5, 260
Shag River  78
shags  114, 143, 145
shanghais  99
sheep  49, 82, 114, 143–4, 196
shelters  69, 136, 257
shepherds' huts  55
Ship Cove  167
shops and shopping  77, 98, 127–8, 131, 166, 174, 231–5
Shortland, Edward  79
shotguns  14, 35, 110, 145, 176, 231–3, 245
Simpson, Dick  147
sinews, deer  164, 167
Sixtus, Jack  223
skin bonuses  152–3, 164, 166, 176, 180, 273
skin hunting  134, 152–4, 222
Skinner, W.H.  79
skins  14, 17, 54, 85, 127, 132, 134, 138, 142, 146–50, 152–6, 160–4, 179–80, 204–5, 224, 245–6
Smith, Doug  261
Smith, Ken  130
Smith, William  246
Smithsonian Institute  36, 239
Smyth, William  173
snaring  65, 78
  methods  65, 78, 80
  pigeons  79, 80, 100
snouts, pig  48, 145–6
social antagonism  40
Soil Conservation and Rivers Control Council  275, 276
South Africa  34, 135, 259
South Hurunui  160
South Island  40, 48, 61, 78–9, 136, 158–9, 168, 205–6, 249, 252, 271, 277
South Mitre Creek  69
South Wairarapa  199
South Westland  82, 168–70, 205, 207, 212, 272
Southern Alps  53, 216, 261, 263, 266
Southern Scenic Air  136
Southland  87, 147, 173, 204
specimen collections  22, 26, 36, 146, 205, 239, 241–2, 245–6, 261
Spencer, E.  173
Splinter Creek  159
Spooner, Neville (Stag)  33, 200
Spooner, Tory  200
*Sport in New Zealand*  167
sportsman's paradise  189–235
sportsmen  33, 56, 62, 128, 189, 196, 211, 253, 258
Stafford, Edward  42
stags — *see* deer
Star, Paul  12, 21, 43, 209, 250, 252, 254–5
Stephenson, Percy  109–10
Stevens, Margaret  70
Stewart, George  147
Stewart, Graham  138
Stewart, W  272
Stewart, William  131
stitchbird (hihi)  60
stoats  43, 261, 286
Stonewall Tent Camp  157

Studholme  109
Styx River  217
suckling pigs  90
Sunday School prizes  228–9
'Sundowner'  228
survey camps  152
surveyors  14, 25, 37, 49, 77–8, 82, 87, 149, 167
survival in the bush  84–5
Sutherland, Alec  168, 199
Sutherland, Ken  168, 199
Swainson, William  87
swamp turkeys  42, 194 *see also* pukeko

tahr  13, 19, 21–2, 38, 53, 67, 72, 130, 205, 212–13, 235, 241–2, 255, 259, 261–2, 273
Taieri Valley  81
tails  26, 146, 156, 158, 160–1, 163–4, 166, 180–1, 224, 245, 257, 273, 280
Takatimu Ranges  183
Talbot, I  173
*Tangataroa*  229
Tangiteroria  245
tapu  250, 257
*Taranaki Herald*  128
Tararua Tramping Club  136, 216
Tararua Ranges  51, 69, 71, 82, 84–5, 179, 200, 205, 213, 216–18
Tate, Frank  205
Tauranga Acclimatisation Society  47
Tawhiao  113
taxidermists  24–5, 127, 164, 172–5, 206, 245–6
Te Ahuru, Sonny  102, 202
Te Awaite Station  168
Te Horo  102, 202
Te Naihi River  138
Te Rena  102
Te Urewera *see* Ureweras
teal  119, 194
tectonic plates  266, 267
tents  108–9, 156–7, 169–70
Thomas, Harold  226
Thomas, R  167, 194
Thomson, GM  147
Thomson, Rev. James Millar  120, 229
Thoreau, Henry  253
Thorpe, Ben  147
tigers  34, 37
*Timaru Herald*  108
timber workers  197
Ting, George  167
tinned quail  44, 127, 131
Tisdall, Sid  199
Toi, Pat  93
Toia, Hone  58
Tokomairiro  197
Tongariro  61, 202, 255, 260
Tongariro National Park  51, 262
tourism  12, 20, 44, 61, 212–13, 228, 241
tourists  26, 39, 168, 172, 189, 208–9, 211, 235, 255, 259, 276
tracks  51, 106, 189, 191, 215–18, 235, 261
trampers  13, 20, 25–6, 68, 71, 87, 114, 161, 189, 191, 194, 197, 213, 216–18, 222, 224–5
tranquilliser darts  135
trapping  78–9, 146, 161, 179
Treaty of Waitangi  56, 58–60, 62, 64
Tripp, Charles  48

**Index 319**

Tripp, Leonard  39
trophies  55, 208, 234–5, 279
trophy heads  36, 54, 138, 193, 214, 279
trophy hunting  26, 197, 205–6, 221, 226
trout  120, 143, 145, 163, 208
Tuatapere  70, 119
tuatara  52, 245, 249
Tuhoe  46, 57, 61–2
Tuhorouta, Rev. Reweti  100
tui  55, 57, 73, 99, 107, 285
Tukino, Te Heuheu  61
Turnbull, Colin  116
tusks, pig  205, 221
Twigg, William  226

United States  19, 21, 36, 44, 73, 134, 147, 153, 228, 234, 258–9
Upper Hollyford Valley  158
Urewera District Native Reserve Act (1896)  61
Urewera  46, 48, 57, 61–2, 167, 231

vegetables  68, 87, 94, 115, 166
*Vegetation of New Zealand*  263
velvet  26, 164, 166
venison  12, 21, 26, 48, 88, 93–4, 106, 118–119, 120–1, 136–7, 139, 163, 184, 193, 199, 215–16
  export trade  125, 131–2, 137, 139–40
  farmed  141
  frozen  132
  hunting  276
  industry  178
  processing  134
  recoveries  111, 129, 135, 140, 167
  stew  13, 119, 213, 222–3
Vercoe, Bert  155, 158, 179
Victoria College  90
Victoria River  180
Vogel, Rt. Hon. Sir Julius  262

wages  25, 88, 125, 132, 138–9, 146, 153, 180, 215
*Waiau Cookery Book*  119
Waiau River  87
Waikanae  182
Waikato  92–3, 246
Waimakariri River  195
Waimate  108–9
Waingawa  82, 84–5, 145
Wainono Lagoon  109
Wainuiomata  198–9
Waiohine  145, 148
Waipoua Forest  260
Wairarapa  88, 99, 113, 168, 197, 199, 202, 219, 246, 260
Wairau  98
Wairoa  57
Wairoa Creek  49
Wairoa River  245
Waitakere  82
Waitangi Tribunal  12, 46, 279
Wakatipu, Harry  163
Wakefield, Edward Jerningham  50, 56, 120
Walker, Cuthbert  109
Wallace, Gavin  205
Wallis, Tim  141, 276
Walsh, Rev. Philip  68, 71, 262
Walter Peak  182
Wanaka  125, 139, 144, 173, 180, 273

Wanganui  14, 41
Wangapeka River  191
wapiti  26, 120, 168–9, 199, 211, 228, 242, 255, 259, 262, 269, 277
Warren, Harold  109–10
Warren, Louis  21
Waterton, Charles  172
weather conditions  86–7, 134, 136–7, 158, 162, 167–8, 170, 191, 223–4, 256
*Weekly News*  228
weka  49, 78, 81, 85–7, 145
Wellington  39, 42, 58, 65, 72, 90, 99, 102, 120, 128, 131, 145, 166–7, 176–7, 198–9, 224
Wellington Acclimatisation Society  132, 145
Wellington Tramping & Mountaineering Club  213
Wenden, Bruce  191
West Coast  149, 167, 246, 252–3
West Taieri  82, 110, 173, 197
Westland  144, 158–9, 261
whalers  31, 47–8, 50, 81
Whangaroa  81
Wharekopae  110
whares  82, 197–9 *see also* huts
White, Rev. William  81
white cranes (kotuku)  149, 246
Whitley, Fred  198–9, 205
widgeons  194
Wiffin, EJC (Ernie)  145, 168–70, 199
Wild Animal Control Act (1977)  141, 214, 278, 279
wild cattle  50–1, 55, 82, 101, 103, 113, 195–6
wild ducks  39, 42, 64–5, 93, 108, 113, 114, 118–19
wild goats  242, 273
wild pigeons  81, 95, 97
wild pigs  25, 31, 42, 48–9, 51, 88, 90, 92, 97, 99, 101–2, 104, 113, 127, 196
wild venison  100, 141
wilderness, relationships with  19, 34–5, 218, 235, 254, 269
wilderness areas  46, 214, 218
wildlife  21, 37, 57, 260, 279
Williams, Murray  280
Wilson, Major Robert  168
Wong, Harry  166–7
Wong Tien  166
wood pigeons — *see* keruru
Woodley, Anne  148
Woodley, Brian  100, 147–8
Woulden, Henry  91
wrens, bush  246

Yardle, Janet  149
Yerex, David  273
Yerex, G.F. (Frank)  152, 155, 159, 161, 179–80, 268, 270–1, 272, 273
Young, David  12, 21, 254, 262, 270